INSIGHT, INTENTION
and
INTEGRITY

Developing the three "eyes" of Emergent Leadership using the Adaptive Learning Map©

Ian Cogdell

Insight, Intention and Integrity: Developing the three "eyes" of Emergent Leadership using the Adaptive Learning Map
© Ian Cogdell 2025

All rights reserved. No part of this publication may be reproduced, stored in a retrieval system, or transmitted in any form or by any means, electronic, mechanical, photocopying, recording or otherwise, without the prior written permission of the author.

Ian Cogdell is recognised as the creator of this content and has asserted the right to be identified as the author of this work.

ISBN: 978-1-923289-97-0 (Paperback)

A catalogue record for this book is available from the National Library of Australia

Cover Design: Ian Cogdell and Clark & Mackay
Format and Typeset: Ian Cogdell and Clark & Mackay
Published by Ian Cogdell and Clark & Mackay

Proudly printed in Australia by Clark & Mackay

CONTENTS

Dedication 5
Observation 7
Acknowledgements 9
The Hierarchy Disconnection Dilemma 11
Some Useful Terms 13
List Of Figures 17

PART 1   **SETTING THE SCENE** 19

Chapter 1   Introduction 21
Chapter 2   The Emergent Leadership Territory 29
Chapter 3   The Foundations Of Self 45

PART 2   **PREPARING TO SEE** 65

Chapter 4   The Adaptive Learning Map© 67
Chapter 5   The Choice Making Drivers 81
Chapter 6   Our Personality Lens 91

PART 3   **UNDERSTANDING BLIND SPOTS** 121

Chapter 7   The Meaning Making Mindset 123
Chapter 8   The Sense Making Mindset 147
Chapter 9   The Connection Making Mindset 163

Part 4	Sight For Fresh 'Eyes'	199
Chapter 10	Insight - The Pathway To Potential	201
Chapter 11	Intention – The Pathway To Priorities	219
Chapter 12	Integrity – The Pathway To Purpose	237

PART 5	**SEEING WITH CLEAR EYES**	**253**
Chapter 13	Our Sensitive Self - Sensitive Energy And The Will To See	255
Chapter 14	Our Conscious Self - Conscious Energy And The Will To Do	275
Chapter 15	Our Creative Self - Creative Energy And The Will To Be	289

Epilogue:	The Emergent Leadership Paradigm Shift	311
Epilogue	The Emergent Leadership Paradigm Shift	313
Tool Kit		351
Reference Sources		381
Author Bio		383

DEDICATION

This book is dedicated to the people I am emotionally connected to and who have inspired me to reflect on my views of the world and question my beliefs and assumptions. First and foremost is my wife and partner Jill who has always been a pillar of support in my life and provided insightful feedback on the early drafts of the book. I have also been inspired by my immediate and extended family with whom I have shared many life experiences. Thank you Lisa, Jody, Kate and Heidi and my grand-children Sam, Jemma, Jacob, Charlotte, Shannon, Lachlan, Callum, Rebecca, Joshua, Dominic, Luke, Sid and Vivienne.

Needless to say, all of my family demonstrate an amazing diversity in abilities and aspirations that are the foundation of the life choices they are making and will continue to make. May all of you achieve happiness in whatever you do.

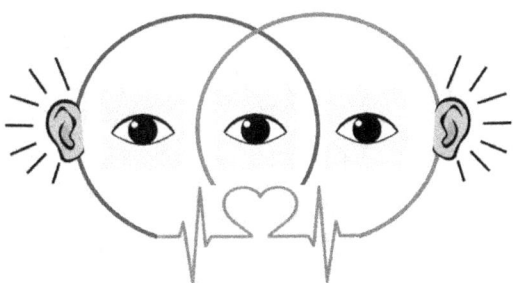

"Empathy is seeing with the eyes of another, listening with the ears of another, and speaking to the heart of another." Anonymous (adapted)

OBSERVATION

In many respects this book is about the difference between management and leadership. Management is about being smart and leadership is about being clever.

Smart refers to someone who is quick in thought, can learn quickly and can make good decisions. Smart is about being intelligent and having the ability to apply the knowledge to practical situations. So a smart person knows how to use their knowledge and to solve problems. So a smart person is practical and problem focussed. It is thinking , analytical and problem centric.

Clever means having or showing the ability to see and understand patterns quickly and easily. Clever refers to originality, inventiveness, and insight. Clever is about the ability to learn things quickly in differing situations by using originality and creativity. So a clever person is tuned into patterns and relationships. It is feeling, intuition and context centric. Emergent leadership and reflective learning are inseparable.

Management has a position based focus to decision making and leadership has a person based focus to influencing choice making.

ACKNOWLEDGEMENTS

I have had a fortunate life in which I have had roles where I was able to interact with a wide diversity of people and had the privilege of being in a range of position-based leadership roles that have given me both an experiential and a conceptual frame of reference for much of what is canvased in this book.

In that context I need to personally acknowledge those colleagues who had a long-lasting impact on my beliefs about leadership. I would sincerely acknowledge the enduring collaborative relationships I have had with Colin Benjamin, Leon Zimmerman, Karl Erik Svieby, Ken Whitters, Graeme Taylor and the late Clarence da gama Pinto, who were valued colleagues at the Mt Eliza Centre for Executive Education, then part of Melbourne Business School. I also want to acknowledge the significant number of colleagues I worked with in roles I have had in Industrial Relations, Human Resources, IT and Sales and Marketing with the SA Public Service, Kimberly Clark, Varian Techtron, Amcor, Australian Cement, Toyoda Gosei and Mitsubishi Motors Australia who contributed to my personal development. Special mention goes to Karina Kerakova, Angie Geldenhuys and the late Louise Davis.

In the 1990's I established my own strategy, leadership and team development consulting and coaching business and for more than fifteen years was a trusted partner of many clients in Australia, China, Hong Kong, Indonesia and Papua New Guinea. I am indebted to them for the faith they showed in me. There are many others who in their own way have helped without knowing it and to those who have provided that "aha" moment I am very grateful.

I acknowledge the work of Jon Husband that introduced the idea of wirearchy I chanced upon a couple of years ago that is a foundational context for what is contained herein. I also acknowledge the genius of the late John Bennett and his work on the idea of energies that puts a structure around the way our will operates.

For the sake of simplicity, I have chosen to use the work of Carl Jung as a foundation for developing the three "eyes" of emergent leadership while acknowledging that there are a wide range of personal behaviour constructs that could be applied to the development of insight, intention and integrity.

Of course, I take the usual responsibility for the content and concepts contained in the book and trust that I have given appropriate recognition to the work of others where I have incorporated their work into the ideas I have developed. There is reference section at the back that attempts to provide a comprehensive source of information that I have found valuable in expanding my understanding of personality constructs and personal development processes that I commend to you as complimentary reading.

THE HIERARCHY DISCONNECTION DILEMMA

Source Unknown

We are all connected to a larger 'whole' whether we recognise it or not!!!

SOME USEFUL TERMS

Adaptive: the behaviours or traits that help an individual adjust and function well within a changing social, technological, economic and political environment and developing the ability and motivation to develop their unique personal disposition in response to their connection with others. The ability to regulate and adapt behaviour to the demands of a situation in order to achieve your potential, priorities and purpose. It is associated with an internal locus of control.

Choice: the act of picking or deciding between two or more possibilities, imagined or real. The opportunity or power to make a decision. It reflects the relationship that occurs between meaning-making, sense-making and connection-making in balancing personal needs and the needs of others.

Emergence: a quality that does not depend on its individual parts, but on their reciprocal relationships to one another. It is non-linear in form and, as a consequence, emergent behaviour cannot be predicted by analysing the individual parts of a system.

Epilogue: a section at the end of a book that serves as a comment on, or as a conclusion to, what has gone before.

Eyes: when you open your eyes, you become aware that something is different from the way that you thought it was. A homophone for the three "I's" of leadership: insight, intention and integrity.

Hierarchy: a system in which members of an organisation or society are ranked according to relative status or authority and are represented as being "above", "below", or "at the same level as" one another.

Homophone: a character or group of characters pronounced the same as another character or group of characters. For example – "eyes" and "I's".

Leadership: the spontaneous assumption of responsibility to contribute to the common good. An emergent quality arising from the synergy between insight, intention and integrity – the 'eyes' of emergent leadership. These three 'eyes' underpin voice, vision and values. It is about responding, rather than reacting, in the moment and being responsible for the choices we make ourselves and influencing responsibility in others for the choices they make.

Learning: the adaptive process of acquiring new understanding, knowledge, behaviours, skills, attitudes, values and preferences. Leadership and learning are indispensable to each other.

Map: a symbolic depiction showing the relationships between elements of some space. The space may be two dimensional, three dimensional, or even more abstract spaces of any dimension, such as complex models with many independent variables.

Wirearchy: a dynamic two-way flow of power and authority, based on knowledge, trust, credibility with a focus on behaviours and outcomes, enabled by interconnected people and technology.

"Everything that irritates us about others can lead us to an understanding of ourselves"

—Carl Jung

LIST OF FIGURES

Figure 1: Hierarchy and Wirearchy
Figure 2: The Adaptive Learning Map©
Figure 3: The Foundations of Self
Figure 4: The Three Mindsets and Styles
Figure 5: The Three Centres
Figure 6: The Core Elements of the Adaptive Learning Map©
Figure 7: The Adaptive Learning Map©
Figure 8: Maslow's Needs as a Hierarchy
Figure 9: The Choice Making Experience
Figure 10: Jungian Function Pairs
Figure 11: The Reactive Self Mindsets
Figure 12: The Meaning Making Mindset
Figure 13: The Sense Making Mindset
Figure 14: Our Sense Making Hierarchy
Figure 15: The Connection Making Mindset
Figure 16: Transactional Analysis Interactions
Figure 17: the Three Reactive Self Mindsets
Figure 18: The Three Eyes of Emergent Leadership
Figure 19: Insight
Figure 20: Intention
Figure 21: Integrity and the Will to Be
Figure 22: The Schwartz Values Circle
Figure 23: The Three Dimensions of the Higher Self
Figure 24: Our Sensitive Self
Figure 25: Our Conscious Self
Figure 26: Our Creative Self
Figure 27: The Full Adaptive Learning Map©
Figure 28: The Adaptive Learning Map© Learning Loops
Figure 29: The Evolution of Leadership

Figure 30: Performance, Capability and Context
Figure 31: Horizontal Development
Figure 32: The Information and Knowhow Transitions
Figure 33: Emergent Leadership Development
Figure 34: Emergent Leadership Role Development
Figure 35: The Three Emergent Leadership Roles
Figure 36: Advocacy and Inquiry Matrix
Figure 37: The Stages of Role Transition

PART 1

SETTING THE SCENE

The first Part sets the scene and the first chapter provides a general introduction to the ideas explored in the book. The second chapter consider the emergent leadership context by exploring the territory that we are now experiencing and being confronted by - the emergence of a tipping point that threatens our way of life and the inability of hierarchy to cope with the rate of change and complexity that is driven by this universal connectedness. The third chapter considers our internal context and how we individually got to where we are by looking at the foundations of self: the relationship between nature and nurture in your early childhood development and how you learned to navigate your way through the territory you were then in.

CHAPTER 1
Introduction

Leadership is probably the most written about topic in the world. It is an elusive subject in many ways and that is reflected in the many adjectives used to describe it. They include democratic, autocratic, laissez-faire, strategic, transformational, transactional, bureaucratic, authentic, servant, visionary, charismatic, situational, authoritative, affiliative, agile, and many more. These descriptions almost invariably reflect leadership in the context of hierarchy and as an extension of a management role.

The aim of this book is to provide a framework for your self-development that does not require you to be in a managerial hierarchy in order to be a leader. You just have to be connected to others and make choices, and influence the choices of others, from a position of insight, intention and integrity. It is a book for everybody who wants to develop their potential, their priorities and their purpose in life.

This book is predicated on the idea that, in a time when we enjoy the benefits flowing from the economic exploitation of finite resources, coupled with massive innovation on many fronts, we have created a "tipping point" that threatens the continuity of our existence on the planet. We have failed to appreciate the nature of the interdependencies between our exploitation and innovation and the natural order of living systems.

Leadership, in this emerging context, is about personal choice-making, and influencing the choices of others, in this new universally, and real time, interconnected world. Fundamentally leadership is embedded in the ways that people make choices, make meaning, make sense and make connections, to share their knowledge and to contribute to the common good. It is a role we can all get to engage in as a situational response to the need to share ideas, knowledge and experiences, and to make and influence choices, in our particular connected spaces.

The approach taken in this book looks at the impact of universal connectedness on how we experience the world around us. It explores the inability of hierarchy to cope with the rate of change and complexity that is driven by this universal connectedness. The ideas of 'wirearchy' and living adaptive systems are introduced as the foundations of the emerging role of leadership as a person-based rather than position-based construct. Wirearchy is defined by John Husband as *"a dynamic two-way flow of power and authority, based on knowledge, trust, credibility and a focus on results, enabled by interconnected people and technology"*.

Consequently, this book seeks to take a somewhat different approach to leadership by considering that we all have the potential to contribute as a leader.

Knowledge is the new renewable capital, and connectedness is the new value creation chain. Knowledge shared is knowledge doubled: I still get to keep all of mine even though I give it away to another, unlike sharing an apple pie! The new knowledge economy paradigm is about abundance rather than scarcity. The shift from non-renewable fossil fuels to various sources of renewable energy is a real-life global example of the abundance economy approach.

Against that background the book encourages you to explore your choice making, meaning-making, sense-making and connection-making mindsets that underpin your Reactive Self - an unconscious, habit based, sense of self that relies on your embedded beliefs and experiences.

In that context the unique Adaptive Learning Map© is introduced to provide a framework to help you understand and explore the interdependencies between the three key personal mindsets that we all use in making choices in our day to day lives: meaning-making, sense-making and connection-making.

This in turn leads to the essence of the book, "The Three 'Eyes' of Emergent Leadership", where "eyes" is a homophone for the three "I's" of insight, intention and integrity that are energised by our 'will to see', our 'will to do' and our 'will to be'.

The book is presented in five parts that are reasonably self-contained but linked to each other.

The first Part sets the scene and the first chapter provides a general introduction to the ideas explored in the book. The second chapter consider the emergent leadership context by exploring the territory that we are now experiencing and being confronted by - the emergence of a tipping point that threatens our way of life and the inability of hierarchy to cope with the rate of change and complexity that is driven by this universal connectedness. The third chapter considers our internal context and how we individually got to where we are by looking at the foundations of self: the relationship between nature and nurture in your early childhood development and how you learned to navigate your way through the territory you were then in.

The second Part is about preparing to see. The first chapter in this part provides the essential structure of the book by developing the rationale behind the Adaptive Learning Map©. In the second chapter in this Part, the role and nature of choice-making, that sits at the centre of our leadership development contribution, is considered. The third chapter in this Part develops the personality lens based on the Jungian personality type model. The personality lens will be used to explore the three "eyes" of emergent leadership – insight, intention and integrity.

The third Part is about understanding the blind spots of our Reactive Self by making you aware of your meaning-making, sense-making and connection-making mindsets. This Part considers the three habit-based mindsets of our Reactive Self:

- Meaning-making (directed by the Feeling Centre and Creative Drive)
- Sense-making (directed by the Thinking Centre and Practical Drive)
- Connection-making (directed the Moving Centre and Instinctive drive)

and how they contribute to our blind spots and those of others we connect and interact with.

The fourth Part looks at the three 'eyes' of emergent leadership - insight, intention and integrity - as foundations for the conscious development of our personal leadership role in the interconnected world of wirearchy.

They each act as the leadership bridge between the three Reactive Self mindsets:

- Insight is the leadership bridge between meaning-making and connection-making
- Intention is the leadership bridge between sense-making and connection-making, and
- Integrity is the leadership bridge between sense-making and meaning-making.

They give us access to the three unconscious emergent leadership qualities:

- Insight gives us access to our potential and voice,
- Intention gives us access to our priorities and vision, and
- Integrity gives us access to our purpose and values.

The fifth Part looks at the nature of our will and the energies that we need to access on our journey of self-development. The Will is described as three separate, but interrelated, higher intelligences. While there is no empirical evidence to support this construct, it serves as a useful way of describing the elusive idea of will in an accessible way. It also sits comfortably with the relationship between the Will and higher life energies.

The three elements of Will and their related energy sources that support them, that will be applied to our self-development, are:

- the 'will to see' and sensitive energy,
- the 'will to do' and conscious energy, and
- the 'will to be' and creative energy.

The three intelligences of our will are the foundation of our three developmental dimensions of Self:

- Our Sensitive Self based on our 'will to see',
- Our Conscious Self based on our 'will to do', and
- Our Creative Self based on our 'will to be'.

The Epilogue looks at the role of emergent leadership as the influencer of choice driven behaviour, and is about the central role of the three "I's" – insight, intention and integrity. Adaptive learning is the new leadership mindset and there are no boundaries to our interpersonal connections and knowledge flows. Even though many still live in the earlier serial world of hierarchical power of position, the emerging new source of power is personal and collective knowledge creation and sharing.

Leadership, in the universally connected context of wirearchy, has an emergent quality that arises from the interaction of the three "eyes" of leadership – insight, intention and integrity. When the three "eyes" are balanced you will naturally lead in any situation that demands it. Hence emergent leadership.

In the Tool Kit a range of tools are introduced to assist in developing insight, intention and integrity, with a significant focus on Jung's model. These approaches are meant to provide an insight into the questions you will be asking yourself as you are faced with challenging your present meaning-making, sense-making, connection-making and choice-making mindsets. These 'personality' constructs provide you with a framework of discovery rather than satisfactory answers to your personal complexity and uniqueness.

When we reflect on our sense of who we are, we begin to see that we have been socialised into a culture of problems and its associated busyness. The universal response to the question "How have you been?" is "Busy!" - busy reacting to the never-ending stream of problems that continually bombard us from multiple sources. We have become aimless problem attractors and problem solvers (and problem forgetters when the next "busy-work" gets our attention), operating inside the boundaries of our experience. We remain stuck in the habit-based Reactive Self. The book seeks to get you to embrace adaptive learning as a pathway out of the busy-ness of your Reactive Self and to take the lead in the world of knowledge creation and knowledge sharing.

In the world of adaptive learning questions are the answers! As Rudyard Kipling said:

> "I keep six honest serving-men
> (They taught me all I knew);
> Their names are What and Why and When
> And How and Where and Who.
> I send them over land and sea,
> I send them east and west;
> But after they have worked for me,
> I give them all a rest."

You are encouraged to question the premises and concepts put forward in this book as much as you are encouraged to question your own premises and mindsets. Learning is about questioning.

The book and its associated Adaptive Learning Map© will, at times, have created its own complexity in your mind, for that is the nature of your Reactive Self in denial, when confronted with ideas that

INSIGHT INTENTION AND INTEGRITY

you have not seen before. However, rather than seeing complexity, stand back and see the simplicity and elegance of the relationships provided by the Map© and reflect on the application of each dimension to your own choice-making approaches to leadership.

While simplicity has its place, the beauty of complexity is that it is the catalyst for curiosity and its partner in crime, creativity. Curiosity thrives on complexity, connectivity and choice.

CHAPTER 2
The Emergent Leadership Territory

Let's set the scene by looking at the territory we are about to explore as the external context for our emergent leadership development trip. The territory provides the constant barrage of 'triggers' that initiate the choices we make as we navigate it. An early childhood experience about Humpty Dumpty provides a useful analogy about the territory we are in.

> *"Humpty Dumpty sat on the wall,*
> *Humpty Dumpty had a great fall,*
> *All the King's horses and all the King's men,*
> *Couldn't put Humpty together again."*
> *Lewis Carroll: The Looking Glass*

While there have been many observations made about the "Humpty Dumpty Effect", the idea that proposes "when doing our best isn't good enough", very little attention has been given to how Humpty found himself on the wall in the first place!

As a metaphor, the "wall" can be seen to represent a "tipping point" that Humpty did not recognise, and his "fall" was inevitable. Then along came those to put things back as they were, using only the things they already knew – their experience of 'horse riding' – all gained in a male dominated hierarchy led by the "King". Sound familiar?

We are faced with a tipping point in human evolution, and we only know how to solve the challenges in the context of hierarchy, managed by the power of position, through "command and control" principles. We are the modern-day Humpy Dumpty's. We are about to relive Humpty Dumpty's fate unless we recognise, we are already sitting on the "wall".

Joseph Campbell in his book, the Myths to Live By, says:

> *"There were formerly horizons within which people lived and thought and mythologised. There are now no more horizons. And with the dissolution of horizons, we have experienced and are experiencing collisions, terrific collisions, not only of peoples but also of their mythologies. It is as when dividing panels are withdrawn from between chambers of very hot and very cold airs: there is a rush of these forces together. And so we are right now in an extremely perilous age of thunder, lightning, and hurricanes all around. I think it is improper to become hysterical about it, projecting hatred and blame. It is an inevitable, altogether natural thing that when energies that have never met before coming into collision - each bearing its own pride - there should be turbulence. That is just what we are experiencing; and we are riding it: riding it to a new age, a new birth, a totally new condition of mankind - to which no one anywhere alive today can say that he has the key, the answer, the prophecy, to its dawn. Nor is there anyone to condemn here (" Judge not, that you may not be judged!"). What is occurring is completely natural, as are its pains, confusions, and mistakes."*

This book is predicated on the idea that, in a time when we enjoy the benefits flowing from the economic exploitation of finite resources, coupled with massive innovation on many fronts, we have created a "tipping point" that threatens the continuity of our existence on the planet. We are in the age of the greatest mass extinction of species ever experienced on the planet.

We have failed to appreciate the impact of our exploitation and innovation on the nature of the interdependencies between ourselves and the natural order of the living system. We have created change at a rate faster than we can manage it.

More than 70 years ago Winston Churchill warned –

> "We are shaping the world faster than we can change ourselves, and we are applying to the present, the habits of the past."

We are the product of the choices we have made, collectively and individually, and the resultant consumerism that reinforces short term satisfaction at the expense of long-term sustainability. The concurrent impact of globalisation has produced its equal and opposite side effect – isolationism, and its close cousin, myopic patriotism. A narrow local focus generated by the fear, perhaps more correctly, the deprivation, that is experienced by those at the powerless bottom of the hierarchy.

The powerful benefit at the expense of the powerless; that is the essence of hierarchy.

Nothing new there except for the one profound emerging power shift from positional power to personal power, facilitated by the technology enabled open real time connections we now have with each other. Up until now the whole concept of leadership has been embedded in hierarchy, using latent "command and control" based positional power, that has its origins in an economic contractual association with some form of impersonal legal entity or another: a corporation or a government agency. This unconscious position-based power approach to leadership inadvertently pervades all management and leadership behaviour and development. It has largely perverted the role of democracy up until now – corporations and lobby groups have more power than individuals.

Connective technology, built on open-source software, is giving democracy, with all of its shortcomings, a new lease of life and we are seeing mass demonstrations being organised digitally, that are challenging the existing power structures and changing the role of position-based leadership in society. On the down side it has led to the emergence of a range of wild conspiracy theories that proliferate the digital space and that exploit naivety, fear and the need to belong. This is the anti-knowledge outcome of universal connection.

At the organisation level we continue to see the emergence of self-directed teams, personal empowerment, multi-faceted diversity, purposeful engagement and knowledge-based autonomy, through the lens of, and hampered by, the positional power of a few at the top and a larger number at the aspiring middle of the hierarchy, who are learning "how to play the game". Power that is manifestly about command and control with compliance consequences for those who don't "toe the line" and rewards for those that have "political or business nous".

Hierarchy thrives on the KISS principle "keep it simple, stupid" – which is primarily about the manager's positional need to demonstrate control. It is a disease of those with a risk averse, low trust mindset. Whenever you hear the plea from a manager to "keep it simple" you can be sure that they are about maintaining control, and at best will humour you, by bureaucratising your idea into their already predetermined "business plan", if they even have one.

While simplicity has its place, the beauty of complexity is that it is the catalyst for curiosity and its partner in crime, creativity. Curiosity thrives on complexity, connectivity and choice. Consequently, curiosity and creativity are the Achilles heel of hierarchy. It is largely the economic power of large organisations to acquire smaller innovative organisations that enables them implement innovative solutions. Their largeness is at best doing the same things a little more cleverly.

In that context it is the emerging 'people to people' and 'people to know-how' connecting technologies that are challenging the way we live and work. We now have work-life integration rather than work-life balance. We now just do stuff and get paid for some of it. In the nineties respected management expert Charles Handy said "the job is dead" yet we still have organisations insisting on job descriptions, almost always by so called Human Resources functions – resources to be exploited as a cost of production. The focus is on managed mandatory performance and totally misunderstands the importance of self-empowered discretionary contribution. People now have roles, not jobs, and need to be adaptable, knowledgeable, connected and responsible to each other, not just please their "boss". Of course some still would rather live in a job-based world where they can control their own "patch" and maintain an "it's not my job" approach to their work environment.

The challenge, as we transition to new ways of designing organisations, is to reflect this shift from positional to personal power. At the core of this power shift is the centrality of personal choice-making, especially in our "at work" roles, and the implications that has for the role of leadership. Leadership has always been a person driven role in a context while management has been position driven in a container, yet that distinction is rarely made.

Leadership is about choice-making at its core. It involves making our own choices and being influenced by the choices of significant others.

Before the determinists call for my head, it needs to be said that this is not a philosophical stance in favour of free will but a pragmatic recognition that people believe they have choice. That belief, like all other beliefs, is based upon their experience in interacting with others in the real world. That is their reality. Exploring the why, how, what, who, where and when of our own choices and their connection to the choices of others can contribute to understanding the power of our habit-based blindness and open us up to the emergent nature of leadership. Leadership is a role anyone can and will play in the new world of voluntary universal connectedness.

The very nature of universal connectedness has created what John Husband has called "Wirearchy", where leadership assumes a personal dimension based on voluntary association. The working definition of Wirearchy is *"a dynamic two-way flow of power and authority, based on knowledge, trust, credibility and a focus on results, enabled by interconnected people and technology"*.

Husband explains that,

> "Wirearchy is an emergent organising principle that informs the ways that purposeful human activities, and the structures in which they are contained, is evolving from hierarchy's command-and-control (top-down direction and supervision) to champion-and-channel ... championing ideas and innovation, and channeling time, energy, authority and resources into testing those ideas and the possibilities for innovation carried in those ideas."

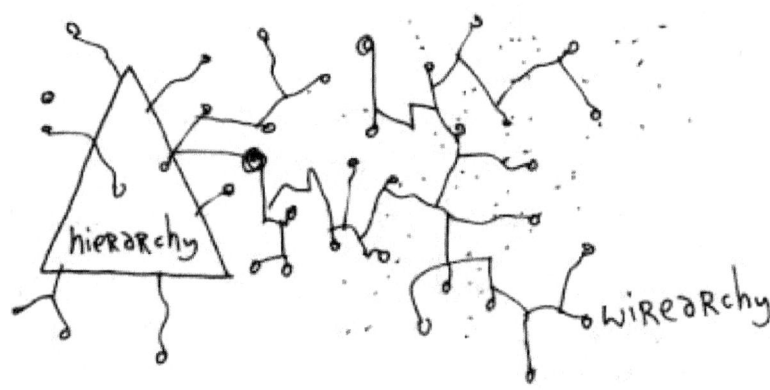

Figure 1: Hierarchy and Wirearchy

The idea of "Wirearchy" can be best understood as a living adaptive system.

Living adaptive systems are neural-like networks of interacting, interdependent agents who are bonded by common goal, outlook or need. They are changeable structures with multiple, overlapping relationships, and like the agents that comprise them, are linked with one another in a dynamic, interactive network. In digital terms it can be likened to the emergence of open-source software development where no one owns the outcomes of the adaptive learning system. In human terms they are about individual and collective meaning-making, sense-making and connection-making.

In the context of organisations, neural-like networks represent real and virtual teams while the interacting and interdependent agents represent individual team members. These teams are now dynamic in nature in that each individual member is working independently as well as interdependently on their own tasks in an effort to contribute to the team's main objective. The emergent role and structure of teams, in a digitally connected world, requires a reconsideration of leadership from power of position in a hierarchy to the influence of person in a wirearchy. So what are the key attributes of living adaptive systems?

Living adaptive systems, aka wirearchy, have six primary attributes: they operate in open systems, they are self-organising, they operate on the *edge of chaos*, they adapt to external changes, and they require interactions among individual agents, ultimately resulting in a new emergent structure.

- Openness - Systems theory and systems thinking operate in closed systems, a change in one part of the system results in an expected and predictable change in another part of the system. Closed systems provide a level of predictability and are partially sheltered from external forces. Open systems are non-linear, unpredictable, in which changes in one part of the system could lead to predictable results just as easy as unpredictable results,
- Self-organising - Operating in open systems requires self-organising systems compared to controlled sys-

tems. Systems that are controlled, or directed every step of the way, are less able to react to multiple threats or opportunities emerging from the environment (external to the system). Systems that are capable of self-organising, and reorganising as needed, are better able to operate in open systems more effectively compared to controlled systems,

- Edge of chaos - The *'butterfly effect'* is about small changes in one part of a system creating dramatic changes in other parts of the system, if not the whole system. Sometimes these changes are planned, but other times they are reactive to external forces (such as governmental policy changes, industry changes, pandemics). Managing these butterfly effects are what living adaptive systems do, they operate on the *edge of chaos*: "they are able to balance order and chaos",
- Adaptability - Being able to adapt to external forces is one requirement when operating in open systems. For a system to self-organise, alter its course and reorganise, it must be adaptable. Adaptive systems have a high degree of awareness to their context as well as a high capability to change internally,
- Emergence - Living adaptive systems operate interdependently in a dynamic manner that facilitates interactions among the system's agents (individual team members) with the potential of producing emergent new structures,
- Interactive - Interactions are a reflection of causal processes at the lower levels, and can represent structural or behavioural processes. When we consider behaviour in a team setting, facilitation of constructive conflict (as opposed to destructive conflict) will improve a team's interactions and help in becoming more adaptive.

The environment we live in is in a constant state of disequilibrium and, as an open living system, is self-organising - there is no one in charge directing the system what to do - apologies to any believers to the contrary. All systems that exhibit disequilibrium and self-organisation are called dissipative - they are continually breaking up and reforming. If you don't believe then just lie on the grass and watch the clouds go by as part of the weather system. Not only is our physical body itself such a dissipative structure, but every organ and cell as well.

Dissipative structures are those which are able to maintain identity only because they are open to flows of energy or information from their environments. More recently, this idea has been expanded to include whole systems, which are labelled dissipative systems. Dissipative systems, rather than responding to disturbance by breaking down into a system of lower order, (as we were taught to believe is an inevitable consequence of Newton's second law of thermodynamics) can, in some instances, respond by re-configuring into a system of higher order.

Understanding how systems are able to do this is a dramatic departure from traditional methods that focus on in-depth analysis. Complex adaptation is characterised not only by a high degree of interaction among component parts but also by the way that the particular nature of this interaction (the way that the system is organised) generates emergent outcomes not related, in a linear way, to the initial conditions. While linear organisation is generally predictable in its consequences, emergence is characterised by a non-linear mode of organisation that can generate non-obvious or surprising consequences, known as emergent properties.

Your brain is a non-linear system that demonstrates emergent properties. "Where did that come from?" is an observation we often make when we see a solution to a problem that bears no relationship to the analysis of that problem or some prior knowledge. Emergence is not easy to understand so let's take the example of sugar.

Sugar is comprised of individual elements of carbon, hydrogen and oxygen and its chemical formula is $C_6H_{12}O_6$. Sugar has the quality of sweetness which cannot be found in the individual elements of carbon, hydrogen or oxygen. Sweetness is an emergent property of sugar that defies explanation. For that matter so is our sense of taste.

Many biological systems commonly exhibit emergent behaviour. The complex behaviour of flocks of birds, colonies of ants, swarms of bees and schools of fish emerge from the interactions of the constituent parts of the respective systems.

Consider an ant colony. In the absence of centralised decision making, ant colonies exhibit complex, problem-solving behaviour. This behaviour emerges from the reaction of individual ants to simple chemical stimuli - from larvae, other ants, intruders, food and waste.

In turn, each ant produces chemical signals, providing a stimulus that other ants respond to. From simple interactions, leading to self-organisation, ant colonies have demonstrated the ability to collectively solve geometric problems, such as optimising their foraging route to and from food resources.

The idea of emergence, though, isn't confined to living systems. It pervades all areas of science and is a manifestation of other complex interactive systems in our daily lives, such as stock markets, the connectivity of the internet, and traffic flow.

Despite the pervasiveness of emergent behaviour there remains no deep understanding of emergence. At each level of complexity, new laws, properties and phenomena arise and herein lies the problem. Living adaptive systems are at the centre of understanding emergence in the universally connected world that we now live in.

A living adaptive system is an open system that describes relationships and transitions, and results in turbulence, or as it has become to be described, VUCA – volatile, uncertain, complex and ambiguous. Emergence suggests a random like, absence of a purposeful nature to evolution, but if we look beneath the surface there is innate purpose in our emergent development: at its most obvious it is to reach the maturity of adulthood. At its most obscure it is to be co-responsible creative agents for the good of the whole system. Complexity, connectivity and creativity have an interdependent relationship in that purpose.

What we are seeking to discover is the nature of the co-responsible creative role for the good of the whole system we are best equipped to engage in. It is in this co-responsible creative agent for the whole system that the new person-based role of leadership happens. It has a quality of emergence, that is not able to be explained in linear cause and effect terms. Our leadership role emerges by us just being there. So how might we recognise it?

The essence of emergent leadership is about the central role of choice-making in all that we do as co-responsible creative "knowledge workers" in the living adaptive system. Leadership now needs to be understood, in the universally connected "knowledge work" world of "Wirearchy", as a personal emergent choice-making role open to all.

This personal role of leadership is no longer a simple extension of management authority, in the closed hierarchic power structures of command and control, that is experienced as position-based leadership. Person-based emergent leadership, in a connected knowledge intensive living system, requires three essential qualities. They are the three "eyes" of emergent leadership:

- Insight - the capacity of seeing your growth potential, by comprehending the inner and outer nature of your voice and developing your influence,
- Intention - the commitment to carry out an action in the future that involves establishing your vison and taking the initiative, and
- Integrity - the consistent and uncompromising adherence to strong ethical principles and values as a foundation of your identity.

The word "eye" is a homophone of "I" - hence the three "Is" of insight, intention and integrity, that are the "eyes" foundation of emergent leadership.

While these personal attributes may have been seen as important qualities in position-based leadership, they were often misapplied in an effort to get "engagement" with remotely developed goals and plans of those in power and failed to recognise the fundamental nature of "connected knowledge work" in a universally connected world of those with energy. Energy is the source of power not the other way around!

To help you explore this territory of "connected knowledge work", and play your leadership role in it, the Adaptive Learning Map© has been developed. The Adaptive Learning Map© allows you to stand back from what you are experiencing so you can "see", then explore, your experience-based lens of personality, that is no longer adequate in the new world of instantaneous universal connection. The Map© is the consistent framework that underpins the entire book and allows you to make your own sense and meaning out of what is presented. For now, it looks like this.

INSIGHT INTENTION AND INTEGRITY

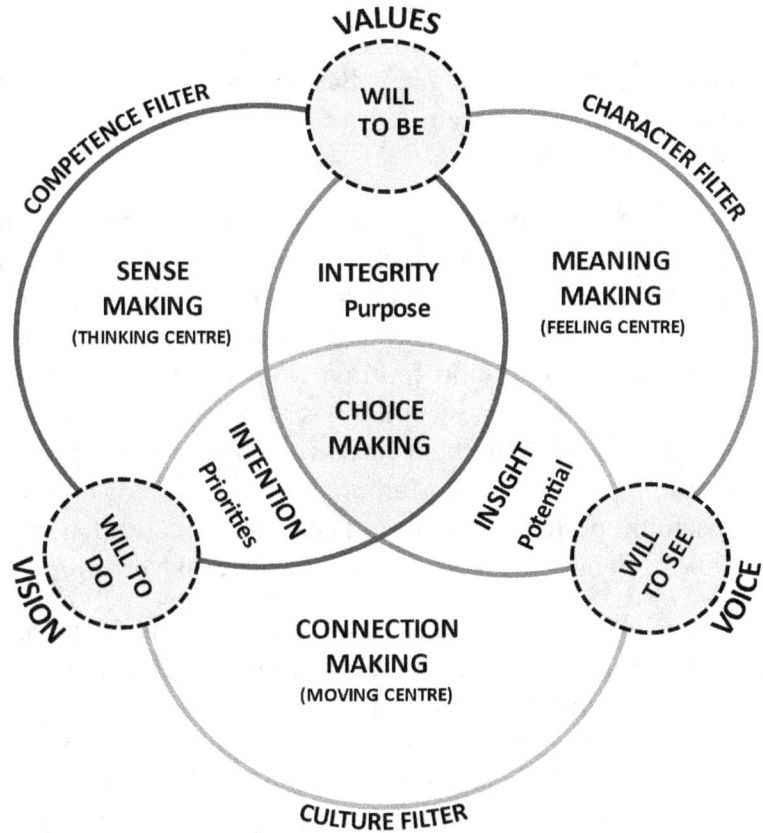

Figure 2: The Adaptive Learning Map©

Learning is a lot like breathing. Breathing just happens by being there. So it is with learning. They are both automatic responses to the 'atmosphere' we find ourselves in. Breathing is about taking in air, (which comprises 78% nitrogen, 21% oxygen and smaller amounts of argon and carbon dioxide) and absorbing the parts we benefit from (oxygen) and discarding the residue. Sometimes the air is polluted, and it can have an impact on our short and long term health.

Learning is somewhat similar. We take in a range of information using our five senses and absorb what we need in that moment and discard the stuff that doesn't fit with our past learning. Sometimes the information contains mysterious beliefs and assumptions, and it can affect or short-term and long-term behaviour, often without us realising it. We develop habit-based responses that becomes our learning "immune system", and they can impact on our short and long-term health.

Our source of information, as learning inputs, has often been prescribed by significant others, such as managers, teachers, trainers and learning and development professionals, in nicely structured and closed boxes that can be controlled, usually prescribed, by job descriptions, curriculum and training workshops. It is called formal, sometimes rote, learning and it has its place when you need to memorise information that may be useful in undertaking tasks that call for technical knowledge. Memorising that one plus one equals two is useful in performing certain tasks that demand that knowledge. Our recall of this knowledge is automatic, like breathing.

Fortunately learning is also different from breathing. It is a reflection of our past experiences. We are inducted into the culture and values by significant others. It is learning by immersion. We may have learned as much in the playground at school as in the classroom. It is the foundation of our beliefs and assumptions that we accumulate through our connection with others. We learn to defend these beliefs and assumptions as "knowledge" and apply them in the same way we apply our formal learning as knowledge. We enjoy the certainty of being correct. The formal and informal learning systems both encourage us to please, or obey, our significant others by being correct and behaving appropriately.

As we mature we begin to realise that we are choice-making beings who engage in meaning-making, sense-making and connection-making in an everchanging environment. Our skills in using judgement, empathy, integrity and influence, for example, are learned in a living, changing environment. We learn to see the interdependencies between problems and opportunities and develop our aspirations, autonomy and acumen. We engage our initiative and demonstrate ingenuity. We understand that learning is situational. We take intentional responsibility for our learning. We are people, connecting with other people, who are learning by interacting.

With the emergence of universal connectedness in the digital age we no longer have to memorise everything and store it in our brain. Of course that has always been the case: we once had volumes of encyclopedias we could laboriously access. However we now have real time access to both stored knowledge on the internet, and to the knowledge of others, through digital connection. Being knowledgeable is now about knowing where to find the information we need in real time. We learn through connection-making. It is called adaptive learning.

The interdisciplinary nature of the problems we face puts a new emphasis on the personal role of knowledge sharing. It is in this connected world of knowledge sharing that we can become adaptive learners in developing our knowledge, and that of others, to solve complex problems. The universally connected space requires personal leadership skills that are not anchored in the position-based hierarchic organisation model. In this new world everyone can be a leader and take the initiative to connect with, and influence others, in solving complex problems. It is about choice-making as a key to exercising leadership through knowledge sharing. Learning and leadership become adaptive and integrated.

In the world of interdependence and emergence (interdependence and emergence always existed in the natural order but was below our consciousness) that we are now more explicitly experiencing, we can now apply the idea of living adaptive systems to our understanding of leadership from both a positional and personal perspective. We can do this in a way that reflects hierarchy and wirearchy as coexisting and complimentary structures in the 'territory' we individually and collectively engage with.

Leadership is not about 'either/or' but 'both/and' choice-making. It is about developing skills in the synthesis of different perspectives, sometimes polar opposites, and these skills can only be developed in interaction with others. We have been taught from an early age that there are 'right' answers to every question and were continuously tested on being correct. As a consequence we even developed the ability to pretend we know and blustered our way through using old hierarchy driven methods that don't work. In a VUCA world it is about responding to complex problems by 'not knowing'. When it comes to emergent leadership 'know-alls' need not apply!

The leadership challenge is now about integrating the creativity that emerges by connecting the knowledge of self and others in your wirearchy and synthesising it to innovate and solve complex problems using the hierarchy. Creativity needs wirearchy and innovation needs hierarchy.

In this context leadership is about understanding your own meaning-making, sense-making and connection-making mindsets and how they impact on your choice-making and that of others. It is people rather than position centred. Against that background let's look at the nature of internal territory that is reflected in the foundations of self.

CHAPTER 3
The Foundations of Self

Now that we have considered the external choice-making territory let's look at our internal choice-making territory so that we can understand the foundations of our self. The complexities of the foundations of self cannot be fully explored in one chapter so this is about providing some touch points on a number of reasonably well-regarded approaches to understanding 'who we are', that have emerged over many years.

Notwithstanding the diversity of views about our sense of self it is clear that there is a general acceptance of the relationship between nature and nurture in almost all discussions about who we are.

Was Humpty Dumpty a product of nature or nurture?

> 'And how exactly like an egg he is!' Alice said aloud, standing with her hands ready to catch him, for she was every moment expecting him to fall. 'It's very provoking,› Humpty Dumpty said after a long silence, looking away from Alice as he spoke, ‹to be called an egg - very!'
>
> 'I said you looked like an egg, Sir,› Alice gently explained. ‹And some eggs are very pretty, you know,› she added, hoping to turn her remark into a sort of compliment.

> *'Some people,'* said Humpty Dumpty, looking away from her as usual, *'have no more sense than a baby!'*

The nature versus nurture debate involves the extent to which particular aspects of behaviour are a product of either inherited (genetic) or acquired (memetic or learned) influences.

Nature is what can be thought of as pre-wiring and is influenced by genetic inheritance and other biological factors.

Nurture is generally taken as the influence of external factors after conception, e.g. the product of exposure, especially to caregivers, life experiences and learning on an individual.

We are all born with specific genetic traits inherited from our parents, such as eye colour, cleft chin and sneezing when exposed to bright sunlight – or being the shape of an egg in Humpty Dumpty's case. Beyond our basic genetic make-up, however, there is a deep interaction between our genes and our environment. Our unique experiences in our environment influence whether and how particular traits are expressed, and at the same time, our genes influence how we interact with our environment. There is a reciprocal interaction between nature and nurture as they both shape who we become, but the debate continues as to the relative contributions of each.

New research into epigenetics - the science of how the environment influences genetic expression - is changing the conversation. As psychologist David S. Moore explains in his book, *The Developing Genome*, this quickly emerging field reveals that what counts is not what genes you *have* so much as what your genes are *doing*. And what your genes are doing is influenced by the ever-changing environment they are in. Factors like stress, nutrition, and exposure to toxins all play a role in how genes are expressed - essentially which genes are turned on or off. Unlike the static black and white conception of nature or nurture, epigenetic research demonstrates how genes and environments continuously interact to produce our individual characteristics throughout our lifetime.

INSIGHT INTENTION AND INTEGRITY

For the longest time, the nature-nurture debate has been cast as a kind of contest between genes and experiences. The thought was that we might have some characteristics that are caused primarily by genetic factors and other characteristics that are caused primarily by experiential factors. What epigenetics is making clear is that's a faulty way to think about the situation, because it's not true that genes do things independently of their contexts. Instead, genes do what they do because of the contexts that they're in. Nature and nurture are always working together to produce all of our traits.

We all begin life connected to our mother by an umbilical cord and inherit our genetic individuality from our biological parents. Connection-making is our primary nature-based foundation. We then find ourselves in the arms of our mother and initially are impacted by touch. We are fed and cuddled and begin to develop our feelings and emotions as our secondary nurture-based self and we develop our meaning-making mindset. We are inducted into the belief systems of our caregiver and family.

Then there is a third, and largely overlooked, stage as we develop an awareness of our surroundings through our sight, hearing, smell and taste senses. We develop our own unique navigation skills as we interact with our environment and those in it. We develop our thinking and gain knowledge about how to operate in our specific environment. As we develop our navigation skills, and its associated knowledge, we begin to question the nurture-based beliefs we adopted from our family context. We develop our sense-making mindset.

As we combine those three experiences of connection-making, meaning-making and sense-making we establish a foundation for our choice-making to meet our needs. We develop a unique sense of self.

The diagram below captures these three experiences and their related mindsets

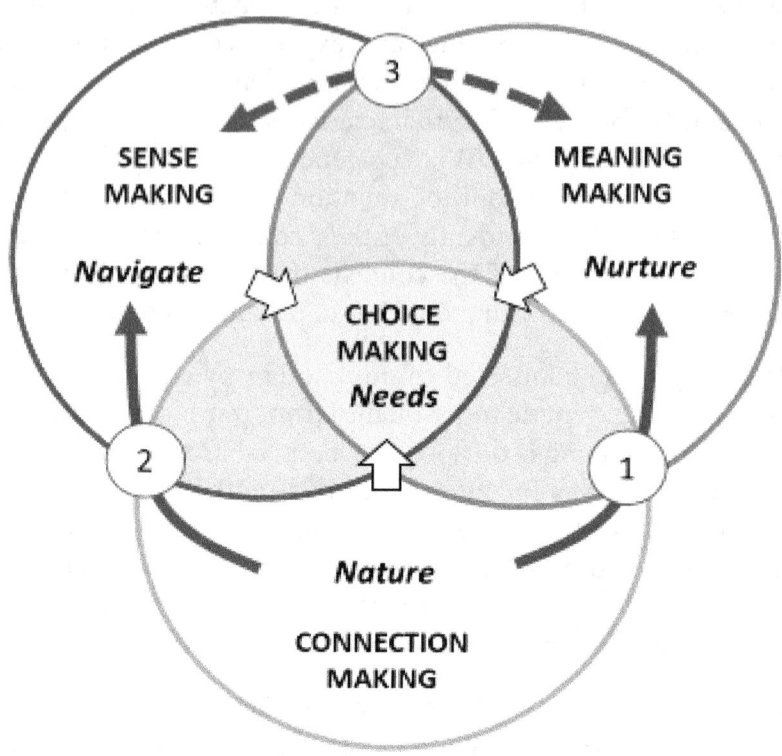

Figure 3: The Foundations of Self

At its most basic our instinctive nature based drive provides us with an internal protective mechanism called "the fight-flight-freeze/fold" response when we are in our connection-making space. This is not a planned, deliberately thought-out reaction, but a rapid-fire, automatic, total body response that we share with other animals. Whenever we perceive that we are in danger our bodies make a heroic and rapid response. Numerous neurotransmitters and hormones produce massive changes in every organ system. The brain sends instantaneous signals to the adrenal glands to secrete epinephrine or, as it is also called, adrenaline. At the same time the brain releases a related substance, norepinephrine, which affects only the brain itself. Simultaneously, increased amounts of steroids flood into the bloodstream, as well as opioid substances that are pain relievers.

In the fight or flight part of the response, heart rate, blood pressure, and respiratory rate increase along with alertness and vigilance. Simultaneously a decrease occurs in feeding, reproductive activity, and immune response. This radical adjustment is in the service of survival, preparing us to make an immediate response to the dangerous situation. When this reaction is a response to a real danger it is time-limited, effective, life-saving and highly adaptive.

If there is no chance for survival if we try to run or fight, we may automatically freeze. The freeze/fold response activates a very different sequence of autonomic nervous system arousal, slowing the heart rate, causing us to fall over and thus preserve blood flow, and even simulate death so that a predator loses interest.

We can now consider the interdependencies between our developmental experiences in our environment. Our first developmental experience is between nature (connection-making) and nurture (meaning-making). Our second developmental experience is between nature (connection-making) and navigate (sense-making). Our third developmental experience is the never-ending reconciliation between nurture (meaning-making) and navigate (sense-making).

These three "learning loops" contribute to our needs as we develop – initially instinctive, then emotional, then rational and ultimately aesthetic and self-actualising. Our needs are both consciously and unconsciously the drivers of our choice-making. Each of these developmental experiences are underpinned by three approaches that have emerged in studies of early childhood development – our nature-based, nurture-based and navigation-based approaches.

Firstly our *nature-based* instincts show up in our connection-making needs. Karen Horney developed a theory of ten relationship driven needs that reflect three behaviour tendencies that impact on our connection-making – moving toward, moving against and moving away from others.

The following table summarises the ten needs Horney identified.

Needs	Behavioural (Connection-making) Tendency and Type
Affection and approval	Movement toward other people (the compliant personality)
A confident partner	
Power	Movement against other people (the assertive personality)
Exploitation	
Prestige	
Admiration	
Achievement	
Self-sufficiency	Movement away from other people (the detached personality type)
Perfection	
Narrow limits to life	

As you can see these connection-making (relationship driven) needs are grouped into three broad categories:

- **Needs that move you *towards* others (compliant types):** these needs cause individuals to seek affirmation and acceptance from others. They are often described as needy or clingy as they seek out approval and love,
- **Needs that move you *against* others (assertive types):** these needs result in aggressiveness and a need to control other people. These individuals are often described as difficult, domineering and unkind,
- **Needs that move you *away* from others (detached types):** these needs create separateness and antisocial behaviour. These individuals are often described as cold, indifferent and aloof.

These needs come into existence because of a person's intensive and compulsive pursuit of their needs as the only way to resolve basic anxiety.

Satisfying these instinctive needs will not help them feel safe and secure but will continue to contribute further to the desire to escape the discomfort caused by their anxiety. They unconsciously seek gratification of these needs to cope with their anxiety and they tend to focus on only one need and compulsively seek its satisfaction in all situations.

In summary, our nature-based instincts, that underpin our connection-making, develop:

- Compliant (move towards people) personalities seek their satisfaction from the affection and approval they receive from the people around them. Compliant personalities tend to achieve a goal through the manipulation of others, and they present themselves as helpless; they tend to hide their desire for control and exploitation.
- Assertive (move against people) personalities find their satisfaction in having their superiority affirmed through others by excelling and receiving recognition.
- Detached (move away from people) personalities get their satisfaction from being self-sufficient and obtaining an emotional distance from everyone around them.

Secondly there are our *nurture-based* development as we interact with significant others, especially in our early infant development. It continues in our childhood development as we are inducted into the beliefs systems and associated behaviours of our family, and later our school, context. It is about our meaning-making centre.

Meaning making is anchored in object relations theory.

The term "object relations" refers to the dynamic internalised relationships between the self and significant others (objects). An object relation involves mental representations of:

- the object as perceived by the self,
- the self in relation to the object, and
- the relationship between self and object.

In the context of object relations theory, the term "objects" refers not to inanimate entities but to significant others with whom an individual relates, usually one's mother, father, or primary caregiver. In some cases, the term object may also be used to refer to a part of a person, such as a mother's breast, or to the mental representations of significant others.

For example, an infant might think:

> *"My mother is good because she feeds me when I am hungry" (representation of the object).*
>
> *"The fact that she takes care of me must mean that I am good" (representation of the self in relation to the object).*
>
> *"I love my mother" (representation of the relationship).*

Object relations theory stresses the importance of the meaning given to early family interactions, primarily the primary carer-infant relationship. It is believed that infants form mental representations of themselves in relation to others and that these internal images significantly influence the meaning given to interpersonal relationships later in life.

Internal objects are formed during infancy through repeated experiences with the primary caregiver. The images do not necessarily reflect reality but are subjectively constructed by an infant's limited cognitive abilities. In healthy development, these mental representations evolve over time; in unhealthy development, they remain at an immature level. The internal images have enduring qualities and serve as templates for future relationships.

INSIGHT INTENTION AND INTEGRITY

Central to object relations theory is the notion of splitting, which can be described as the mental separation of objects into "good" and "bad" parts and the subsequent repression of the "bad," or anxiety-provoking, aspects. Infants first experience splitting in their relationship with the primary caregiver: the caregiver is "good" when all the infant's needs are satisfied and "bad" when they are not.

Initially, these two aspects of the object (the caregiver) are separated in the mind of the infant, and a similar process occurs as the infant comes to perceive good and bad parts of the self. If the caregiver is able to satisfactorily meet the needs of the infant or - in the language of object relations - if the caregiver is "good enough," then the child begins to merge both aspects of the caregiver, and by extension the self, into an integrated whole. If the caregiver does not satisfactorily meet the infant's needs, the infant may repress the "bad" aspects of the caregiver and of the self, which may cause difficulty in future relationships.

There are three fundamental "affects" that can exist between the self and the other as a result of their early childhood development – frustration, rejection or attachment.

People with the frustration object relations affect know what will make them happy, but they feel they seldom have it. However, once they find the source of their happiness, they tend to become disappointed and disillusioned with it. As a result, they become frustrated as they begin their search again. Their sense of self is based on the search for an ideal. These types need to remember that they can find contentment by accepting their present experience.

People with the rejection object relations affect feel that they have been rejected by others. Others don't care about their needs, so they reject their own needs too. Consequently, their relationships often have issues of not wanting to be nurtured or touched. Despite feeling rejected, they feel they only have one gift to offer to prevent future rejection. Their sense of self is based on countering this rejection by offering their talent.

People with the attachment object relations affect tend to have a sense of contentment that their needs (with people, situation, things) are being met. Their sense of self is based on being deeply attached to things perceived as good. To attach themselves, these types adapt their ways to be consistent with important people or things. Attachment also has further styles that reflect avoidance and anxiety.

Let's look at attachment more closely. The four child/adult attachment styles are:

- Secure – autonomous;
- Avoidant – dismissing;
- Anxious – preoccupied; and
- Discordant – unresolved.

The table below shows the four adult attachment styles based on different levels of avoidance and anxiety:

INSIGHT INTENTION AND INTEGRITY

	High		
AVOIDANCE		**Avoidant:** Uncomfortable with closeness and primarily values independence and freedom; not worried about an other's availability. "I am uncomfortable being close to others. I find it difficult to trust and depend on others and prefer that others do not depend on me. It is very important that I feel independent and self-sufficient.	**Discordant:** Uncomfortable with intimacy, and worried about an other's commitment and love. "I am uncomfortable getting close to others and find it difficult to trust and depend on them. I worry I will be hurt if I get close to my partner."
		Secure: Comfortable with intimacy; not worried about rejection or preoccupied with the relationship. "It is easy for me to get close to others, and I am comfortable depending on them and having them depend on me. I don't worry about being abandoned or about someone getting too close to me."	**Anxious:** Crave closeness and intimacy, very insecure about the relationship. "I want to be extremely emotionally close (merge) with others, but others are reluctant to get as close as I would like . My inordinate need for closeness scares people away.
	Low	ANXIETY	High

Thirdly, there is the development of *navigation-based* approaches as we acquire knowledge and skills in our interactions with our environment and those in it. It is about our approach to problem solving.

Navigation is underpinned by our Harmonic coping (problem solving) style. There are three coping styles: reactive, positive outlook and objective.

People whose dominant coping style is the *reactive* approach are expressively reactive under stress. They tend to work themselves up when a problem happens and have a hard time containing their feelings. This emotional intensity allows them to feel the "realness" of the problem, even if it is a relatively small one. Venting their frustration allows them to move on to dealing with the issue. Wanting others to see the realness of the problem, they expect others to react. Such a reaction would confirm that others agree that indeed this is a big deal. If others don't respond in the way the reactive approach types want, they may become even more frustrated. The reactive approach is not naturally trusting of others. They have strong opinions and tastes and want to know where others stand. Their desire for a strong response from others may also be a test of trust.

People whose dominant coping style is the *positive outlook* approach are generally optimistic and tend to avoid negative thoughts or situations. Under stress, they seek to avoid the problem, distract themselves with something else, or minimise the problem. These types want to feel good and want others around them feel good. They would rather have everyone happy (including themselves) than to deal with problems or negativity (especially in themselves). Unfortunately this approach can lead them to deny the existence of their problems and therefore delay addressing them. These types also have issues with finding a balance between meeting their own needs and meeting the needs of others.

People whose dominant coping style is the *objective* approach try solving problems in an objective, unemotional manner. Unlike people of the reactive approach, they don't get worked up when problems happen, they remain cool and emotionally detached from them. When confronted by a problem, these types have issues about wanting everyone to work within a framework or structure.

These various dimensions of our foundations of self are shown in the diagram below which forms the underlying framework for our Adaptive Learning Map© that will be explored in the next chapter.

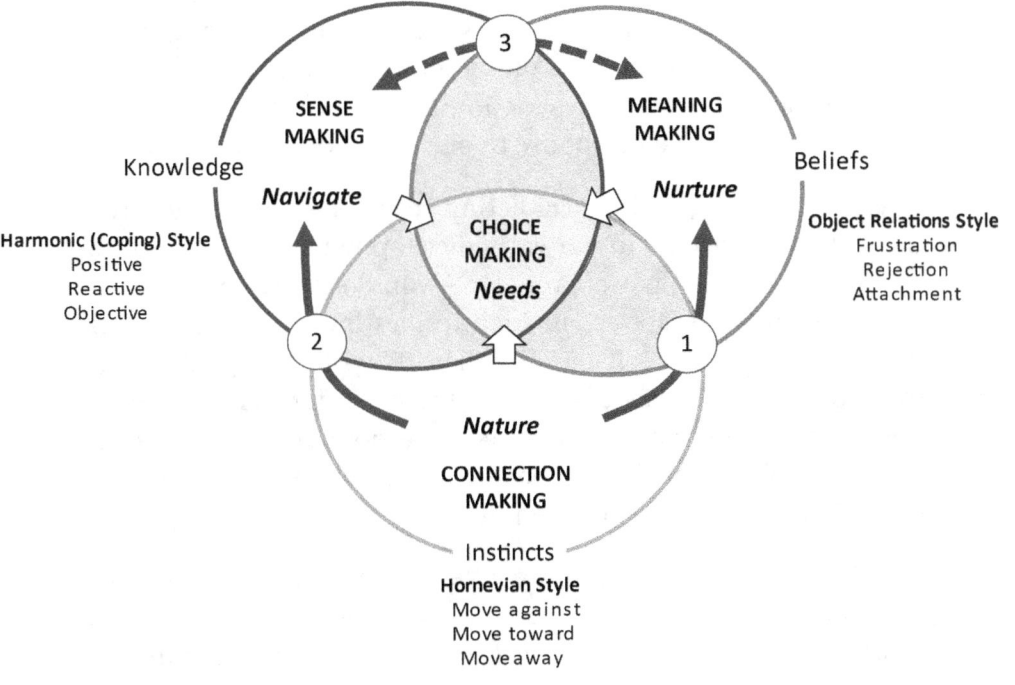

Figure 4: The Three Mindsets and Styles

It needs to be said that there is a significant degree of overlap between Hornevian, object relations and harmonic coping (problem solving) styles. These approaches are by no means meant to be more than a simplified way of providing some insight into the complex internal territory of self.

As we develop through childhood into adulthood our choice-making becomes the vantage point where the outside world confirms or contradicts the behaviour we have undertaken based on our choices.

If the outside world and others in it confirm our behaviour, it reinforces our self-identity and we come to define ourselves by what others expect of us and confirm as "true".

If the outside world and others in it contradict our behaviour, we tend to interpret their response as an attack on our self-identity and defend it. In primal terms we react by engaging in our preferred styles and our unconscious instinctive fight, flight or freeze behaviour. Invariably we come to reinforce our self-identity through the perceived response to our behaviour by others.

These confirming and contradicting responses that we get from the significant people in our early development shape our socialised choice making patterns – some would say create them. The scripts we develop about our identity destine us to become role players, acting out a self-identity that fits with the signals we get from the world "outside". We are truly "performers" – unconscious actors who have abandoned our spontaneity and genuine potential. We adopt the language of those in power and become slaves to the prevailing culture in all its forms.

Paradoxically we are very "creative" in maintaining this roles-based sense of self. Once we have become absorbed in our fixated roles we will defend it as our "real" identity without any conscious effort. However, deep down inside we recognise the debilitating nature of the mechanical and predictable conversations we engage in. We become creatures of our all-consuming economic and cultural context. As Louis Dumont says we are now members of the species *homo economicus* and consumers of the marketing images that sustain us. We develop what Jung calls a persona.

Persona is the Greek word for an actor's mask - the face shown to others. The word "persona" comes from the Greek word for the large masks that early Greek actors would use to portray their characters. With audiences in the big Greek amphitheatre the nuances of performances could easily be lost. The primary function of the mask was not to hide the actor but give information about the character.

INSIGHT INTENTION AND INTEGRITY

It reveals certain selected aspects of the individual and hides others. Jung saw the persona as a vital part of the personality which provides the individual with a container, "a protective covering for his or her inner self". A well-developed individual may have several personae appropriate to business and social situations. The problem comes not in having a persona but in identifying with it to the neglect of our inner life.

Jung said that the persona is that which in reality we are not, but which we, as well as others, think we are. The persona can be seen as our "psychological clothing." The persona refers to that aspect of the self that we present to the world for its approval. It is like a mask, and we can hide behind it. The persona is the mask or role that a person plays in society. While it gives information it can be used to hide the inner sense of who we are, to others and often, our self.

As a social role the concept of the persona is useful in allowing an individual to move in and out of relationships without being too vulnerable. A persona can be the oil to ease potential social friction.

A persona, as a social role, provides for some predictability of relationship. For example, the personas of doctor and patient or of student and teacher can be useful in knowing what to do, when, and where. Other examples of the persona are mother, father, husband, wife, lawyer, judge, policeman and baker.

Our persona becomes a problem only when a person becomes too attached to it and cannot put it aside, for example, when someone who is a judge is a "judge" all the time at work and at home, or perhaps, a teacher, or parent, who is in that role all the time. When a person cannot move flexibly between roles then the persona not only hides the person from others but also from themselves. It is difficult for such a person to have appropriate self-insight.

The idea of Transactional Analysis, developed by Eric Berne, proposes that we develop three ego states or personas, called Parent, Adult and Child that impact on every interaction we have with others.

Parent is a state in which people behave, feel, and think in response to an unconscious mimicking of how their parents (or other parental figures) acted, or how they interpreted their parent's actions.

Child is a state in which people behave, feel, and think similarly to how they did in childhood. The Child is the source of emotions, creation, recreation, spontaneity, and intimacy. When we are in the Child ego state we act like the child we once were.

In the Adult ego state the person uses logical thinking to solve problems making sure that Child or Parent emotions do not contaminate the process. Berne took the view that these ego states or personas were very difficult to change, especially when they occurred in stressful situations.

We will revisit this idea again when we look at connection-making in Chapter 9.

Consequently, we develop a sense of our self from our social, family, school and later, work context in a way that is sometimes not obvious to us. We get to unconsciously define our self-identity in power relations terms. Maturana says of power relations:

INSIGHT INTENTION AND INTEGRITY

> *"Power is action through obedience. ...We always concede power in order to conserve something - company, things, prestige, appearances, life ..... Obedience always gives rise to emotions of self-depreciation in the person that obeys.... Being obeyed gives rise to the emotion of pride and delusion of ownership of the transcendental right to be obeyed, emotions that unavoidably lead to blindness with respect to the other and to abuse. .... relations of power are not social relations because they always entail the mutual negation of the subordinate and the master as human beings. .... relations of power are defined by obedience, and, as I said above, obedience does not entail mutual acceptance. On the contrary, obedience entails mutual negation and pertains to a power system as a para-social system, not to a social system."*

Kurt Vonnegut gives us sound advice:

> *"...that we should be careful what we pretend because we become what we pretend. And something like that, a sort of self-depreciation, occurs in all organisations and human cultures. What people presume to be "human" is what they build in as the assumptions underpinning their social arrangements, and what they build in is sure to be learned by them: is sure to become a part of their character as they participate in that power relations context."*

The relationship between nature, nurture and navigate forms the three centres of intelligence we have:

- the Feeling Centre,
- the Thinking Centre, and
- the Moving Centre.

The diagram below shows the relationship between the three centres.

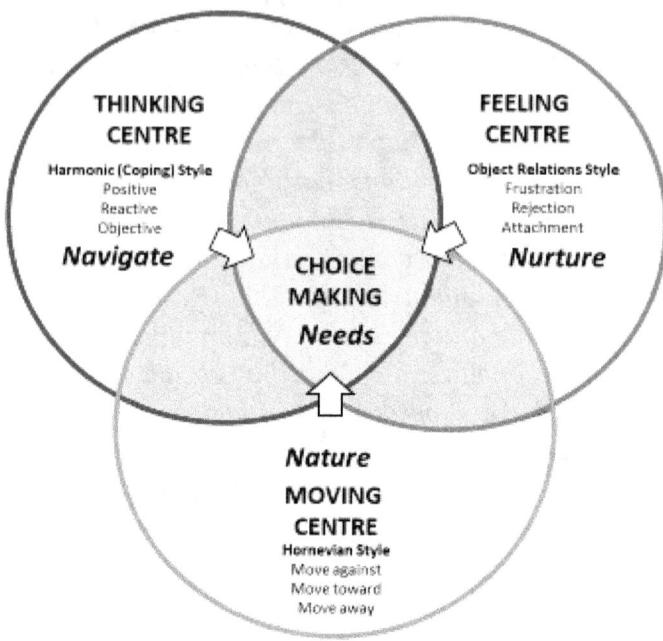

Figure 5: The Three Centres

Our Feeling Centre is a reflection of how we have used our feelings to inform our choices and to give energy to our meaning-making. Our Feeling Centre prefers to work in short sessions rather than finishing a task all at once, is interested in people and how they feel, is in tune with both its own emotions and those of other people, bases decisions on immediate feelings, and generates excitement and enthusiasm in group settings and enjoys new connections, experiences, and situations.

Our Feeling Centre is moderated by the choice-making function of feeling and has a values-based connection with past emotional experiences. The Feeling Centre is triggered by our information gathering function of intuition (a belief in possibility and future).

On the other hand, Thinking Centre is about the clarity of our sense-making. It is about our competence to solve problems. It is very much about objective evidence and facts informing our choices. It struggles with the idea of emergence that we discussed earlier because it cannot analyse and define it in linear ways. It is underpinned by our competence and knowledge. It pretends it knows even when it doesn't. The Thinking Centre likes to be in total control until you actively remind yourself to stay in the moment.

Our Thinking Centre is moderated by the choice-making function of thinking and has a logic-based connection to present problems. The Thinking Centre is triggered by our information gathering function of sensing (a sense of practicality and physical reality).

The Moving Centre is both a genetic and a socialised function, that operates automatically. It makes both the "instinctive at birth" and "learned through imitation" decisions open to it in the moment, then adopts those as its reference point for taking immediate action. It is reflexive in nature and operates without immediate reference to the other choice-making functions of thinking and feeling. It accesses these thinking and feeling functions "after the event" in order to confirm its initial response. The moving function is the missing automatic Jungian choice-making function.

The Moving Centre is essentially neural and chemistry system based and probably basal brain related, as that is said to be the centre of instinctive/automatic reactions to stimuli, and when aroused, sets of a series of chemical reactions that are highly focused on the immediate external environment. As it is socialised, and 'learns', the basal brain develops neural connections to the amygdala and cortex that manage feeling and thinking functions. It is concerned with outputs and gathers information through either a sensing or intuition function. It is triggered by external events unlike thinking and feeling which can have an internal or an external source. The instinctive moving function is automatic (internal to us in regulating breathing, digestion, etc.) and the learned moving function is triggered (needing external connection to operate in the moment). It is the function that is the foundation of connection-making.

In the Part 2 the ideas of instinctive drives, temperament, Maslow's needs and Jung's attitudes and functions model will be explored in relation to our meaning-making, sense-making and connection-making mindsets that are central to understanding the Adaptive Learning Map©. Let's look at how we might 'prepare to see' so we can make conscious choices that contribute to the greater good of the living adaptive system we are part of.

PART 2

PREPARING TO SEE

The second Part is about preparing to see. The first chapter in this part provides the essential structure of the book by developing the rationale behind the Adaptive Learning Map©. In the second chapter in this Part, the role and nature of choice-making, that sits at the centre of our leadership development contribution, is considered. The third chapter in this Part develops the personality lens based on the Jungian personality type model. The personality lens will be used to explore the three "eyes" of emergent leadership – insight, intention and integrity.

CHAPTER 4
The Adaptive Learning Map©

If we return to Humpty Dumpty we can see that before his fall from the wall he was also renowned for his understanding of the meaning of names of things.

"Must a name mean something?" Alice asked doubtfully. "Of course it must," Humpty Dumpty said with a short laugh; "my name means the shape I am - and a good handsome shape it is, too. With a name like yours, you might be any shape, almost."

Source: Through the Looking Glass: Lewis Carroll

Like Humpty Dumpty and Alice, no two people can have exactly the same version of themselves. While we all have similar neurological structure, it functions differently in all of us. This is the basis of our problems in communication when we try to impose our version of the 'territory' upon another person, as though it is a "shared map". Learning to recognise the structure of another person's 'territory' allows us to "see the world through their eyes" and therefore understand and relate to others respectfully, and perhaps, more accurately.

Our personal version of the external and our internal 'territory' has been created through gathering data through our five senses. Our senses bring certain aspects of the world to our attention, which go through neurological processes or filters, forming our values, beliefs, rules of conduct, and capabilities. These are often expressed consciously, yet most of the time they operate outside of our awareness, and we don't realise that they can be changed to serve us in better ways.

Generalisation is the basis for the formation of your beliefs. What you believe about the world is how you interact within it. It becomes your unique view of the territory - your personal mind map. However, your mind map always comes with certain inherent problems:

- it can be wrong without you realising it,
- it is by definition a reduction of the territory, which means it leaves out certain important information,
- it needs interpretation, which is a process that often leads to mistakes, and
- it can be outdated and represent something that has changed or no longer exists.

The distinction between map and territory is a useful metaphor of the differences between perception and reality. Your embeddedness in your own personality lens does not allow you to 'see' what others 'see'.

The father of general semantics, Alford Korzybski stated:

> "A map is not the territory it represents, but if correct, it has a similar structure to the territory, which accounts for its usefulness".

A properly constructed map is a representation of a particular area such as a city, a country, or a continent, showing its main features, as they would appear if you looked at them from above. It can be very useful in understanding where you are in the surrounding territory. What it does is provide a framework for understanding the relationship between places and spaces. And that's a better foundation for making situationally conscious choices than just relying on the experience-based habits of your own mind map, especially when you are in uncharted territory.

INSIGHT INTENTION AND INTEGRITY

Concepts can be seen as maps. Maps depict important information of reality. They show the roads that lead to our destination. They serve as orientation. When moving around as a stranger in unfamiliar surroundings, it is good to have helpful information for your orientation.

In this context, there is significant benefit from having a more generic map we can use to share our perception of the territory: a map that captures our experience and potential, and also that identifies our personal mindset locations and pathways. A map that shows the interrelationships between choice-making trigger locations that better enables you to understand your personal mindset and allows you to describe your collective reality. A map that enables you to explore the territory of adaptive learning.

Being an adaptive learner is about understanding the behaviours or traits that help you adjust and function well within a changing social, technological, ecological, economic and political environment and developing the ability and motivation to challenge your unique personal disposition in response to your connection with others. It involves the ability to regulate and adapt your behaviour to the demands of a situation in order to achieve your potential, priorities and purpose. It is associated with an internal locus of control. You move from being an outside-in responder to an inside-out initiator.

Learning is the adaptive process of acquiring new understanding, knowledge, behaviours, skills, attitudes, values and preferences. Leadership and learning are indispensable to each other.

The generic map we will be using is a in the form of a Venn diagram based on the Foundations of Self framework that was developed in the previous chapter and is called the Adaptive Learning Map©.

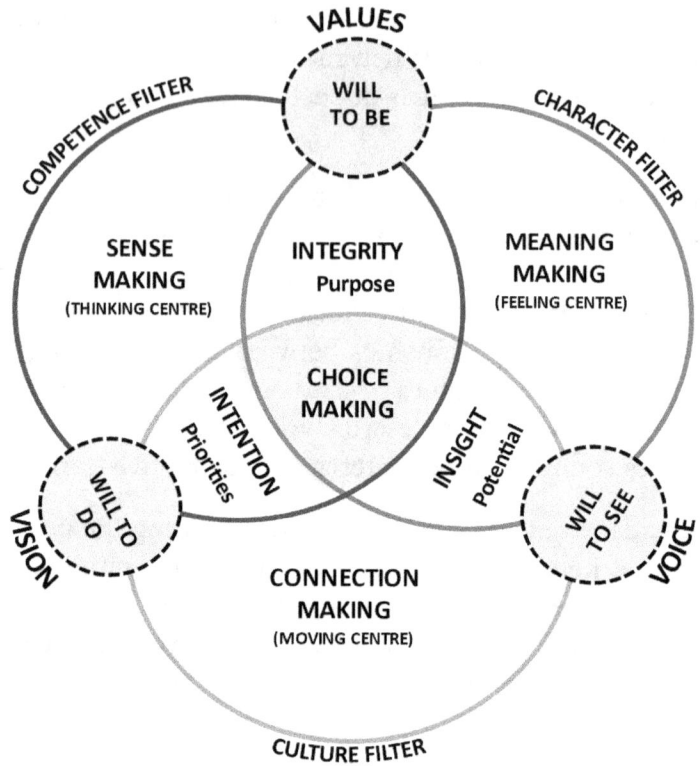

Figure 6: The Core Elements Adaptive Learning Map©

At the centre of the map is choice-making. Choice-making is the process we engage in as we experience the world in which we live: the territory. Mature choice-making is about making conscious and meaningful decisions to act or not. Our conscious choices generate new knowledge, new ideas and new behaviours that emerge from our connection to others. Mature choice-making sits at the centre of emergent leadership.

Reactive choice-making is messy and inevitably suffers from post-event rationalisation. When we are asked "why did you do that?", mostly we don't know, as our choices, as many as a thousand a day, are not made consciously but out of habit. Choices also have emergent properties, like the sweetness of sugar. We sometimes call it luck and other times attribute it to our cleverness.

Choices are based largely on our socialised human instincts as we adopt (or reject) beliefs in our interactions with significant others – parents, siblings, teachers, peers, friends, etc. Socialisation involves imitation, instruction and indoctrination, the three early childhood 'eyes' of our developing Reactive Self, as we interact with our external world. While those processes are never over it is our early development that provides the foundations of the three key mindsets of our Adaptive Learning Map© - meaning making, sense making and connection making.

We naturally need to give meaning to our experiences, to make sense out of what we experience and to have the experience of connecting with others, as we act upon the choices we make. We get feedback that provides 'pleasure or pain' responses and develop attraction and avoidance behaviours that influence how we see ourselves and how others see us. Sometimes we are in the third dimension of 'peace' which is an absence of pleasure or pain. Despite our obsession with duality there is always a third dimension – remember thesis, antithesis and synthesis or me, you, us.

Our choices become consistent over time as a product of our embedded meaning-making, sense-making and connection-making mindsets – there's that threeness again.

We notionally have three reactive choice making mindsets:

- Meaning-making - our emotional and intuitive responses which reflect our character - underpinned by our Feeling Centre,
- Sense-making - our logical and practical responses which reflect our competence – underpinned by our Thinking Centre, and
- Connection-making - our instinctive and interactive responses which reflect our culture – underpinned by our Moving Centre.

We generally have a preference for one of these three mindsets that works for us most of the time. Distortions in any of these mindsets, usually under some form of stress, is where most of us encounter our limitations.

Just being aware of these three distinct, but integrated, reactive mindsets can be a major challenge to those who choose not to be responsible for their behaviour, attribute blame for their circumstances to others, have a sense of entitlement and self-centredness, or need to have absolute control over their situation and those they interact with. We will look more closely at these three mindsets in subsequent chapters.

Reflecting on the map at Figure 6 we can see the three dimensions of reactive choice-making are integrated and informed by the three I's ('eyes') of emergent leadership which underpin the adaptive learning practices that are a natural situational response to the world of complexity that we inhabit, once we let go of our habit-based reactive mindset.

These adaptive learning practices are:

- Insight – which surfaces our Potential and supports the development of Influence and self-Image,
- Intention – which surfaces our Priorities and supports the development of Initiative and Ingenuity, and
- Integrity – which surfaces our Purpose and supports the development of Inspiration and Identity,

Insight is the reflective act of seeing into a situation, or the act or result of comprehending the inner and outer nature of things, or of seeing intuitively. It underpins mature meaning-making and engaged connection-making.

Intention is a mental state that represents a commitment to carrying out an action or actions in the future. Intention involves mental activities such as planning and forethought. It underpins mature sense-making and valued connection-making.

INSIGHT INTENTION AND INTEGRITY

Integrity is the practice of being true to self and showing a consistent and uncompromising adherence to strong moral and ethical principles and values. It underpins mature meaning-making and sense-making.

There are three higher level "learning loops" between the three "eyes" – between insight and integrity (I will do what I say I will do), between intention and integrity (I am competent to do what I say I will do) and between insight and intention (I understand what I need to commit to).

Reflecting back again on Figure 6, sitting in the overlap (unconscious) spaces between the three mindsets, are the three dimensions of our will – that are the energising essence of our personal potential, our personal priorities and our personal purpose.

Our will is an emergent quality of being human. Consequently, the will cannot be observed or analysed. Confused? Don't be, as that observation is just meant to provide some appreciation of the elusive quality of will. Understand that the will is the emergent choice-shaping and energising source of meaning-making, sense-making and connection-making even though the will itself does not have a causal explanation; it just is. Embracing the idea of our will is about having an internal freedom to act that challenges the way we have learned to apply our unconscious learned habits. The will is about an absence of external constraints. Our will enables us to own our choices as scary as that may be.

The will has three 'intelligences' that provide the adaptive learning source of the three "eyes" of emergent leadership. They are:

- the Will to See – the 'intelligence' to develop our Insight,
- the Will to Do - the 'intelligence' to develop our Intention, and
- the Will to Be – the 'intelligence' to develop our Integrity.

These three 'intelligences' of our will are connected to non-visible sources of energy that induce choice-making. To put these energies into context let's look at the insightful contribution of John G Bennett who developed a scale of twelve universal energies that contribute to the infinite (cosmic), living and material processes we are a part of.

His scale of energies provides us with a conceptual framework for seeing the unseen, and for understanding some of the hidden forces that are at work as we become more self-aware, and eventually at one with life itself.

The table below shows his twelve energy types and their basic descriptions.

Level	Energy Type	Description	Category	Awareness
E1	TRANSCENDENT	Energies of the divine	INFINITE (COSMIC)	SUBJECTIVE
E2	UNITIVE			
E3	CREATIVE	Energies of being		
E4	CONSCIOUS			
E5	SENSITIVE	Energies of responding	LIVING	
E6	AUTOMATIC			
E7	VITAL	Energies of growth		OBJECTIVE
E8	CONSTRUCTIVE			
E9	PLASTIC	Energies of form	MATERIAL	
E10	COHESIVE			
E11	DIRECTIVE	Energies of movement		
E12	DISPERSED			

Our externally triggered and habit-based Reactive Self is underpinned by automatic (E6) energy. This is the energy that underpins our present meaning-making, sense-making and connecting-making mindsets. However, the three 'intelligences' of will that underpin our freedom to make our own conscious, rather than externally triggered and habit-based choices, are underpinned by three higher energies:

INSIGHT INTENTION AND INTEGRITY

- the Will to See by sensitive (E5) energy – that enhances our choice-making by enabling us to be aware of our thoughts, feelings and bodily states. It allows us to say yes and no when we react to a situation - to develop insight and reflect upon the nature of our potential,
- the Will to Do by conscious (E4) energy – is of a higher order and underpins our choice-making by enabling us to be "aware of our awareness". It is about self-observation and allows us to give voluntary attention to any situation - to develop intention and activate our priorities, and
- the Will to Be by creative (E3) energy – is an energy beyond consciousness (it has an elusive quality) and underpins our choice-making by enabling us to be creative agents in our own transformation. It allows us to integrate our potential and priorities that are underpinned by our creativity and enables us to become whole - to develop integrity and a sense of purpose.

The will and the related higher energies will be considered in more depth in subsequent chapters suffice to say that accessing these energies involves the process of transformation that applies our 'will to see', our 'will to do' and our 'will to be' to our three mindsets of meaning-making, sense-making and connection-making. Our framework provides an integrated map for exploring those territories.

Sitting on the outer limits of our map are Voice, Vision and Values – the three macro drivers of adaptive learning.

Voice is our personal way of expressing our potential and is anchored in personal insight. It is our unique way of being situationally aligned with others and speaking our mind in ways that contribute to the common good in our connectedness with others. It represents the influence you want to have consistent with your values and vision. When you have insight you find the source of your voice.

Vision is what you want to create for yourself and contribute to the world around you. It is the long-term foundation of your intentions and enables you to have clarity about your priorities. It enables you to take the initiative when opportunities and problems present themselves. It requires ingenuity in order to create imaginative and even somewhat unrealisable intentions when based on your current sense of self and competencies.

Values are a reflection of the way we choose to live. Identifying your personal core values is one of the critical choices that shape the way we behave and live our life. Values reflect our sense of purpose and underpin our integrity. In the flow of connected choices, they provide the foundation that should influence all of our personal interactions. We derive a sense of fulfilment when living our personal values because our energy and behaviour is aligned with our purpose.

Let's just refresh our view of the Adaptive Learning Map©.

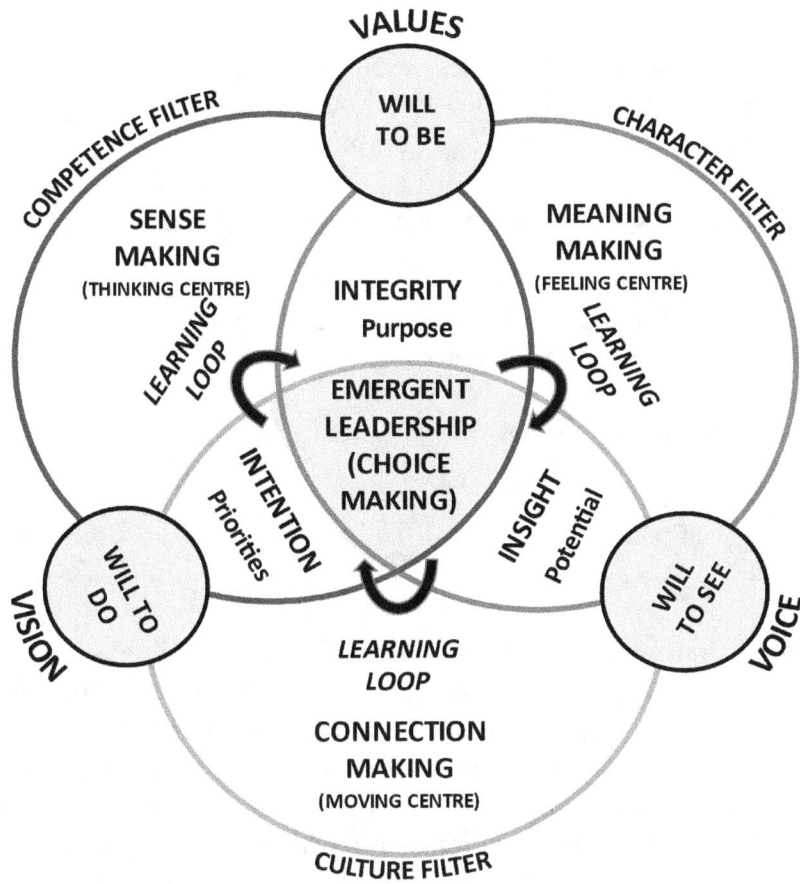

Figure 7: The Adaptive Learning Map©

So, the key locations identified in the Adaptive Learning Map© are:

The three reactive mindsets:

- Meaning-making and the Feeling Centre,
- Sense-making and the Thinking Centre, and
- Connection-making and the Moving Centre.

The three adaptive learning practices (the 'eyes') and their related learning loops:

- Insight that focuses on our potential,
- Intention that focuses on our priorities, and
- Integrity that focuses on purpose.

The three 'intelligences' of will and their energising elements:

- Will to see and sensitive energy,
- Will to do and conscious energy, and
- Will to be and creative energy.

The three macro drivers:

- Values
- Vision
- Voice

Rather than seeing complexity, stand back and see the simplicity and elegance of these relationships and reflect on the application of each dimension to your own choice-making approaches. This will be the map you are invited to use as you are provided with some more detail about each location on the map. You will be able to use the map to explore your personal development journey in life so far, by initially describing your meaning-making, sense-making and connection-making territory that determine what you are experiencing right now.

Remember the map is not the territory. It won't tell you when there will be sheep on the road, when an attraction is closed or when the winter menu at a local café is being offered. Just as it won't tell you if you believe in UFO's, grew up on a farm or are afraid of heights.

However, it will provide a structure for engaging your Feeling Centre, developing your Thinking Centre, and exploring your Moving Centre, and uncovering your habit-based blindness, that flow from your familiarity with your own territory. You will begin

INSIGHT INTENTION AND INTEGRITY

to see your territory, and that of others, through three new lenses – a new set of glasses – leading to the development your emergent personal leadership role in the new world of wirearchy.

You will understand the limitations of your present approach to choice-making and lay the foundations for engaging with the three 'eyes' of emergent leadership – insight, intention and integrity.

We are going to look at each location on the map separately in the following chapters.

Now that we have a map to guide us we can now get a deeper understanding of our choice-making territory that is central to our emergent leadership journey.

CHAPTER 5

The Choice Making Drivers

"We are our choices."
—Jean-Paul Sartre

Back with Humpty Dumpty again.

"I mean, what is an un-birthday present?" asked Alice. "A present given when it isn't your birthday of course." said Humpty Dumpty. Alice considered a little. "I like birthday presents best," she said at last. "You don't know what you're talking about!" cried Humpty Dumpty. "How many days are there in a year?" "Three hundred and sixty five," said Alice. "And how many birthdays have you?" asked Humpty Dumpty. "One!"

Source: *Through the Looking Glass: Lewis Carroll*

Alice and Humpty Dumpty had a different view of choice-making.

Choice-making is fundamental to emergent leadership in a wirearchy and sits at the centre of the Adaptive Learning Map©. Emergent leadership is about personal choice-making in emerging contexts: both your own and influencing those of others.

Choice is both our friend and enemy. It pervades all that we are and do. It can include judging the merits of multiple options and selecting one or more of them. We can make a choice between imagined options or between real options followed by the corresponding action. The arrival at a choice engages our mindsets of sense-making, meaning-making and connection-making and their underpinning thinking, feeling and moving centres.

Choice theory provides an explanation of motivation which is markedly different from what many of us have been taught. A central aspect of choice theory is the belief that we are internally, not externally motivated. While other theories suggest that outside events "cause" us to behave in certain predictable ways, choice theory proposes that outside events never "make" us to do anything.

What drives our behaviour are internally developed notions of what is most important and satisfying to us. Our internally created notions of how we would like things to be, are related to certain basic needs built into the genetic structure of every human being.

Choice theory is based on the idea that all behaviour represents our constant attempt to satisfy one or more of our basic needs. While our behaviour is often 'triggered' by external events no behaviour is 'caused' by any situation or person outside of us. Accepting this idea requires a paradigm shift on the part of those who view life according to stimulus-response theory. According to the stimulus-response theory, we answer the telephone because it rings and stop the car because the traffic light is red. From the stimulus-response perspective, behaviour is caused by someone or something (the stimulus) outside the individual; the action following is a response to that stimulus.

Choice theory says people or events outside us never cause us to do anything. Rather, our behaviour always represents the choice to do what we believe most satisfies our need at the time. From this perspective, we follow the rules of a game to achieve a meaningful outcome. We answer the phone because we choose to do so in order to communicate, not because we react to the ring. We stop at a red light because we choose to avoid risking a traffic ticket or an accident, not because the light turned red.

When we repeat a choice that is consistently satisfying, we exercise less deliberation in making that choice when a need arises.

INSIGHT INTENTION AND INTEGRITY

We have no choice but to feel pain when a need is frustrated and pleasure when it is satisfied. When any need goes unsatisfied, there is a continual urge to satisfy it. This urge is as much a part of human genetic instructions as is eye colour. Biological or primal needs related to survival - such as hunger, thirst, and sexual desire - are relatively distinct. We quickly learn that there is a particular discomfort attached to a survival need, and it is plain what we must do to satisfy that need.

The non-survival, or higher level psychological, needs are more challenging because it is often less clear what we must do to satisfy them. Psychological needs, like biological and physiological needs, have their originating source in the genes, even though they are much less tangible, and the behaviours that fulfil them are more complex than the physical behaviours used to fulfil survival needs.

The diagram below illustrates our latent needs based on Maslow's expanded model. This model is illustrative only as Maslow did not express them in this form. There remains some conjecture over the validity of these needs as they were not anchored in any serious research. However, they are a way of prompting you to reflect on their relevance to you, and as a recognition of a way of thinking about needs that have been a part of our belief system.

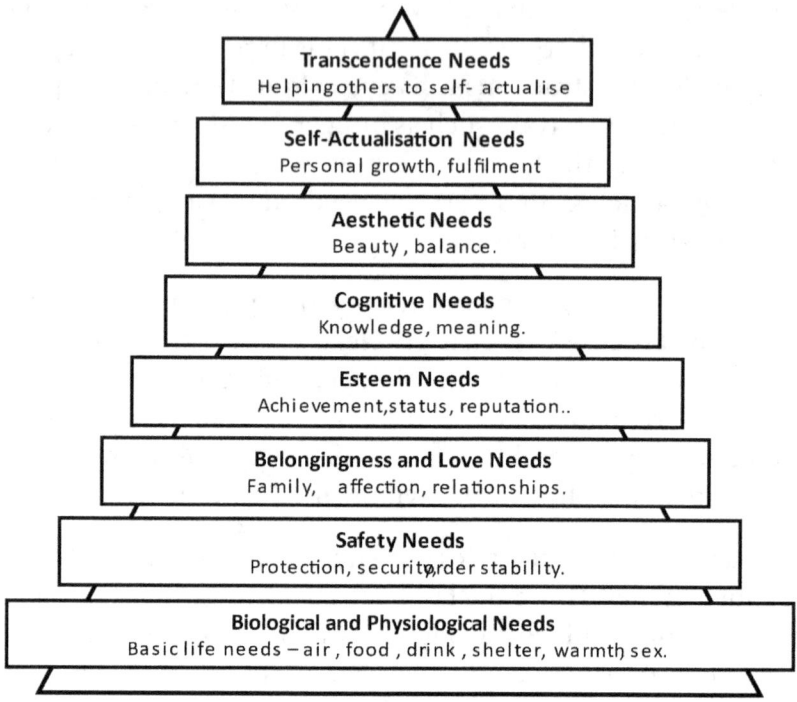

Figure 8: Maslow Needs as a Hierarchy

At different levels of needs-based maturity we attend to what we find attractive or aversive, as triggers of our choice-making. In their book, The Attention Economy, Thomas H Davenport and John C Beck identify the sorts of things that will grab our choice-making attention at each of Maslow's levels of bio-psycho-social needs in two ways: triggers that may be *aversive* or *attractive*.

The table illustrates Maslow's Attention Hierarchy based on this neat duality.

INSIGHT INTENTION AND INTEGRITY

	Biological and Physiological Needs	
PRIMAL INSTINCTS	*Aversive Attention* Hunger and thirst Sexual rejection Any threat to one's children Disease	*Attractive Attention* Food and water Sexual activity Caring for children Good health
	Safety Needs	
	Aversive Attention Suspicious strangers Weapons (other people's) Bad weather (hurricanes, blizzards) Natural disasters (fire, earthquakes)	*Attractive Attention* Trusted friends and family Weapons (one's own) Shelter from the elements Resources to cope with disaster
	Belongingness Needs	
CULTURAL EMBEDDEDNESS	*Aversive Attention* Loneliness Ostracism Disagreement Cruelty	*Attractive Attention* Intimacy Popularity Consensus Kindness
	Esteem Needs	
	Aversive Attention Subordination to others Captivity Low rank Bad reputation	*Attractive Attention* Authority above others Freedom High rank Good reputation
	Cognitive Needs	
	Aversive Attention Boring repetitive facts Information about unknown Incorrect information Lies	*Attractive Attention* New or interesting facts Information about self Accurate information Truth
	Aesthetic Needs	
	Aversive Attention Ugly objects Traffic noise Tasteless food Bad fashion sense	*Attractive Attention* Beautiful objects Music Haute cuisine Stylishness

INDIVIDUATION	Self-Actualisation Needs	
	Aversive Attention Ignoring personal potential Refusing to go out Fearing new ideas Clinging to social labels	*Attractive Attention* Developing talents Seeking adventures Expanding mind Defining individual identity
	Transcendence Needs	
	Aversive Attention Unethical behaviour Massive inner conflict Self-destruction	*Attractive Attention* Ethical behaviour Perfect inner peace Personal enlightenment

There are three levels in the hierarchy: primal instincts, cultural embeddedness and individuation that reflect our hierarchy of personal development through nature, nurture and navigation dimensions we discussed earlier. Even though human needs are essentially the same for everyone, the behaviours through which individuals choose to satisfy those needs may be quite different.

Beginning at birth, individuals have unique experiences that feel either pleasurable or painful. Through these experiences, individuals learn how to satisfy their needs. Because individuals have different experiences, the things they learn to do to satisfy their needs will be different as well. Each individual has memories of need-fulfilling behaviours specific to their unique life experiences.

These pleasurable memories constitute our choice-making world and become the most important part of our life. For most of us, this choice-making world is composed of perceptions representing what we have most enjoyed in life. These perceptions become the standard for our behavioural choices. Unlike the basic biological and physiological survival needs, which are the same for everyone, the perceptions in each person's choice-making territory are very specific and completely individual. We choose to behave in different ways to fulfil our needs because our choice-making territories are different.

INSIGHT INTENTION AND INTEGRITY

To satisfy our basic needs, we must exhibit behaviours. This means acting, thinking, feeling, and moving our body, all of which are components of the behaviour we exhibit in the effort to get what we need or want. Whenever there is a discrepancy between what we need or want and what we have, our behaviour shows it. Our motivation is always to behave in a way that meets present needs, often based on past experience, and, after those are satisfied, to meet future needs.

To satisfy our higher-level needs, we must be able to sense and feel what is going on both around us and within us, and then be able to make choices based on that information. When we notice a discrepancy between what we have and what we need or want, we behave by acting upon the world and upon ourselves as a part of the world. If we examine this behaviour, we will discover that there are four unconscious drives of that influence our choice-making behaviour.

These four drives, which often occur in an integrated way, are:
- Moving (e.g. walking, gesturing, resting),
- Thinking (e.g. reasoning, problem solving, analysing),
- Feeling (e.g. disliking, enjoying, anticipating), and
- Instinctive (e.g. fearing, cooperating, belonging)

In most interactive situations, we tend to be more tuned in to, and responsive to, our feelings than our actions, thoughts, or instincts. On the other hand, when we reflect on a situation, most of us are much more likely to apply one drive, such as thinking, than other drives, and, therefore, we tend not to view it as just one part of our integrated conscious choice-making behaviour. When we are asked to talk about a complex situation, we tend to describe the most obvious or recognisable factor, rather than see the whole choice-making picture.

Mature choice-making has a more conscious awareness of the connection to our potential, our priorities and our purpose that are surfaced if and when we begin to develop the three aligned conscious qualities of acumen, aspiration and autonomy.

Acumen, aspiration and autonomy underpin our mature choice-making self-belief. Without any one of them we will not be able to effectively operate with the confidence that underpins emergent person-based, rather than authority position-based, leadership.

Each of these mature choice-making attributes are at the centre of our Adaptive Learning Map© and integrate each of our mindsets of meaning-making, sense-making and connection making with each other and influence our preferred choice-making approach as shown below:

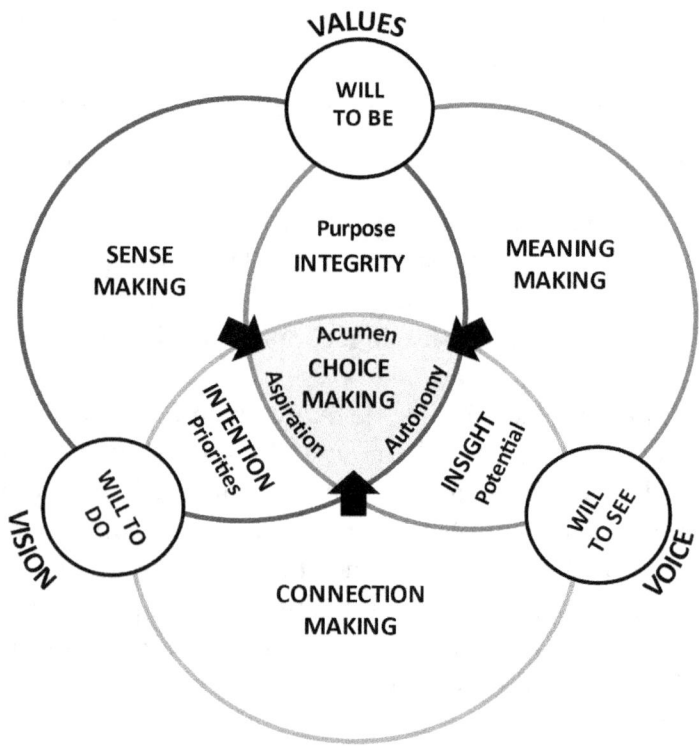

Figure 9: The Choice Making Experience

Acumen is quite elusive and is the intuitive foundation of wisdom. It is keenness and depth of perception. It is about seeing the interdependencies between things and the ability to quickly and accurately understand and make sound judgements about a situation requiring choice. While it is founded in our technical or intellectual ability it also reflects our intuitive and contextual know how rather than just our technical depth. Personal acumen means clearly seeing the integrated nature, or wholeness, of a situation and this can be difficult because of our blind spots. Blind spots are blinkers that we all have that prevent us from seeing the full picture. Acumen underpins integrity and integrates meaning-making and sense-making.

Aspiration gives energy to our intentions. Aspiration is future-oriented, driven by conscious and unconscious motivations and they are indicative of our commitment to a particular approach or end point. Aspirations are dynamic and are often connected to other aspirations held by us as well as to those held by others. Aspirations are multi-dimensional, varying in importance and timescale. They may be latent (unarticulated, evolving, abstract and uncertain) and can surface suddenly, or emerge slowly. Aspirations may be institutional, political, social or legal and can be both personal and shared. They may relate to home, school, work, national or international life. Whilst aspirations are future-oriented they may also pertain to the continuity of a present state of being. Aspiration underpins intention and integrates sense-making and connection-making.

Autonomy is generally understood to refer to the capacity to be your own person, to be directed by considerations, desires, conditions, and characteristics that are not simply imposed externally upon you, but are part of what can somehow be considered your conscious self. Autonomy in this sense seems an irrefutable value, especially since its opposite, being guided by forces external to the self and which we cannot authentically embrace, seems to be the height of oppression. Personal autonomy should also be distinguished from freedom. Generally, we can distinguish autonomy from freedom in that the freedom concerns the ability to act, without external or internal constraints and also with sufficient resources and power to make our desires effective. Autonomy concerns the independence and authenticity of the desires (values, emotions, beliefs, etc.) that move us to act in the first place. Autonomy underpins insight and integrates meaning-making and connection-making.

Our Adaptive Learning Map© provides the framework for exploring and developing the behaviour that allow us to live and lead with insight, intention and integrity and take responsibility for our choice-making behaviour.

As discussed earlier, our approach to choice-making our behaviour is influenced by three reactive key *habit-based* mindsets that attribute our behaviour to external forces, and three key *will-based* higher intelligences that attribute our behaviour to conscious choice and internal forces – our insight, intentions and integrity.

The three reactive habit-based mindsets that underpin reactive choice-making are:

- Connection-making (alignment of the instinctive-moving centres), that asks 'where am I?'
- Meaning-making (alignment of the intuitive-feeling centres), that asks 'who am I?', and
- Sense-making (alignment of the sensing-thinking centres), that asks 'how do I operate?'

The three emergent will-based higher intelligences that underpin emergent choice-making, which we will explore in later chapters, are:

- Will to See (Insight and the associated sensitive energy),
- Will to Do (Intention and the associated conscious energy) and,
- Will to Be (Integrity and the associated creative energy).

Now we have an understanding of our choice-making drivers let's look at the personality lens we use to make choices and influence the choices of others.

CHAPTER 6

Our Personality Lens

Let's go back to Alice in Wonderland.

"Would you tell me, please, which way I ought to go from here?" "That depends a good deal on where you want to get to," said the Cat. "I don't much care where –" said Alice. "Then it doesn't matter which way you go," said the Cat. "– so long as I get SOMEWHERE," Alice added as an explanation. "Oh, you're sure to do that," said the Cat, "if you only walk long enough."

Unlike Alice, before we explore the territory using the Adaptive Learning Map© we would benefit from having a deeper look at our personality lens so that we can know where we are and understand where we are going in the particular territory we are in. We need to make the unconscious conscious.

Our personality lens is the collective term for the instincts, temperament, social style and beliefs that each of us has developed that impacts, usually unconsciously, on our choice-making. It guides us in applying the embedded meaning-making, sense-making and connection-making mindsets we bring to the emergent leadership territory.

While there are a number of approaches that can be used to explore our instincts, temperament, and personality type, such as DISC, the Enneagram and Brain Dominance, we will be using the Jungian model, adapted by Myers Briggs, to understand our personality lens in more depth.

In their approach to personality type they identified two dimensions that interact with each other. They are attitudes and functions.

Attitudes that underpin our temperament are comprised of:

- *Extraversion,*
- *Introversion,*
- *Judging and*
- *Perceiving.*

Functions that underpin our social style are comprised of:

- *Sensing,*
- *Intuition,*
- *Thinking and*
- *Feeling.*

The four attitudes interact to create four dimensions of our embedded temperament:

- *Extraverted Judging (the Challenger temperament),*
- *Extraverted Perceiving (the Experimenter temperament),*
- *Introverted Judging (the Organiser temperament), and*
- *Introverted Perceiving (the Maintainer temperament).*

To moderate our temperament, we all have developed our own preferred and distinct centre pair (functions) *that reflects our particular learned Social Style:*

- *Sensing and Thinking pair (the Specialist style),*
- *Sensing and Feeling pair (the Harmonist style),*
- *Intuition and Thinking pair (the Catalyst style), and*
- *Intuition and Feeling pair (the Synergist style).*

While we have four social styles that reflect the four Jungian functions there is a fifth function that reflects our instincts and temperament drives as the unconscious, largely genetic, source of our identity that is the Moving function (or Centre). It is the instinctive "focal point" around which our personality lens operates. It unconsciously shapes the way the four Social Styles (Jungian function pairs) behave in their connection-making context.

Let's look at the Moving Centre in some more depth.

In his book Deeper Man, John Bennett discusses what he calls the three centred man and identifies the three centres as the moving, thinking and feeling centres or "brains". He says that generally speaking, everyone tends to have one of their centres of moving, thinking or feeling more active than others, which is consistent with the Jungian dominant function approach.

Bennett says:

> *"It is not immediately clear what forms the bodily or moving intelligence might take. Our difficulty in visualising the intelligence of the body brain arises because we think somehow it must be similar to the intelligence that we are aware of in the thinking brain. But it is not at all the same. The moving brain is associated with parts of the nervous system, the spinal cord and parts of the head brain, that do not work in the same way as those parts which operate in mental association. Our thinking intelligence is very much engaged in connecting past and future, but this does not enter the experience of the moving part. The intelligence of the body is almost wholly concerned with the immediate present. It does not make plans. It is not concerned with results in the future or correcting something that has happened in the past. Things are registered by the body, but not as memories the mind knows. They are either active or latent, but not yesterday or last year"*

and he goes on to say:

> "The activities of the moving centre are not already prepared. It is the moving centre which gives us the power of dealing with the world. We are able to move in most of the ways that animals can, apart from flying. We can climb, we can crawl, we can walk, hop and run and jump and dance, we can tumble and toss and turn. But it takes time to acquire these skills. Much of a child's learning consists of the recognition of objects and how to handle them, how to produce sounds; and how to walk and make other movements. For the most part these things are **learned by imitation**, which is a power of the moving centre." (the emphasis is mine)

The moving centre is both a genetic and a socialised function, that operates through automatic energy. It makes both the "instinctive at birth" and "learned through imitation" decisions open to it in the moment, then embeds those as its latent reference point that is available for future action. It is reflexive in nature and operates as a choice-making function without immediate reference to the other choice-making brain functions of thinking and feeling. When you have an itch you scratch it! It accesses these thinking and feeling functions "after the event" in order to confirm its initial response. "Ahh, that feels better!" The moving function is the missing automatic Jungian choice-making function.

The moving centre is essentially neural and chemistry system based and probably so-called R-brain related, as that is said to be the centre of instinctive/automatic reactions to stimuli, and when aroused sets of a series of chemical reactions that are highly focused on the external environment. As it is socialised, and 'learns', the R-brain develops neural connections to the cortex that exercises thinking and feeling functions. It is concerned with outputs and gathers information through the sensing function. It is triggered by external events unlike thinking and feeling which can have an internal or an external source. It is instinctive rather than intuitive.

Consequently, there are two dimensions to the Moving Centre. We have an *automatic or instinctive* moving function we cannot control and largely operates in the background to control our breathing, digestion, blood circulation, cell renewal, etc. and a *socialised or learned* moving function that operates in response to our environment as a survival mechanism to engage our socialised self-preservation, self-renewal and social primal instincts that form our instinctual stack. The instinctive moving function is automatic (internal to us in regulating breathing, digestion, etc.) and the learned moving function is triggered (needing external connection to operate in the moment).

Our Moving Centre has evolved, and in part continues to evolve, in a natural and organic way that has been shaped by three related capacities:

- our three primal instincts of self-preservation (security), self-renewal (continuity) and social (belonging),
- our temperament, which is our predisposition to respond to events in a specific extraverted/introverted and judging/perceiving driven way,
- our learned strategies for interacting with the world and others in it that reflect our social development – moving towards, moving against, moving away from and moving with others.

Our genetic disposition includes our three primal instincts (instinctive action/reaction drives) that operate to ensure our basic survival. These three primal instincts are our inheritance of our evolution from lower order to higher order beings and relate to the survival of our species: they are "hard wired" into our brain and related systems.

The three primal instincts are the self-preservation instinct (concerned with security), the self-renewal instinct (concerned with continuity) and the social instinct (concerned with belonging). It is worth mentioning that there are said to be five primal instincts: self-preservation, reproductive, territoriality, hierarchy and ritualism. They have been reduced to three by incorporating the last three, territoriality, hierarchy and ritualism, into one social instinct that reflects the nature of our belongingness to a group in terms of place, pecking order and custom-based behaviour. It needs to be said that these primal instincts are not to be confused with personality type or sub-type. They are the evolutionary heritage upon which our neural intelligence has evolved. They can be observed in many other forms of animal life.

Our human primal, or innate, instincts get socialised in context-specific ways based on cultural rituals, family traditions and geographic conditions. We develop an "instinctive stack" that reflects the way that our three instincts operate as a dominant, supporting and under-developed instinct, that are used to navigate our environment and interact with the people in it.

The brain's neural network connections, which develop through our interactions with our external environment, provide the socialised genetic expression of our dominant instinct. While the filters that decide what gets through to our brain are complex, and indiscriminate in many ways, it is useful to see our underdeveloped socialised instincts as a primary influence of our connection-making behaviour.

For instance, people for whom self-preservation is the least developed tend to have little instinct for how to take good care of themselves, perhaps putting themselves at risk for health problems or being financially inept. Their challenge is to learn good self-care and skills for managing their resources. Their challenge is to learn how to recognise risks associated with their personal well-being and be more aware of the potential of their habits to cause longer term harm to them and others.

An underdeveloped self-renewal instinct leaves a person uneasy in really close relationships, feeling vulnerable and exposed in intimate situations. It is hard for these people to sustain passionate feelings, and they lose energy in the midst of what they are doing, whether it is a relationship, a project, even a conversation. Their challenge is to learn to explore feelings, to allow themselves to feel exposed, and to consciously invest themselves deeply in whatever they are doing.

If the social instinct is the least developed, individuals have little instinct for how to engage with other people, often feeling awkward and getting into problem situations because of misunderstandings about social norms of behaviour. They need to learn how to value and respond to other people's need to belong, to engage with the group and to meet social norms.

A summary of these three primal instincts – self-preservation, self-renewal and social, and their attributes that have been developed by Katherine Fauvre, are shown in the table below:

Instinct	SELF-PRESERVING "I/me"	SELF-RENEWAL "You and me"	SOCIAL "All of Us"
Drive	The search for survival	The search for intimacy	The search for community
Focus	Self My Personal World	One other Our Intimate World	Others Our Collective World
Desire	Desire for Security Personal well being Food–Comfort–Safety Protection–Conservation	Desire for Mate Pair bonding Affinity–Closeness–Wholeness Attractiveness–The other half	Desire for Group Social acceptance People–Recognition Popularity–Honour–Status

	Fear of not surviving	Fear of undesirability	Fear of not belonging
Fear	Suspense-Poverty Illness-Endangerment Loss-Annihilation	Unworthiness-Letting go Disconnection-Incompleteness Loss of Appeal-Invalidation	Loneliness-Low Ranking Failure-Outcast Inferiority-Isolation
	Physical Issues	**Intimacy Issues**	**Relating Issues**
Issues	To be or not to be present How to be secure	To be or not to be intimate How to be intimate	To relate or not to relate How to relate
	Coping	**Connection**	**Cooperation**
Approach	Anxiety-Mortality-Vigilance Diets-Obesity-Time-Energy Finances-Insurance Hoarding-Essentials	Intrigue-Encounters-Rivalry Sex Appeal-Impulse-Passion Best Friend-Revealing Self Eye Contact-Union-Glamour	Fellowship-Events-Cooperation Admiration-Pecking Order-Clubs Prestige-Glory-Causes Companionship-Superiority-Fame

	Caution or Self-destruction	Promiscuity or Abstinence	Social or Anti-social
Strategy	Aggressive-Defensive Logistics-Health Fanatic Constriction-Accumulating Conservation-Fearful	Power-Submission Responsiveness-Gender Roles Provocative-Possessive Imagination-Search-Curiosity	Approval-Shame Philanthropy-Misanthropy Rigidity-Companionship Friendliness-Enmity-Achievement
Disposition	**Responsible** Grounded-Solid-Serious Sombre-Heavy-Consistent	**Intimate** Intense-Penetrating-Vibrant Playful-Lyrical-Passionate	**Engaging** Scattered-Personable-Cursory Inconsistent-Superficial-Cooperative
Theme	**How am I?** I am my body I sacrifice for myself I must make it on my own	**What am I?** I am my relationship I sacrifice for the relationship You and me against the world	**Who am I?** I am my group I sacrifice for the group We can make it if we cooperate

We need all three instinctual drives in order to function in a healthy way, ready to respond to the variety of phenomena life brings into our awareness. In connection-making our focus is on bringing the three instincts into balance.

The second dimension of our Moving Centre is temperament. Temperament theory describes four organising patterns of personality and is based in descriptions of behaviour that go back over twenty-five centuries. It answers the "how do I?" question of behaviour, our way of interacting and sources of stress. Knowing our temperament patterns tells us about the reactive behaviour style we are more likely to be drawn to as we develop our underlying innate drives of extraversion, introversion, judging and perceiving.

Ornstein in his book The Roots of Self describes temperament as:

> *"a person's predisposition to respond to specific events in a specific way; thus, temperament refers to the style rather than the content of behaviour. Temperament is the 'how' of behaviour, not the 'what'".*

He goes on to say:

> *"Temperament is more general (than personality), more basic than is the whole personality: it concerns whether one does everything slowly or quickly, whether one seeks excitement or sits alone, whether one is highly expressive or inhibited, joyous or sullen. Temperament is the basic rootstock of individuality, our basic shape, which is ready to be moulded into different characteristics by other forces."*

He then describes three dimensions of temperament and the brain-based systems that they are anchored in. These are:

- The system that has the task of alerting the cortex, sending a stream of arousal messages to the higher parts of the brain. Many of these messages travel through the limbic system in the midbrain where emotions are controlled. He refers to this as amplification (the need

- for stimulation or not) – similar to extraversion and introversion,
- The system that involves the interplay between the ancient lower brain centres, which have precise pre-programmed plans of action, and the more recently evolved higher brain centres, which try to regulate these spontaneous actions and make plans of their own. He refers to this as deliberation or liberation (the need for structure versus spontaneity) – similar to judging and perceiving,
- The system that governs the overall feeling and tone of the person – whether a thing is sweet or sour, warm or cold; whether the person characteristically approaches the world or withdraws from it. He refers to this as positive approach versus negative withdrawal (move towards versus move away).

Consistent with Ornstein's work, it is our view that temperament (our innate drives), based on the Jungian/Myers Briggs orientations, has extraversion and introversion as a genetic element. Jung was clear about the pre-eminent role of extraversion and introversion in determining the way preferences were formed. Jung also regarded the four functions – sensing, intuition, thinking and feeling – as mental functions rather than aspects of temperament.

The orientation of judging and perceiving, that was given a specific role by Myers and Briggs, is also a temperament-based function, again consistent with Ornstein's work. While Jung did not give these orientations a specific place in temperament, he was clear about the relationship judging had on the rational choice-making functions of thinking and feeling, and perceiving had on the information gathering functions of sensing and intuition.

Let's go back to basics for a moment to get an understanding of these four orientations of extraversion and introversion and judging and perceiving.

EXTRAVERSION	INTROVERSION
• Prefers action over reflection • Talks things over in order to understand them • Prefers oral communication • Shares thoughts freely • Acts and responds quickly • Extends self into the environment • Enjoys working in groups	• Prefers reflection over action • Thinks things through in order to understand them • Prefers written communication • Guards thoughts until they are almost perfect • Reflects and thinks deeply • Defends self against external demands • Enjoys working alone
Key words: initiating, expressive, gregarious, active, enthusiastic, external, outside thrust, talk thoughts out, interaction, action, do-think-do	**Key words**: responding, contained, intimate, reflective, quiet, internal, inside pull, keep thoughts in, concentration, reflection, think-do-think

JUDGING	PERCEIVING
• Likes things to be settled and ordered • Finishes tasks before the deadline • Focuses on goals, end results and closure • Establishes time-based deadlines • Is structured about outcomes • Prefers no surprises • Prefers to be conclusive • Quickly commits to plans	• Likes things to be flexible and open • Finishes tasks at the deadline • Focuses on processes, options and openings • Dislikes time-based deadlines • Is flexible about outcomes • Enjoys surprises • Prefers to be open-ended • Reserves the right to change plans
Key words: systematic, planned, early starting, scheduled, methodical, regulate, control, closing off, organised, structured	**Key words**: casual, open-ended, pressure-prompted, spontaneous, emergent, flow, adapt, opening up, flexible, unstructured

INSIGHT INTENTION AND INTEGRITY

The terms *extravert* and *introvert* are used in a special sense when discussing the Jungian psychological types. People who prefer extraversion draw energy from action: they tend to act, then reflect, then act further. If they are inactive, their level of energy and motivation tends to decline, and they need stimulation from outside. Conversely, those who prefer introversion become less energised as they act and they prefer to reflect, then act, then reflect again. People who prefer introversion need time out to reflect in order to rebuild energy – they get stimulation from inside.

As mentioned, the extraverted-introverted attitude as highly correlated with the amplification function of the reticular activating system, discussed by Ornstein, which alerts the cortex to arriving information and controls our general level of arousal. It is in the thalamus that the information is amplified or reduced. The "average setting" for this amplification system differs in all of us and the amount of amplification influences everything we do. For introverts the world is very loud and for extraverts it is subdued. So introverts, who are highly aroused internally, seek little external stimulation and extraverts, who have a quiet inner world, need external stimulation and often produce the "noise" themselves.

The extravert's flow is directed outward toward present stimuli, people and objects, and the introvert's is directed inward toward past experiences, ideas and thoughts. There are several contrasting characteristics between extraverts and introverts: extraverts are action-oriented and desire breadth, while introverts are thought-oriented and seek depth. Extraverts often prefer more frequent interaction, while introverts prefer more substantial interaction. Extraverts are initiators, introverts are responders.

The judging-perceiving orientation on the other hand is considered to be strongly influenced by the frontal lobe and limbic system neural connections. The judging orientation has closed boundaries and is deliberate and the perceiving orientation has open boundaries and is spontaneous and they represent a continuum. This capacity to focus sharply and cleanly on one thing (judging) or to see options and possibilities (perceiving) seems to be "neurally" independent of our thinking and feeling and sensing and intuiting functions even though they are highly influential in the way those functions are expressed.

Judgers are very organised and seek closure. They like to "plan their work and work their plan." A Judger most likely has a day planner or if they don't have one, they carry one around in their head. Work is carried out in an orderly fashion. There is a place for everything, and everything should be in its place. Judgers like things to be in order. The Judging person likes everything put away. They don't get side-tracked by other issues. They decide then act, then they just keep moving.

Perceivers are very flexible and like to go with the flow. If they have a "to do" list, it will likely be just a scrap of paper. They are always looking for new information. They put off making decisions because there might just be that last little bit of information that would help them make a better decision. Perceivers follow an "event" schedule. They are waiting for everything to come together, and then at the right moment, they are energised to make their move. They seize the moment.

The four temperament drives that emerge from these orientations are shown below.

INSIGHT INTENTION AND INTEGRITY

Challengers (Extraverted Judging): Depend on rational predictability for their primary experience of life and make it their business to know how things are supposed to happen. Are directed and organised and know how to set goals and meet them. Cannot rest until they know the situation is under control and hence find it hard to contend with the unpredictable or irrational side of life. Spend much of their time trying to keep things under control, opting for perfectionism when the situation requires risk or making the most of opportunities. Standards in public life have no bearing on private life. When mature they understand their impact on others, begin to take the immediate experience into account, and develop the ability to see with clarity.

In summary Challengers:

- are proactive
- are rational
- are restless
- find it difficult to relax unless tired
- are "calmly energetic" with few intense variations in the level of energy during the day

Experimenters (Extraverted Perceiving): React to immediate stimulation and depend on direct experience for their primary understanding of life. Are likely to be accomplished change masters and a very good at improvising as the situation is happening. Adapt to reality by participating fully in whatever turns up, and invest as much time, energy and attention as they have, until it runs out, when they then need to escape from the expectations of others. They get irritated and bored with ongoing pursuits whose rewards are not immediate. When mature they see things from a broader perspective, recognise their very real power to affect others, and make a difference in the world.

In summary Experimenters:

- are flexible
- are mobile
- are impulsive, shifting from apparent inactivity to bursts of energy, often several times a day, showing impatience during them
- are optimistic and open-minded
- entertain people easily and naturally

Maintainers (Introverted Perceiving): Are immediate and contextual and encourage the recognition of underlying patterns of an ongoing situation, and respect its implications. Sense that their own actions are part of a larger pattern, or have a role in its unfolding, which results in an appreciation for intricacy and aesthetic aspects of things. They do not count on things staying the way they are each time they are repeated, and regard every moment as unique, with its own character and possibilities. May not focus their attention, unless they are engaged by something that compels or obliges them. They tend to ritualise daily routines and become quite protective of their personal space. When mature they engage in experiences that have real meaning for them and recognise their own strengths and boundaries.

In summary Maintainers:

- are relaxed
- go-with-the-flow
- find it easy to spend long periods of time in no activity, or at very low levels of energy
- are flexible and unhurried

Organisers (Introverted Judging): Feel most comfortable when they can establish predictable reference points in the outside world. Have interest in represented experience in the form of numbers, words, facts, signs and symbols – the kind of data that can be explored in the mind - rather than direct experience. Constantly taking in new information and are single-minded in their attempts to accommodate it into existing procedures, or to change the system to fit. Constantly analysing what others believe and think in terms of their own reflective process. Are exacting about time, plans and goals when dealing with others, but may struggle to set personal priorities, or pursue their own ambitions. When mature they provide new ways and insights about issues that make a genuine contribution to society.

In summary Organisers:

- are calm, balanced and inert
- are "unflappable"
- may appear passive-aggressive
- are usually very stable mood
- are more reactive than active

While our instincts and temperament drives provide the anchor point of our connection-making it is also fundamentally influenced by our social development; the third dimension of our Moving Centre.

The third dimension of our Moving Centre is based on our *social style*, identified by Karen Horney, and also mentioned in part by Ornstein, which emphasises the three ways in which we solve our inner and outer conflicts to maintain our stable sense of self: moving against people (confronter) style, moving away from people (withdrawer) style and moving towards people (embracer) style.

There is a fourth style that is evident that I have called the moving with (adapter) style which has been largely overlooked in the hierarchy driven nature of our social development but has emerged as we become immersed in social networks.

The four connection-making styles (that correlate highly with the four temperaments) are:

- People with a *confronting (move against people) style* are independent, directive and strong willed. They meet life head on and are unwilling to withdraw. They know what they want and go directly after it. They have a sense of importance and feel that they are the centre of things, often insisting that their demands are met. When under pressure they push back against obstacles and reinforce their position. They see opportunities and seek to take advantage of them. They identify with order, achievement and power.
- People with a *withdrawing (move away from people) style* are quiet and introspective. They enjoy spending lots of time alone and feel uncomfortable in large groups. They don't directly seek attention and feel uncomfortable taking charge. They are excited by their own imagination and have a sense of being different from others. When under stress they withdraw into their inner space and prefer to work alone. They will generally not present their ideas or assert themselves until they are confident of their position. They identify with their own needs, knowledge and harmony.

- People with an *embracing (move toward people) style* are responsive, warm and comply with what others want from them. They will do what they believe is best, even if it means sacrificing their own wants. They are committed to their promises, work hard to finish what they said they would do, and seek affirmation from others about what they have done for them. They have a subtle sense of superiority over others. Under pressure they seek advice from their own feelings to determine the right thing to do. They work well in groups where the plans and procedures are agreed upon – within a structure they work tirelessly. They identify with other's needs, authority and variety.
- People with an *adaptable (move with people) style* are spontaneous, engaging, and values oriented and seek alignment with others. They share their ideas and dreams openly and energetically. They are persuasive and collaborative with a strong commitment to the development of others and themselves in a flexible rather than structured way. Under pressure they tend to become reserved and self-questioning to determine how to re-engage with valued colleagues. They work well when given the freedom to develop their ideas and potential. They identify with others who have a similar disposition, and this may lead to many initially exciting plans remaining incomplete.

Against that Moving Centre background let's look a little more closely at the four other Jungian functions that we have called the Practical Drive, the Creative Drive, the Thinking Centre and the Feeling Centre.

Practical Drive (Sensing) (S): is about experiencing the world as it "is" - through using the five senses. It is about attending to the here and now, being aware of the tangible sensory impressions of the moment. It is about trusting most your direct experiences as a guideline for future action. Sensing is about being literal, concrete and practical, noticing "what is" as opposed to what "could be." It is about remembering, cataloguing and recalling, often with great detail, a wide variety of experiences and information.

Creative Drive (Intuition) (N): is about understanding, exploring, creating patterns, noticing relationships, and imagining new possibilities. It is a 'sixth' sense that involves an unconscious awareness of facts, events, happenings, and the whole of experience to produce insights about complex relationships, concepts, future possibilities, and trends. The Intuitive mind automatically links the past and present to forecast the future, speculates about possibilities, looks at the "big picture," and seeks to grasp the general context of an idea, concept, or a situation. It learns to trust its hunches.

Thinking Centre (T): is about order and organisation, being objective, detached, being able to discriminate, and using logic. Thinking preference people naturally seek to understand cause and effect - using an orderly chain of reasoning to establish the relationships. The Thinking mind seeks the truth, getting to the heart of the matter in an objective way. We experience our Thinking function when we are being dispassionate and are able to make decisions at arm's length from whatever emotional turmoil may surround a situation. Thinking is about principles and well-organized foundations for beliefs. It is the engine that devises strategies and creates organized, conceptual structures.

Feeling Centre (F): is about values, beliefs, moral foundations, and the human condition. It is about being open to emotions, sensations, needs, and thoughts. It is about being subjective, valuing the conclusions that arise from within. The Feeling mind desires harmony, values being attached rather than being detached, and is sensitive to one's inner self as well as sensitive to others and their needs. This attachment to people, ideas, and moral foundations directs action and decisions. The Feeling function is an internalized moral and spiritual compass that provides direction and guidance - without the need to consciously analyse or understand why.

Your unique Social Style is a combination of the information gathering functions of sensing (S) and intuition (I) and the decision-making functions of thinking (T) and feeling (F). These two Jungian functions operate in pairs – you can't have one without the other.

The four descriptive characteristics of the Social Styles (Jungian function pair) are:

- The NT Catalyst (focused on strategy) social style - relating to initiative, control and ingenuity,
- The NF Synergist (focused on vision) social style - relating to optimism, ideas and compassion,
- The SF Harmonist (focused on values) social style - relating to patience, duty, and cooperation,
- The ST Specialist (focused on standards) social style - relating to correctness, predictability and standards.

The figure below illustrates the relationship between the four Social Styles (Jungian function pairs):

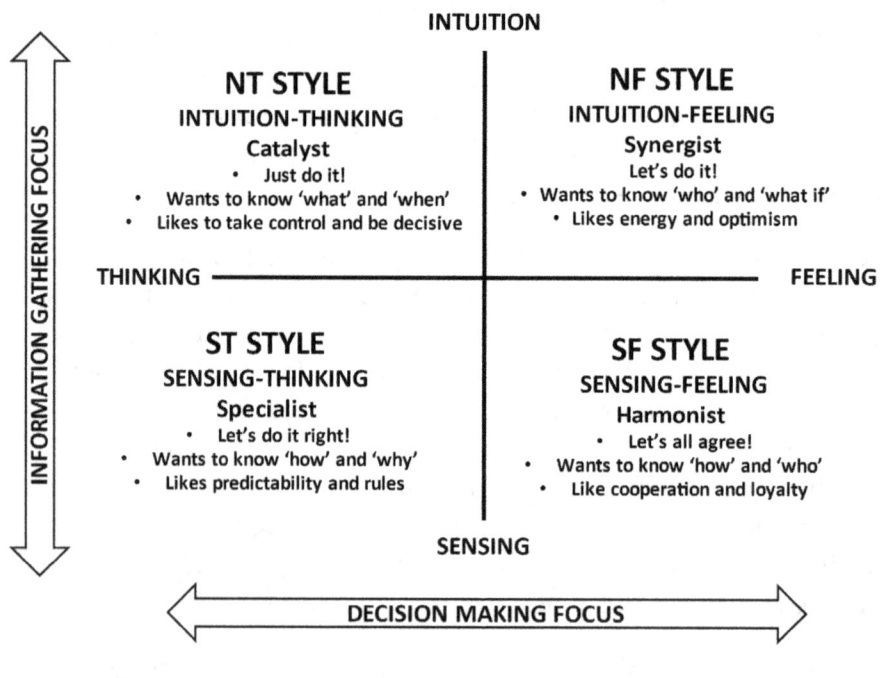

Figure 10: Jungian Function Pairs

INSIGHT INTENTION AND INTEGRITY

Catalyst style - NT (Intuition and Thinking): tend to approach others in a single-minded and objective manner, and like to make use of their ingenuity to focus on strategic and technical possibilities. They prefer to undertake tasks that that require an impersonal and analytical approach to ideas, information and people, and they tend to avoid tasks that require a warm, sympathetic, and hands-on approach to helping people.

In summary Catalyst style NT's:

- are competitive, strategic and idea-focused,
- want to know the gist of what is expected, while having room to design their own logical systems and pursue their personal vision,
- place great value on competence, expertise, and the logical soundness of ideas,
- will critique and improve ideas and strategies, with an eye on the big picture and sound models,
- are single-minded and may struggle to see ideas, realities, and details that do not fit with their visions, systems, and plans,
- might struggle with interaction in emotionally charged situations and taking the emotions of others into account.

Synergist style - NF (Intuition and Feeling): tend to approach others in a warm and enthusiastic manner, and like to focus on ideas and possibilities, particularly "possibilities for people." They are big picture oriented and are stimulated by change. They prefer tasks that require interaction with others, a focus on the abstract, and an empathy for others and tend to avoid tasks that require an impersonal or technical approach to things and factual data.

In summary Synergist style NF's:

- are people-oriented and idea-focused,
- want to know the gist of what is expected, while having room to do things in their own way, while helping others,

- will place great value on genuineness, empowerment, and meaning in work and in life,
- want to help others find their passions and reach their potential, while allowing others' voices and opinions to be heard,
- are sensitive to criticism and may react impulsively to feedback,
- might miss details and current realities while carrying out their own ideas and working towards desired change.

Harmonist style - SF (Sensing and Feeling): approach tasks in a warm people-oriented manner, liking to focus on realities and hands-on tasks. They prefer tasks that require a sympathetic approach to people. They are practical will tend to use their beliefs first and then seeks data that confirms their beliefs. They tend avoid tasks that require an analytical and impersonal approach to information and ideas.

In summary Harmonist style SF's:

- are people-oriented and practical,
- want to know detailed expectations for completing tasks and helping others up front,
- will place value on consistency, harmony, and good relationships in their environment,
- want to help people get through their tasks with as little difficulty as possible,
- may take criticism too personally but will brood on it rather than reacting immediately,
- might avoid conflict to preserve harmony, even when conflict may improve the situation in the end

Specialist Style – ST (Sensing and Thinking): approach tasks in an objective and analytical manner and like to focus on realities and practical applications in their work. They are upholders of standards and rules that are logical and universal. They prefer tasks that require a technical approach to things, ideas, or people, and avoid tasks that require nurturing of others or attending to their growth and development.

In summary Specialist style ST's:

- are logical and practical,
- want to know detailed expectations for completing tasks and projects up front,
- will place value on having, knowing, and consistently following standard operating procedures for tasks that are to be repeated,
- want to know the outcome required and get things done in the most efficient, simple way possible… no fuss, no drama,
- may struggle to adjust to change that seems unneeded and/or happens quickly,
- might struggle with interaction in emotionally charged situations and considering others' emotions.

Our temperament shapes the way our social style is expressed, and is especially noticeable when we are under pressure. For example, the NT – Catalyst social style can be shaped by the EJ – Challenger temperament that creates an assertive, even aggressive, moving against way of behaving whereas when the NT – Catalyst social style is shaped by the EP – Experimenter temperament it creates a more adaptable, even political, go with the flow way of behaving.

The integrated personality lens that illustrates the various implications of the way temperament shapes social style are shown below.

				SOCIAL STYLE (FUNCTION PAIRS)			
				NT	NF	SF	ST
				Strategy	Vision	Values	Standards
				CATALYST	SYNERGIST	HARMONIST	SPECIALIST
TEMPERAMENT (ATTITUDES)	EJ	Moving against	CHALLENGER	EJ.NT (ENTJ) Strategist	EJ.NF (ENFJ) Mentor	EJ.SF (ESFJ) Facilitator	EJ.ST (ESTJ) Implementer
	EP	Moving towards	EXPERIMENTER	EP.NT (ENTP) Explorer	(EP.NF) ENFP Visionary	EP.SF (ESFP) Motivator	EP/ST (ESTP) Pragmatist
	IP	Moving with	MAINTAINER	IP.NT (INTP) Designer	IP.NF (INFP) Mediator	IP.SF (ISFP) Loyalist	IP/ST (ISTP) Protector
	IJ	Moving away	ORGANISER	IJ.NT (INTJ) Conceptualiser	IJ.NF (INFJ) Foreseer	IJ.SF (ISFJ) Analyst	IJ.ST (ISTJ) Logician

The Jungian Myers Briggs personality types that flow form the temperament and social styles interaction are shown below:

EJ Challenger instinctive drive with related Social Style:

- **EJ.NT (ENTJ) – Strategist: Frank, decisive, assume leadership readily. Quickly see illogical and ineffi-**

cient procedures and policies, develop and implement comprehensive systems to solve organisational problems. Enjoy long-term planning and goal setting. Usually well informed, well read, enjoy expanding their knowledge and passing it on to others. Forceful in presenting their ideas. Value action.

- **EJ.NF (ENFJ) – Mentor:** Warm, empathetic, responsive, and responsible. Highly attuned to the emotions, needs, and motivations of others. Find potential in everyone, want to help others fulfill their potential. May act as catalysts for individual and group growth. Loyal, responsive to praise and criticism. Sociable, facilitate others in a group, and provide inspiring leadership.

- **EJ.SF (ESFJ) – Facilitator:** Warm-hearted, conscientious, and cooperative. Want harmony in their environment, work with determination to establish it. Like to work with others to complete tasks accurately and on time. Loyal, follow through even in small matters. Notice what others need in their day-by-day lives and try to provide it. Want to be appreciated for who they are and for what they contribute.

- **EJ.ST (ESTJ) – Implementor:** Practical, realistic, matter-of-fact. Decisive, quickly move to implement decisions. Organize projects and people to get things done, focus on getting results in the most efficient way possible. Take care of routine details. Have a clear set of logical standards, systematically follow them and want others to also. Forceful in implementing their plans.

EP Experimenter instinctive drive with related Social Style:

- **EP.NF (ENFP) – Visionary:** Warmly enthusiastic and imaginative. See life as full of possibilities. Make connections between events and information very quickly, and confidently proceed based on the patterns they see. Readily give appreciation and support to others. Spontaneous and flexible, often rely on their ability to improvise and their verbal fluency. **Value variety.**

- **EP.NT (ENTP) – Explorer:** Quick, ingenious, stimulating, alert, and outspoken. Resourceful in solving new and challenging problems. Adept at generating conceptual possibilities and analysing them strategically. Good at reading other people. Bored by routine, will seldom do the same thing the same way, apt to turn to one new interest after another.
- **EP.SF (ESFP) – Motivator:** Outgoing, friendly, and accepting. Exuberant lovers of life, people, and material comforts. Enjoy working with others to make things happen. Bring common sense and a realistic approach to their work and make work fun. Flexible and spontaneous, adapt readily to new people and environments. Learn best by trying a new skill with other people.
- **EP.ST (ESTP) – Pragmatist:** Flexible and tolerant, they take a pragmatic approach focused on immediate results. Theories and conceptual explanations bore them - they want to act energetically to solve the problem. Focus on the here-and-now, spontaneous, enjoy each moment that they can be active with others. Enjoy material comforts and style. Learn best through doing.

IP Maintainer instinctive drive with related Social Style:

- IP.SF (ISFP) – Loyalist: Quiet, friendly, sensitive, and kind. Enjoy the present moment, what's going on around them. Like to have their own space and to work within their own time frame. Loyal and committed to their values and to people who are important to them. Dislike disagreements and conflicts, do not force their opinions or values on others. Value loyalty.
- **IP.ST (ISTP) – Protector:** Quiet, friendly, responsible, and conscientious. Committed and steady in meeting their obligations. Thorough, painstaking, and accurate. Loyal, considerate, notice and remember specifics about

people who are important to them, concerned with how others feel. Strive to create an orderly and harmonious environment at work and at home.

- **IP.NT (INTP) – Designer:** Seek to develop logical explanations for everything that interests them. Theoretical and abstract, interested more in ideas than in social interaction. Quiet, contained, flexible, and adaptable. Have unusual ability to focus in depth to solve problems in their area of interest. Sceptical, sometimes critical, always analytical.
- **IP.NF (INFP) – Mediator:** Idealistic, loyal to their values and to people who are important to them. Want an external life that is congruent with their values. Curious, quick to see possibilities, can be initiators for implementing ideas. Seek to understand people and to help them fulfil their potential. Adaptable, flexible, and accepting unless a value is threatened.

IJ Organiser instinctive drive with related Social Style:

- **IJ.ST (ISTJ) – Logician: Quiet, serious, earn success by thoroughness and dependability. Practical, matter-of-fact, realistic, and responsible. Decide logically what should be done and work toward it steadily, regardless of distractions. Take pleasure in making everything orderly and organised - their work, their home, their life. Value correctness.**
- **IJ.SF (ISFJ) – Analyst:** Tolerant and flexible, quiet observers until a problem appears, then act quickly to find workable solutions. Analyse what makes things work and readily get through large amounts of data to isolate the core of practical problems. Interested in cause and effect, organise facts using logical principles, value efficiency.
- **IJ.NT (INTJ) – Conceptualiser:** Have original minds and great drive for implementing their ideas and achiev-

ing their goals. Quickly see patterns in external events and develop long-range explanatory perspectives. When committed, organize a job and carry it through. Sceptical and independent, have high standards of competence and performance.

- **IJ.NF (INFJ) – Foreseer:** Seek meaning and connection in ideas, relationships, and material possessions. Want to understand what motivates people and are insightful about others. Conscientious and committed to their firm values. Develop a clear vision about how best to serve the common good. Organised and decisive in implementing their vision.

We will look more deeply at each of these Social Styles (function pairs) when we consider the three 'eyes' of emergent leadership in Part 4.

In summary, our personality lens provides us with an integrated understanding of:

- the Moving Centre that has three interrelated dimensions that form the embedded dimensions of our personality lens:
  - Our primal instincts of self-preservation, self-renewal and social
  - Our temperament reflected by our preference for the instinctive drives of extraversion or introversion, and judging or perceiving,
  - Our basic tendencies of moving against, moving away from, moving towards and moving with others,
- the four Jungian functions that underpin our two Practical (Sensing) and Creative (Intuitive) information gathering Drives and our two Thinking and Feeling decision making Centres,
- the four Social Styles that reflect the four Jungian function pairs of Intuitive Thinking (Catalyst), Intuitive

INSIGHT INTENTION AND INTEGRITY

Feeling (Synergist), Sensate Feeling (Harmonist) and Sensate Thinking (Specialist),

You might like to go to the Tool Kit and complete the Temperament and Dominant Function questionnaire to provide you with an appreciation of your likely temperament, Jungian function pair preference and personality type that you will find useful as you go through the following chapters.

And a word of caution that these constructs are just entry points for self-discovery that enable you to explore the territory of your meaning-making, sense-making and connection-making mindsets.

You will come across many other points of interest in your self-development travels that will make your learning journey worthwhile – and many more that will emerge as you begin to understand the emergent nature of your choice-making mindset.

Now that we have an overview of the choice making territory let's take a closer look at the three Reactive Self habit-based mindsets in the next Part called Understanding Blind Spots.

PART 3

UNDERSTANDING BLIND SPOTS

The third Part is about understanding the blind spots of our Reactive Self by making you aware of your meaning-making, sense-making and connection-making mindsets. This Part considers the three habit-based mindsets of our Reactive Self:

- Meaning-making (directed by the Feeling Centre and Creative Drive)
- Sense-making (directed by the Thinking Centre and Practical Drive)
- Connection-making (directed the Moving Centre and Instinctive drive)

and how they contribute to our blind spots and those of others we connect and interact with.

CHAPTER 7

The Meaning Making Mindset

> *"When I use a word" Humpty Dumpty said in a rather scornful tone, "it means just what I suppose it to mean – neither more nor less." "The question is," said Alice, "whether you can make words mean so many different things." "The question is," said Humpty Dumpty, "which is to be master, that is all."*

Let's begin by considering our Reactive Self. It is our master and contributes to the certainty of Humpty Dumpty when he expresses what words mean to him. Meaning-making is personal, and we are all unconsciously certain about what we mean when we use words (and behaviour) as a reaction to the words (and behaviour) of others. This is the nature of our Reactive Self.

Our Reactive Self comprises the three mindsets of meaning-making, sense-making and connection-making. They are the three mindsets that impact directly, and disproportionately on our choice-making, both reflexively and intentionally.

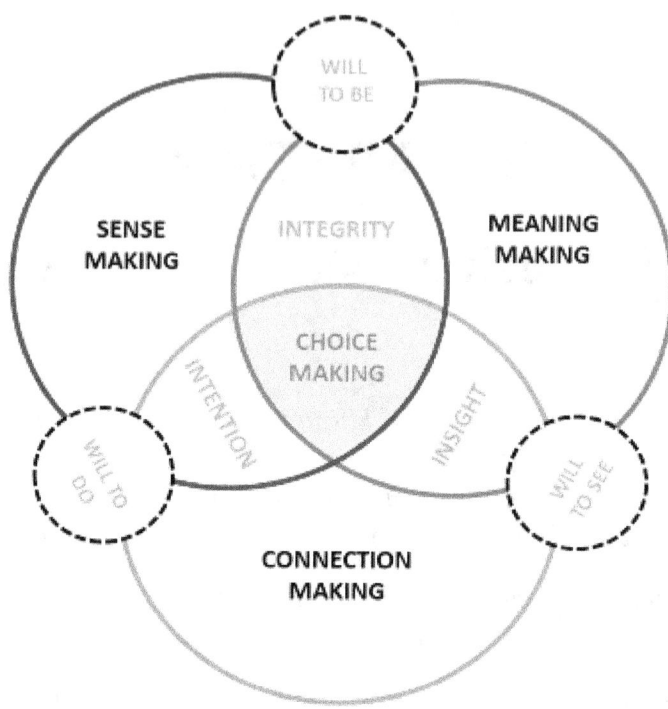

Figure 11: The Reactive Self Mindsets

When we reflect on our sense of who we are, we begin to see that we have been socialised into a culture of problems and with its associated busyness. The universal response to the question "How have you been?" is "Busy!" - busy reacting to the never-ending stream of problems that continually bombard us from multiple sources. We have become aimless problem attractors and problem solvers (and problem forgetters when the next "busy-work" gets our attention) operating inside the boundaries of our experience. Our experience dominates our Reactive Self.

We are continuously confronted with complex problems that are beyond our personal capacity to solve: climate change, economic crises, poverty, terrorism, pandemics, etc. These problems are seen through the "lens" of our experience and beliefs. Very few people can transcend that "lens" and become conscious, and then connect to the inherent creative, self-generating qualities of the natural living order. Sadly, for many, life is about just coping with this raft of overwhelming problems - we know too much about problems and have no personal capacity to deal with them other than to engage in material escapism, romantic idealisation of a past simpler life or ideological closed mindedness. Happiness becomes an absence of unhappiness.

The sense we have of our identity is based on the way we have learned to classify and solve problems that arise from the interactions we engage in with others. Our habitual patterns of meaning-making, sense-making and connection-making reactions to the world are our unconscious blind spots. We are the 'prisoner' of our Reactive Self, and it attributes our success to our own capabilities and failure to our circumstances, or by blaming others. Our experience dominates our Reactive Self.

The Reactive Self is the self that you know and rely on. It is the self that maintains your sense of control in a turbulent world and is based on the three formative 'eyes' of imitation, instruction and indoctrination of and by others, that are anchored in your primal instincts. It values striving. It serves you well in reacting unconsciously to the day-to-day problems you encounter but it is not open to personal development and engages in blame and self-justification when under pressure.

In a healthy sense our Reactive Self is protective in that it provides us a capacity to cope with life's problems and gives us a sense of control: a haven against the intrusion of external forces. This is the coping (problem solving) level of our Reactive Self, called our Constructive Self, because it constructs a view of reality based on our experience and does have the value of giving us a sense of stability in an otherwise turbulent world.

There is also a deterioration of our Reactive Self that occurs when we are highly stressed and struggle to cope. We get into self-defeating thoughts and feelings that lead to what we experience as our

Destructive Self: that part of our Reactive Self that does damage to us (and others) as it struggles to cope with those thoughts and feelings and the associated brain chemistry that reinforces this unhealthy state, beginning with neurosis and developing into psychosis.

Against that general background let's now consider the deeper nature of the meaning-making mindset of our Reactive Self.

The most prevalent view among contemporary philosophers is that meaning is not something you stumble upon, find or discover, but something you fashion, invent or create. Meaning is relative to your own desires, attitudes, beliefs, interests, wants, needs and preferences. Meaning is constructed by individual human minds and varies between people. It poses the reactive 'who am I?' question of choice-making.

In his book *The Evolving Self*, Robert Kegan explores human life problems from the perspective of a single process, which he calls meaning-making: the activity of understanding experience through discovering and resolving problems.

Kegan says:

> *"Why is the state of a person's evolution so crucial to understanding him or her? Because the way which the person is settling the issue of what is "self" and what is "other" essentially defines the underlying logic (or "psychologic") of the person's meanings. Since what is most important for us to know in understanding another is not in the other's experience but what the experience means to him or her, our first goal is to grasp the essence of how the other composes his or her private reality. The first truth we may need to know about a person, in other words, is how the person constructs the truth."*

> *and,*

INSIGHT INTENTION AND INTEGRITY

> *"It is not that a person makes meaning, as much as that activity of being a person is the activity of meaning-making,"*

He says that meaning-making is a lifelong activity that begins in earliest infancy and can evolve in complexity through a series of "evolutionary balances".

The six "evolutionary balances" that Kegan proposes are:

- Incorporative – influenced by primary caregiver,
- Impulsive – influenced by family triangle,
- Imperial – influenced by institutions of authority,
- Interpersonal – influenced by mutual reciprocity in one-to-one relationships,
- Institutional – influenced by personal sense of identity in groups, and
- Interindividual – influenced by intimacy relationships.

Each stage represents a level of truce between self and others as reflected below.

Incorporative: At this point there is in a beginning no sense of self, because the baby has no sense of self. The baby is embedded in the sensory experience, and that is all that it is aware of. Babies get practice of using their senses and reflexes, and therefore develop mental representations of those reflexes. The sense of self then emerges from the knowledge or the intuition that there are things in the world that are not the self (like a reflex and a sense). The culture of embeddedness is thus a mix of the sensory experience plus the care-giver influences.

Impulsive: In this second stage, it is called the impulsive stage. This suggests that the child is embedded in its impulses (those things that coordinate reflexes). The self in this stage of life would be comfortable expressing impulses like "hunger" or "sleep". Babies, whilst aware that they can fulfill a need by actions, are not yet aware that other people exist as independent creatures.

Imperial: The child realises now that it has needs and therefore starts manipulating in order to fulfil them, however the realisation that other people have needs is not there yet. This stage sees the emergence of self-concept and involves a capacity to take command of our impulses rather than just be them giving a sense of freedom, power and independence. Everything is projected through :my needs" – rather than see my needs, I see 'through' my needs.

Interpersonal: This stage starts when the children becomes aware that there are other people in the world whose needs have to be taken into account. This expansion of perspectives starts with the inclusion those people close and important to the child, and to progressively include more and more people. The fact that the child is aware that those needs exist does not mean that it will take the needs into account. Some children will conclude that their own needs are more important, whilst others will conclude that other people's needs should take priority over them.

Institutional: This stage begins when the child realises that there exists some sort of guiding principle that can be established to determine which needs take priority over others. These become the first values of the child and involve a commitment to ideas and beliefs. The sense of self becomes "institutionalised" and can be expressed for example as "being honest". For many people, social maturity can stop at this stage: this is the stage of conventional adult social maturity.

Interindividual: The last evolution of social maturity occurs when the child (or most likely an adult) begins to realise that there is more than one way of being "honest" (for example). This means that someone that has reached the interindividual stage, is able to hold both generic and counter-cultural or counter-intuitive value systems at the same time, or at least understand that they exist and accept this.

Each evolutionary balance is both an achievement of, and a constraint on, meaning-making, possessing both strengths and limitations. Each evolutionary balance presents a new solution to the lifelong tension between how people are connected, attached, and included (integration), on the one hand, and how people are distinct, independent, and autonomous (differentiation), on the other. In this context meaning-making is the foundation of our personal growth and underpins our depth of connection to others.

As a cautionary note it must be said that most adults do not slowly and steadily move forward, one evolutionary balance at a time toward more sophisticated, complex habits of mind. Their development isn't smooth. And it's rarely a one-way process towards more complex and sophisticated modes of meaning-making. Rather, most adults seem to consistently move forwards and backwards along their own highly idiosyncratic developmental path. It is highly likely that each of us moves backward along our own developmental trajectory at least as often as we evolve forward and upward.

In today's evolutionary context we need to recognise that the existential threats that exist in today's globalised and universally connected world - climate change, terrorism, pandemics and nuclear war - are phenomena that are consistently influencing each of us. These threats are deeply anchored triggers for our habitual modes of thinking. And right now, at this point in time, it seems like they're more likely to trigger regression than they are to activate development.

It is also likely that these existential threats are exactly the kinds of triggers that are powerful enough to catalyse large numbers of today's adults into deeply regressing backwards into their habitual modes of meaning-making, backwards into what we have defined as our Destructive Self, with its associated mental health consequences.

Our meaning-making mindset is one of the keys to unlocking our capacity to respond to change as it reflects the way we use our past experience to understand these threats to our sense of the present and future. Developing your understanding of your meaning-making mindset will provide you with an appreciation of the question 'who am I?' when you react to the proliferation of information about these potential threats that you are bombarded with on a daily basis.

At its most basic level meaning-making is about our beliefs and values. It is about our justification of why we feel the way we do about things we experience or have experienced.

The meaning-making mindset has several key characteristics. It is:
- about the development of our Attitude,
- about our Character, Curiosity and Continuity,
- informed by our Creative (Intuitive) Drive,
- anchored in our Feeling Centre,
- supported by Emotional Intelligence, and
- develops from our Identification (object relations) Style.

Meaning-making is subjective. It is about feeling and intuition. It is about attitude and character. Meaning-making forces us to focus on the individuality and the uniqueness of the meaning-maker.

As you can see with Humpty Dumpty, the meaning-maker has no limitation in their ability to know the "truth" in that moment. Paradoxically, there is also no end to the intuitive and emotive process of the meaning-maker as we continue to create new meanings by interacting with our environment and those in it.

Let's look more closely at the meaning-making mindset of our Adaptive Learning Map©.

INSIGHT INTENTION AND INTEGRITY

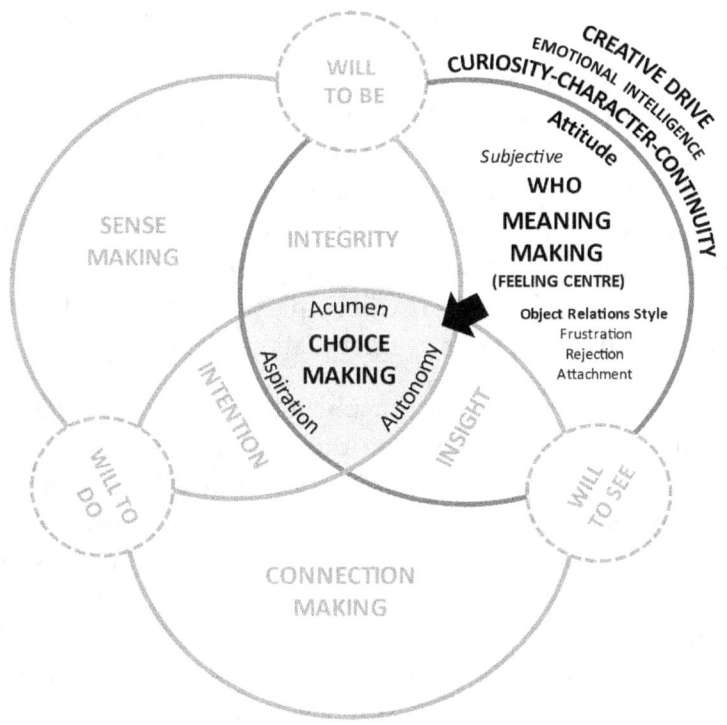

Figure 12: The Meaning Making Mindset

Meaning-making is underpinned by assumptions and beliefs about oneself and the external world. These assumptions and beliefs underpin our character: the source of emotional and motivated responses to triggers we get from our environment. Meaning-making is reflected in our attitude.

Attitude can be defined as our response to people, places, things, or events in life. It can be referred to as a person's viewpoint, mindset, beliefs and perception. Our attitude towards people, places, things, or situations influences the choices that we make.

Churchill said:

> "Attitude is a little thing that makes a big difference."

Attitude is informed by our character, our curiosity and our continuity.

Character in humans is learned and ensures we are adaptable in our environment. Character begins to develop early in life. Extremely sensitive, young infants learn by how they are touched and held. Later they learn through what they see, hear, taste and smell. All these inputs are processed as feelings and emotions. Through many interactions with care givers and siblings, young children learn what behaviour will help them survive and succeed. They also learn what works against their success.

By the age where we can reason, a belief pattern has already been deeply embedded in our meaning-making structure by significant others, who have also learned by the socialisation 'eyes' (imitation, instruction and indoctrination), and is largely unconscious. That is, until we realise that not everything we learned in our early years is appropriate in all settings and we begin to reject aspects of our family upbringing. However, the ability of our Feeling Centre to respond much more quickly to triggers in our environment, in a habit-based way, keeps much of our early learning in place. This socialisation of meaning-making beliefs often pervades generations of families.

As we mature, we may begin to develop the capacity to be more aware of the impact that our emotion and intuition-based responses have on our success in new situations. Maturity is an option some people do not develop and they become addicted to 'their way', and lack both empathy toward others and openness to their intuition.

Without developing a mature character everything we seek to do is draining and ultimately futile, and we become trapped by the roles others expect us to play. With maturity we become inquisitive about our past experiences, expand our relationships and seek to discover new places. It is about engaging our curiosity.

Curiosity is a fundamental human trait. Everyone is curious, but the focus and degree of that curiosity is different depending on the person and the situation. When our curiosity is triggered, we are less likely to fall prey to confirmation bias (looking for information that supports our beliefs rather than for evidence suggesting we are wrong) and to stereotyping people (making broad judgments based on superficial cues). Curiosity has these positive effects because it leads us to generate alternatives. Curiosity is the engine that drives meaning-making. Once you abandon your curiosity your meaning-making becomes stagnant and narrow-minded. That is the challenge of religious belief when it is the foundation of your meaning-making Reactive Self.

This curiosity based, higher level of meaning-making maturity is a reflection of our Creative Drive – that sense of self that has the capacity to intuitively attach itself to our life experiences and future possibilities and which engages our creativeness as we evolve over time. Without a sense of future possibilities, we are very good at extrapolating our experience as worse case scenarios, that reflect our capacity to make the specific general ("they always do that"), and the general specific ("that will happen to me").

We attribute cause externally when we are in our unconscious reflexive mode. For meaning-making to be conscious we need to understand the way that we presently interpret and react to the varied and unrelenting triggers in our ever-changing life conditions, and find ways to realise our purpose and potential.

Meaning-making is a subjective activity. Subjective things depend on our own values: there isn't any universal truth about values. Subjective is the opposite of objective, which refers to things that are more clear-cut. That Earth has one moon is objective – it is a fact. Facts are objective, but values are subjective. To say that values are subjective is to say that they vary from person to person, that they cannot be referred to without reference to an individual. It leads us to say that your values are personal and unique to you. They provide a personal sense of continuity for us in our day-to-day interactions with others. Values can be egocentric or other centric.

We achieve continuity because our meaning-making focuses mainly on the things we care about: our needs and values. Our needs and values make up much of the terrain of our inner worlds and are anchored in our beliefs. Our beliefs, in turn, provide us with a sense of continuity in an ever-changing environment across our life.

There is an ongoing balancing act going on between continuity and change over our life. We are an open (living adaptive) system and we exhibit both continuity and change in our beliefs throughout our life. The "six evolutionary balances" referred to by Kegan are largely in place by early to mid-adulthood in most of us. While the effects of psychological, social, and cultural factors do tend to diminish as we grow older, often as a result of insight and intention, our beliefs tend to remain the bedrock of our meaning-making.

Beliefs are assumptions we hold to be true. When we use our beliefs to make decisions, we are assuming the causal relationships of the past, which led to the belief, will also apply in the present and future. In a rapidly changing world where complexity is increasing day by day, using information from the past, to make decisions about the future, may not be the best way to support us in meeting our needs.

Two long-standing observations about human behaviour provide us with some understanding of how people form beliefs. One is our readiness to perceive patterns even in random phenomena. The other is our readiness to nominate our intentional action as the cause of what are really natural events.

Consequently, once we form our beliefs we then look for evidence in support of them. It is this 'pattern seeking' and 'intentionality attribution' capacity that underlies the diverse reasons why we form particular beliefs. They arise from subjective, personal and emotional prompts, in our unique social and historical context, that give them power over our day to day lives.

Our mind is always seeking to find meaning in the information that pours into it. Once it has constructed a belief, it rationalises it with explanations, almost always after the event. The mind thus becomes invested in the beliefs, and reinforces them by looking for supporting evidence while blinding itself to anything contrary.

We develop a belief-dependent reality - what we believe determines our reality, not the other way around.

Beliefs thus involve at least two properties:

- experiential content (we have seen it before or significant others informed us), and
- assumed truth (they provide us with a sense of certainty about perceived outcomes).

It is important to note, however, that beliefs need not be conscious or verbally articulated. The majority of our beliefs remain unconscious, or outside of our immediate awareness, and are of relatively mundane content. Through our beliefs, our five senses reveal an environment that is physically real to us, and determine our actions in the present, and influence outcomes in the future.

Beliefs are best considered as being multidimensional. Beliefs share a number of common properties but can vary across dimensions within these properties. These include the following:

- Beliefs have different origins. Beliefs, for example, can be formed through direct experience or by accepting information from a trusted or authoritative source,
- Beliefs vary in terms of the level of evidence and support they command. Some beliefs have high levels of evidence, while others appear to be accepted without requiring much evidential support,
- Beliefs vary considerably in generality and scope. Beliefs may refer, for example, to specific objects or individuals, groups of objects and people, or whole classes of objects and people,
- Beliefs vary in their degree of personal reference. A belief can be limited to the specific individual holding

the belief, extend to friends, relatives and other in-group members, or apply to other groups of people or all people equally,
- Beliefs can be held with different degrees of confidence. This can range from firmly held (e.g. in the case of basic physical laws) to relative uncertainty (e.g. in the case of unfamiliar topics),
- Beliefs vary in their resistance to change in response to counter-evidence and social pressure. People can also vary in how open they are to disconfirming evidence toward their beliefs and to considering alternative points of view,
- Beliefs can vary in their impact on how we think and behave. This may be influenced by our degree of conviction. While people may act on some beliefs, they may fail to act on other beliefs that they verbally endorse,
- Beliefs can produce different emotional consequences. While some beliefs may be relatively innocuous or even self-serving, other beliefs may cause considerable distress,
- Beliefs vary in the degree to which they are shared by other people. While some beliefs are very common, other beliefs may be comparatively unusual such as in the case of some delusions.

Beliefs are contextual. They arise from learned experiences, resulting from the cultural and environmental situations we have faced. They can be distinguished from values.

When we think of our values, we think of what is important to us in our lives (e.g. security, independence, wisdom, success, kindness, pleasure). Each of us holds numerous values with varying degrees of importance. A particular value may be very important to one person, but unimportant to another.

Shalom Schwartz identified ten motivationally distinct, broad and basic values that are derived from three universal human needs: needs of individuals as biological organisms, needs for coordinated social interaction, and the survival and welfare needs of groups. Values influence most if not all motivated behaviour. Schwartz makes it clear that behaviour entails a trade-off between competing values.

Each of the basic Schwartz values can be characterised by describing the central motivational goal of each value that underpins our meaning-making.

Value	Motivational Goal
Power	The attainment of social status and prestige, and the control or dominance over people and resources.
Achievement	Personal success through demonstrated competence. Competence is evaluated in terms of what is valued by the group or organisation in which the individual is located.
Hedonism	Pleasure or sensuous gratification for oneself. This value type is derived from physical needs and the pleasure associated with satisfying them.
Stimulation	Excitement, novelty, and challenge in life. This value type is derived from the need for variety and stimulation in order to maintain an optimal level of activation. Thrill seeking can be the result of strong stimulation needs.
Self-Direction	Independent thought and action (for example, choosing, creating, exploring). Self-direction comes from the need for control and mastery along with the need for autonomy and independence.
Universalism	The understanding, appreciation, tolerance, and protection of the welfare for all people and for nature.

Benevolence	Preserve and enhance the welfare of people with whom one is in frequent personal contact. This is a concern for the welfare of others that is more narrowly defined than Universalism.
Tradition	Respect, commitment, and acceptance of the customs and ideas that one's culture or religion imposes on the individual. A traditional mode of behaviour becomes a symbol of the group's solidarity and an expression of its unique worth and, hopefully, its survival.
Conformity	Restraint of action, inclinations, and impulses likely to upset or harm others and violate social expectations or norms. It is derived from the requirement that individuals inhibit inclinations that might be socially disruptive in order for personal interaction and group functioning to run smoothly.
Security	Safety, harmony, and stability of society or relationships, and of self.

Needs and values are highly interconnected. There will be times, in the process of gaining deeper understanding of another person, when it won't be important to distinguish whether you are exploring a need or a value. But there is an important distinction between the two: needs tend to be very similar for all people, whereas values tend to be highly individualised.

Another way to state this distinction is in the negative: when someone is not meeting one of their needs, they will have a hard time *functioning well* - getting up in the morning, holding down a job, maintaining relationships. When a person is not honouring one of their values, they will function fine by all outward appearances, but they will not *feel well* in their life.

Needs are the things that almost all people fundamentally require to function in life - but this doesn't mean we don't frequently deny or ignore them. Values, on the other hand, are the aspects of life that you choose to invest in to create your own special meaning.

INSIGHT INTENTION AND INTEGRITY

Needs and values show themselves in a variety of ways. Each has some characteristic patterns that make it possible to distinguish one from the other, even in casual conversation.

The tell-tale signs of an unmet need are:

- Complaining
- Blaming and name calling
- Fearfulness, feeling threatened
- Gossiping (when in teams or groups)

Needs are a set of impulses and responses based on our conditioning and make-up. When we think about 'now' - we look to the immediate urges or impulses that are pushing and pulling us from the inside. These are needs. When we discuss needs we are usually focussing on the present. We're not looking at past patterns or thinking about our identity, just on what's going on for us right now, in this moment.

An unmet need - for food, water, rest, breathable air - produces an irritation, a drive to let others know you are not getting what you need.

The tell-tale signs of a disregarded value are:

- Withdrawal
- Disappointment
- Agitation or anxiety
- Frustration, the source of which remains vague

It is less common for values to manifest as complaints. When people have an unmet value they don't feel well but don't know how to articulate what's wrong, they tend to say nothing. A disregarded value produces a malaise, a more vague sense of discontent.

In short, an unmet need shouts for attention; the disregarded value slinks into the shadows.

Beliefs, values and needs at the collective level are interpreted at the individual level having regard to our social development (our experience of similar situations in the past) and interpretation of the present situation that we find ourselves in.

With that background to our meaning-making mindset let's look a little more closely at Feeling Centre and meaning-making in the context of our Adaptive Learning Map©.

Our Feeling Centre is anchored in our early social development. The social development perspective that underpins our meaning-making is anchored in our *identification style* (based on object relations theory that we looked at earlier). Our unconscious emotional reaction developed in very early childhood relationships when we didn't get what we wanted or couldn't solve a problem our way: frustration, rejection and attachment.

- People with *frustration identification style* know what will make them feel happy but seldom feel they have it. Even when they find the source of their happiness, they often become disillusioned with it which induces further frustration and they begin their search again. Their sense of self is based on the search for an ideal.
- People with *rejection identification style* feel that they have been rejected by others. They feel that others don't care about their needs, so they reject their own needs too. Consequently, their relationships often have issues of not wanting to be nurtured or touched. Despite feeling rejected, they feel they only have one gift (love, knowledge or power) to offer to prevent future rejection. Their sense of self is based on countering possible rejection by offering their particular talent.
- People with *attachment identification style* need to have a feeling of contentment that their needs are being met. To attach themselves, they adapt their ways to be consistent with important people, groups or things. Their sense of self is based on being deeply attached to things perceived as good.

INSIGHT INTENTION AND INTEGRITY

Our Feeling Centre is also underpinned by emotional intelligence that gives you both empathy for another person's thoughts and feelings, and a greater compassion for and understanding of your own. Emotional intelligence seeks to surface unconscious motivations, where you excel and where you have an opportunity to grow.

Harvard psychologist Howard Gardner came up with the concept in his book, Multiple Intelligences. His research questioned whether human intelligence could be measured or defined by a single factor. He concluded that we have multiple intelligences, including emotional intelligence (EQ). He says:

> *"Your EQ is the level of your ability to understand other people, what motivates them and how to work cooperatively with them".*

There are said to be five major categories of emotional intelligence (EQ) skills recognised by researchers in this area.

- **Self-awareness** - the ability to recognise an emotion as it "happens" is the key to your EQ. Developing self-awareness requires tuning in to your true feelings. If you are aware of your emotions, you can manage them.
- **Self-regulation** - you often have little control over when you experience emotions. You can, however, have some say in how long an emotion will last by using a number of techniques to alleviate negative emotions such as anger, anxiety or depression. A few of these techniques include recasting a situation in a more positive light, taking a long walk and meditation.
- **Motivation** - to motivate yourself for any achievement requires clear intention and a positive attitude. Although you may have a predisposition to either a positive or a negative attitude, you can with effort and practice learn to think more positively. If you catch negative thoughts as they occur, you can reframe them in more positive terms.

- **Empathy** - the ability to recognise how other people feel is important to success in your life and career. The more skilful you are at discerning the feelings behind others' behaviour the better you can control the signals you send them.
- **Social skills** - the development of good interpersonal skills is tantamount to success in your life and career. In our always-connected world, everyone has immediate access to technical knowledge. Consequently, social skills are even more important now because you must possess a high EQ to better understand, empathise and connect with others.

With emotional intelligence, you are completely aware of who you are and can appreciate yourself fully. You can embrace your feelings, fears and motivations without hesitation.

Our meaning-making is influenced by the impact of our Creative Drive on our Feeling Centre. It is a reflection of how we have used our intuition to inform our feeling to give meaning and energy to our choice-making. Our Feeling Centre prefers to work in short sessions rather than finishing a task all at once, is interested in people and how they feel, is in tune with both our own emotions and those of other people, bases decisions on immediate feelings, and generates excitement and enthusiasm in group settings and enjoys new connections, experiences, and situations.

Our Feeling Centre, in Jungian terms, moderates the choice-making function of feeling (a values-based connection with past emotional experiences). In the context of meaning-making our feeling function is triggered by our Jungian information gathering function of intuition (a sense of possibility and future).

- Feeling is about deciding based on values, beliefs, moral foundations, and the human need to belong. It is about being open to emotions, sensations, needs, and thoughts. It is about being subjective and valuing the conclusions that arise from within. The Feeling function desires harmony, values being attached rather than being detached, and is sensitive to one's inner self as well as sensitive to others and their needs. This attachment to people, ideas, and moral foundations directs choice-making. The Feeling function is an internalised moral and beliefs-based compass that provides direction and guidance - without the need to consciously analyse things.

- Intuition is conceptual and is about understanding, exploring, seeing patterns, noticing relationships, and imagining new possibilities. It is a 'sixth' sense that involves an unconscious awareness of signals, events, happenings, and the whole of experience, to produce insights about complex relationships, concepts, future possibilities, and trends. The intuitive function automatically links the past and present to forecast the future, speculates about possibilities, looks at the "big picture," and seeks to grasp the general context of an idea, concept, or a situation. It learns to trust its hunches.

When we bring the information gathering functions of intuition and the judging function of feeling

together what emerges is a Jungian function pair social style that informs our meaning-making.

- **Intuitive-Feeling (NF)** – is a big picture meaning-making approach that focuses on imagination and experience, and portrays personal views as the facts. There are few rules in their decision-making and they rely on intuitive perception. They will construct open ended, non-linear, and ill-defined problems and seek fresh, human possibilities. Their focus is more on the broad themes than on specifics and they see information in the context of longer-term goals. They are subjective and may test their hunches as an iterative response to what they are feeling. They are "open-minded" and 'warm-hearted'.

The two functions of feeling and intuition, in the context of meaning-making, can be expressed with an extraverted or introverted orientation.

- **Extraverted Feeling**: reaches out to attach and interact with other living things . . . nurturing relationships. It is about validating and valuing others, encouraging, coaching, educating and motivating. It is protecting, helping, and caretaking. The Extraverted Feeling mind organizes action consistent with values, beliefs, spiritual foundations, and sense of humanity - how people (and other living things) ought to be treated. Extraverted Feeling promotes collaboration, a shared sense of community, and harmony in interpersonal relationships.
- **Introverted Feeling** is being aware of and cherishing one's own mental framework of values, beliefs and sense of self. It is being open to emotions and inner sensations. It is also being sensitive to others in an empathetic way. It is about knowing what is right and wrong according to one's personal moral and spiritual compass. It is being authentic. As a gatekeeper of the mind; it admits what is consistent with one's value and belief framework and rejects what is repulsive or draining. Introverted Feeling seeks harmony with others and harmony within.
- **Extraverted Intuition**: scans the external world to explore new ideas, new people, and emergent possibilities. The Extraverted Intuitive mind is imaginative, inventive, and innovative - seeing and describing ways things can be reshaped, altered, or improved. It naturally energizes people and engages action towards a vision of what could be - of future possibilities.
- **Introverted Intuition**: reflects on patterns, relationships, symbols, meanings, and perspectives on matters from complex phenomena to magical connections to practical problems. The Introverted Intuitive mind typically creates a unique vision and arrives at unique insights about things, phenomena, or people. It strives

to discover the essence of things and fill in the missing pieces of a puzzle. Introverted Intuitive types frequently will have complex visions or perspectives that they are unable to explain with clarity to others.

The two Jungian function pairs of intuition and feeling provide the lens that we use to unconsciously give meaning to our relationships and experiences. They are the people focussed and subjective 'who am I?' functions that underpin our sense of self and provide the meaning-making foundation for our connection to others. They are to be distinguished from the task focused and objective 'what is it?' function of our sense-making lens that will be discussed in the next chapter. The level of development of these two functions (intuition and feeling) will impact upon the balance we have between meaning-making and sense-making.

Some of the abilities popularly associated with the Jungian intuition-feeling function pair include:

- Recognising faces
- Expressing and reading emotions
- Using imagination and creativity
- Seeing possibilities
- Testing hunches

A person with a dominant Feeling Centre is likely to focus on beliefs, values and their emotional connection to others and place less weight on evidence based and practical explanations for their behaviour and that of others. They become adept at confusing meaning-making and sense-making and consequently engage in emotional explanations that can often see them blaming and criticising others rather than reflecting on the internally generated causes of their own behaviour. They reinforce emotional Reactive Self in their meaning-making role

In summary, meaning-making is said to be subjective. It is about the integration of feeling and intuition. It is about attitude and character. Meaning-making forces us to focus on the individuality and the uniqueness of the meaning-maker. Paradoxically, there is also no end to the intuitive and educative process of the meaning-maker as they continue to create new meanings by interacting with their environment and those in it.

Let's now consider the sense-making mindset of our Reactive Self.

CHAPTER 8
The Sense Making Mindset

The second mindset of our Reactive self is sense-making.

Let's have a look at what Humpty Dumpty says about sense-making.

> *"If you take one from three hundred and sixty five what remains?" asked Humpty Dumpty "Three hundred and sixty four of course." said Alice. Humpty Dumpty looked doubtful, "I'd rather see that done on paper." he said.*

Sense-making is objective. It is about evidence and analysis. It is about the "What is it?" question. It is about knowledge and competence. It is about our Practical (Sensing) Drive.

Julie Buxbaum in 'What to Say Next' says:

> *"I ask this question a lot - Does that make sense? - usually to my family, because I appreciate clarity and assume others do as well... we just assume other people understand what we are talking about. That we are, as the idiom goes, on the same wavelength. In my experience, we are not."*

Sense-making is a process of clarifying and removing ambiguity and uncertainty by searching for and organising similarities and differences from data sources through which intention-directed interpretations for choice-making are established. Therefore, sense-making as a process is the foundation of knowledge creation, where the quality of sense-making affects the quality of knowledge produced, and the outcome of choices based on that knowledge.

Brenda Dervin in a paper entitled Sense Making Theory and Practice, An Overview of User Interests in Knowledge Seeking and Use, says:

> *"..knowledge is the sense made at a particular point in time-space by someone. Sometimes, it gets shared and codified; sometimes a number of people agree upon it; sometimes it enters into a formalised discourse and gets published; sometimes it gets tested in other times and spaces and takes on the status of facts. Sometimes, it is fleeting and unexpressed. Sometimes it is hidden and suppressed. Sometimes, it gets imprimatur and becomes unjust law; sometimes it takes on the status of dogma. Sometimes it requires reconceptualising a world. Sometimes it involves contest and resistance. Sometimes it involves danger and death.*
>
> *In this view, sense-making and sense unmaking is a mandate of the human condition. Humans, sense-making assumes, live in a world of gaps: a reality that changes across time and space and is at least in part "gappy" at a given time-space; a human society filled with difference manifested in madness, culture, personality, inventiveness, tentativeness and capriciousness; a self that is sometimes centred, sometimes muddled, and always becoming. In this view, the sense-making and sense unmaking that is knowledge is a verb, always an activity, embedded in time and space, moving from a history toward a horizon, made*

INSIGHT INTENTION AND INTEGRITY

at the juncture between self and culture, society, organisation."

Acquiring knowledge is the "gap-filler" for each individual when they encounter a discrepancy between what they know and what they are experiencing in their connected context.

With that background let's look at where the sense-making mindset of our Adaptive Learning Map© is located.

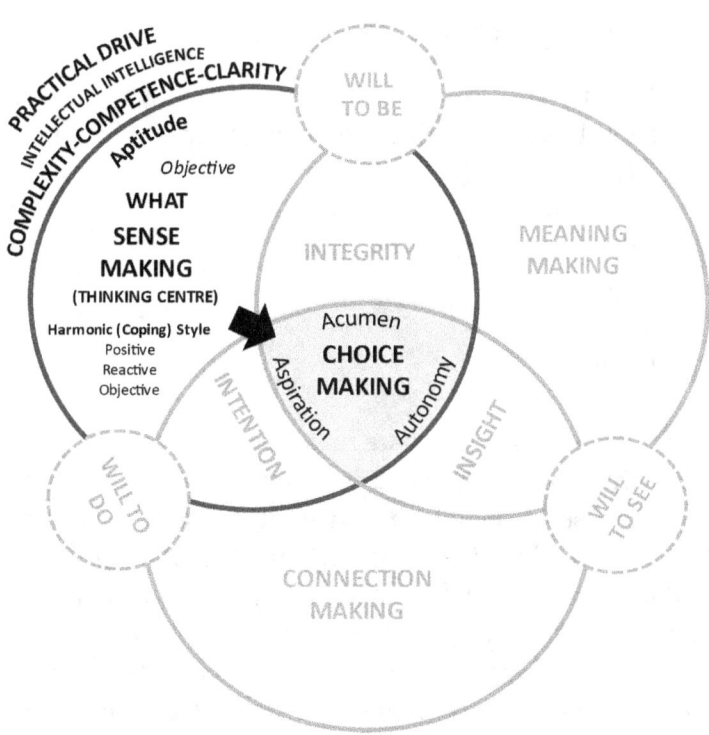

Figure 13: The Sense Making Mindset

The sense-making mindset has several key characteristics. It is:

- about the development of our Aptitude,

- about Competence, Clarity and Complexity
- informed by our Practical (Sensing) Drive,
- anchored in our Thinking Centre,
- supported by Intellectual Intelligence, and
- develops from our Harmonic coping (problem solving) style.

Aptitude is our natural ability to learn or excel in a certain area. It is often the case that a person has a group of aptitudes that fit together and helps them succeed at specific tasks.

There are many types of aptitude, including:

- Linguistic
- STEM (science, technology, engineering and mathematics)
- Artistic
- Mechanical
- Musical
- Physical
- Spatial
- Logical

Intellectual intelligence (IQ) is a measure of a person's growth in their reasoning ability. In short, it is supposed to gauge how well someone can use information and logic to answer questions or make predictions. *It is the combination of verbal, numerical and spatial abilities which includes visualising, use of memory, word fluency, verbal relations, perceptual speed, induction and deduction. Our ability to discern and make sense out of the triggers from our environment is underpinned by our present level of competence.* Sense-making competence indicates sufficiency of knowledge and skills that enable someone to act in a wide variety of situations.

Let's first look at the sense-making hierarchy that our knowledge sits in so we can have some context for the way we progressively make sense of what we are experiencing.

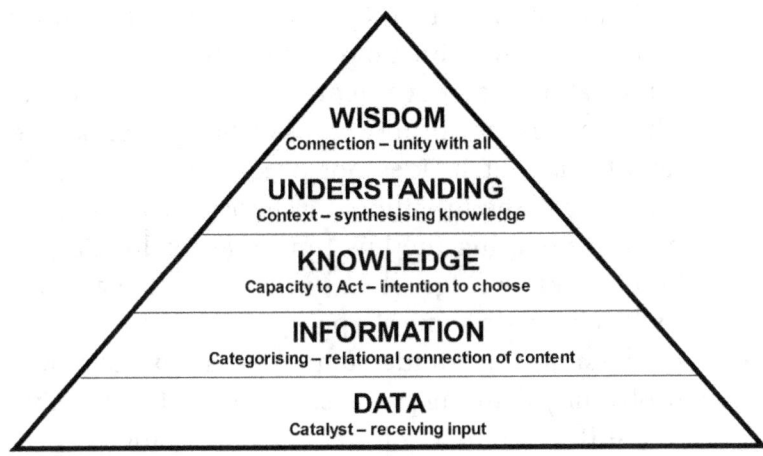

Figure 14: Our Sense-Making Hierarchy

The first four levels relate to the past and the present; they deal with what has been or what is known. Only the fifth level, wisdom, deals with the future because it incorporates vision and design. With wisdom, people can shape the future rather than just grasp the present and past. To achieve wisdom people must move successively through the other levels.

Let's have a closer look at the attributes of each level.

- **Data** - data is raw. It simply exists and has no significance beyond its existence (in and of itself). It can exist in any form, usable or not. It does not have meaning of itself. It may act as an external "trigger". It is often experienced as "noise". For example a bus just went past me is data.
- **Information** - information is data that has been made sense of by way of relational connection. Information can be useful, but does not have to be. It may enable us to classify a data "trigger". For example a bus timetable is information.
- **Knowledge** - knowledge is the capacity to act in a context and involves the appropriate collection of infor-

mation, such that its intent is to be useful. Knowledge involves a deterministic process. When we 'memorise' information, we have acquired potential knowledge. This knowledge in and of itself has potential usefulness to us, but it does not become actual knowledge until I have the intention, or choose, to act. For example remembering the bus timetable (or looking it up) becomes knowledge when I intend to catch a bus to go to the city to do some shopping.

- **Understanding** - understanding is an explanatory and probability defining process. It is mental and analytical. The difference between understanding and knowledge is the difference between 'learning' and 'memorising'. People who have understanding can undertake useful actions because they can synthesise new knowledge, or in some cases, at least new information, from what is previously known and understood. That is, understanding can build upon currently held information, knowledge and understanding itself. For example I have understanding when I recognise that the bus may be late at my bus stop because of situational factors I am aware of, such as an accident or heavy traffic, and can have contingency plans.

- **Wisdom** - wisdom is an inferential, interpretive, and somewhat intuitive process. It calls upon all the previous levels of consciousness, and specifically upon special types of human characteristics such as moral and ethical codes. It seeks to give us understanding about which there has previously been no understanding, and in doing so, goes far beyond understanding itself. It is the essence of philosophical probing. Unlike the previous four levels, it asks questions to which there is no, or no easily-achievable, answer, and in some cases, to which there can be no humanly-known answer. Wisdom is therefore, the process by which we also discern, or judge, between right and wrong, good and bad.

INSIGHT INTENTION AND INTEGRITY

Wisdom is a uniquely human state. For example I have wisdom when I realise that there is more than one way to get to the city after I reflect on the decision I made to accept a ride from the bus stop with a friend who stopped and offered me a lift to the city, and realised the value of our friendship, when they said call me anytime you may need a lift to the city.

Each of these sense-making elements can be looked at in terms of the aim, the learning mode, the attention timeline and the nature of the energy output in the following table:

DATA
Aim: Gathering information - receiving input, registering data without reflection
Learning mode: Instinctual reaction - the data mode of learning is at sensory or input level. Little actual learning takes place.
Attention: Immediate moment
Energy output: Automatic (Instinctive)
INFORMATION
Aim: Procedural efficiency - doing something the most efficient way: Conforming to standards or making simple adjustments and modifications.
Learning mode: Single-loop learning - action without reflection: Procedural learning entails redirecting a course of action to follow a pre-determined course.
Attention: Very short (present – now)
Energy output: Automatic (Practical)
KNOWLEDGE
Aim: Functional effectiveness - doing it the best way: evaluating and choosing between two or more alternative paths. Goal is effective action and resolution of inconsistencies.
Learning Mode: Double-loop learning - self-conscious reflection: a larger perspective that involves evaluation and modification of the goal or objective, as well as design of the path/process to get there.
Attention: Short (immediate past and present)
Energy: Sensitive (Self-reflection)

UNDERSTANDING
Aim: Synthesis - understanding what promotes or impedes integration of knowledge into action : strategic management and allocation of resources, using conceptual frameworks to track multiple events, encompasses attending to work roles and team climate.
Learning mode: Triple loop learning – "learning how to learn" by understanding context, relationships and trends: learning requires the making of meaning, which includes understanding context, seeing trends, comprehending roles and relationships and generating alternatives.
Attention: Medium to long term (historic past, present and near-term future)
Energy: Conscious (Contextual)
WISDOM
Aim: Integrity - Finding or reconnecting to one's purpose: defining or reconnecting with values, vision and mission. Understanding purpose and deep awareness of ecology, community, and ethical action.
Learning mode: Generative learning - values driven: learning for the joy of learning in open interaction with the environment. It involves creative processes, open-ended explorations and profound self-questioning.
Attention: Long term (distant past, to distant future)
Energy: Creative (Purposeful)

In summary, our five senses give us Data inputs (signals from the environment that are not capable of inducing a response alone – data is neutral) which we either ignore (as noise) or turn into Information (using our internal categorisation system to put the data into a useful response structure) which we then convert into to Knowledge (by applying an intention and capacity to act – our competence - from our repertoire of learned responses).

Knowledge, in our interactions with our context, may become Understanding (a recognition that our repertoire of learned responses is situational and will not necessarily serve us well next time) which may in time become Wisdom (by connecting us to our purpose and the living natural order). Of course it is not a sequential as that – our millions of neural pathways and complex brain chemistry operate in a much more holistic, intuitive, self-generating and emergent way.

Sense-making, at the lower levels, is highly valued in organisational hierarchy and is reinforced by position descriptions and "performance" management. It strongly supports the measure and control principles that underpin a results focused business model. It is mostly driven by the first three levels of data, information and knowledge, and in the new interrelated digital world, has become obsessed with 'big' data to support so called 'customer' driven marketing initiatives (many of which may annoy potential customers rather than attract them!).

Wirearchy demands that we understand all five levels of sense-making competence in order to contribute in the context of a world of increasing complexity. Complexity characterises the behaviour of a system whose component parts interact in multiple ways, culminating in a higher order structures or qualities that are greater than the sum of its parts. This means that there is no reasonable capacity to define the various possible interactions, or the nature of the emergent structures they create, in a linear problem-solving, so called 'root cause analysis', way that our sense-making mindset prefers. Emergence is a non-linear quality and defies step by step analysis. We can recall the sweetness in sugar example. The same could be said of the saltiness of salt.

Complex systems are not only non-linear but also adaptive. Chaos and complexity theory focuses on relationships and transitions - turbulence being the relational state of a system in transition - be it a weather system, stock market prices, molecular biology or technology development.

Emergence describes the ability of individual components of a large system to work together to give rise to dramatic and diverse behaviour. Emergence is the quality of non-linear organisation that arises in complex systems. Our brain is the most complex system in our known universe from which the mind is an emergent outcome that defies explanation, notwithstanding two thousand years of philosophical debate. In a similar way personal leadership in the context of wirearchy is emergent. It emerges from the demands of the context and defies 'after the event' analysis.

Paradoxically, the sense-making mindset is about the clarity of our thinking. It is about our competence to solve problems. It is very much about a focus on objective evidence and facts. It struggles with emergence because it cannot analyse and define it in linear ways. It thrives on position-based management in a power hierarchy – nation, organisation or family.

The problem with the Thinking Centre is that it likes to be in total control until you actively remind yourself to stay in the moment. It diverts your attention from everything important to the noise, stops you from creating, and sometimes poses as reality and causes fear and anxiety. Mental chatter doesn't deserve the attention it demands.

In our increasingly busy and connected world, brain fog is becoming far more common. When you spend a lot of time in your head, it becomes difficult to think. A cluttered mind is disruptive and frequently hinders critical thinking and causes mental fog. Common conditions of brain fog include poor memory, difficulty focusing or concentrating, and struggling with communicating.

Clarity (of thought) is one›s ability to gather and differentiate all incoming data and information into a clear definition so you can make, or not to make, choices. Clarity of thought also includes the ability to consider actions of self and others intentionally, rather than reflexively, and to understand that rational thinking is only one way to experience the world. Sense-making in the Reactive Self relishes problems that require objective analysis.

Our Practical (Sensing) Drive is a reflection how we have learned to give clarity to, and cope with, problems in our early social development of navigation.

INSIGHT INTENTION AND INTEGRITY

As mentioned earlier the social development perspective that underpins our sense-making is based on our coping (problem solving) style developed in our early childhood which suggests that we have three differing approaches to dealing with problem solving: positive, reactive and objective.

- People with a *positive problem-solving style* are generally optimistic and avoid negative thoughts or situations. Under pressure they seek to avoid the problem and distract themselves with something else, or minimise the importance of the problem. They want to feel good and have others around them feel good which often leads them to deny the existence of problems and therefore delay addressing them. They believe that they need to be upbeat about their own circumstances and often deny their own feelings.
- People with a *reactive problem-solving style* are reactive under pressure. They tend to work themselves up when a problem happens and have a hard time containing their reactions. This reactive intensity enables them to sense the "realness" of the problem even if it is only a small one. Venting their views enables them to move on to dealing with the issue. They believe others should react with the same intensity about the realness of the problem in a way that would suggest to them that others agree that it is a big deal too.
- People with the *objective problem-solving style* try to solve problems by being detached. Under pressure they remain cool and stay at arm's length from the problem. They value competence and knowing the right way to solve the problem. Their detachment from the problem can cause them to be seen as wanting to work outside of agreed frameworks or structures. They believe that they have the mental resources to deal with problems and even see emotional issues as having logical solutions.

Our Practical (Sensing) Drive, the source of our sense-making that underpins our competence, is a reflection of how we have used our

Jungian thinking function in a practical way to apply competent analysis to our choice-making. At its best sense-making focuses on the present, is practical and reasonable, utilises experience and 'common sense' to solve problems, keenly observes the surrounding world, is interested in logic and analysis, dislikes basing decisions on emotions and bases decisions on objective reasoning.

Our Thinking Centre, in Jungian terms, operates as a logic-based connection to present problems. In the context of the sense-making mindset our thinking function is triggered by our Jungian information gathering function of sensing (a sense of practicality and physical reality).

- **Thinking** is about order and organisation, being objective, detached, being able to discriminate, and using logic. Thinking preference people naturally seek to understand cause and effect - using an orderly chain of reasoning to establish the relationships. The Thinking mind seeks the truth, getting to the nub of the matter in an objective way. We experience our Thinking function when we are being dispassionate and are able to make decisions at arm's length from whatever emotional turmoil may surround a situation. Thinking is about principles and uses well-organised foundations of knowledge. It is the engine that devises plans and creates organised structures.
- **Sensing** is concrete and is about experiencing the world as it "is" - using the five senses. It is about attending to the here and now, being aware of the tangible sensory impressions of the moment. It is about trusting most one's direct experiences as a guideline for future action. Sensing is about being literal, concrete and practical, noticing "what is" as opposed to what "could be." It is about remembering, cataloguing and recalling, often with great detail, a wide variety of experiences and information,

INSIGHT INTENTION AND INTEGRITY

When we bring the information gathering function of sensing together to influence the judging function of thinking what emerges is the Jungian sensing-thinking function pair that is the foundation of sense-making.

- **Sensate Thinking** – stress systematic decision-making with quantitative, not qualitative data. They establish order, set up control and manage with certainty. They prefer tasks that are structured and prefer to take very few risks. There is a focus on immediate problems, the use of standard processes and playing by the rules. ST's dive into the details and look for specifics and to make step-by-step progress. Once set with a decision, doubt and opposition do not deter them, and they may resist a reanalysis. They are objective. They are "level-headed" and 'hard-hearted'.

The two functions of thinking and sensing, in the context of sense-making, can be expressed with an extraverted or introverted orientation.

- **Extraverted Thinking:** has its focus on order. It is about organizing and ordering the outside world; organizing both people and things to achieve a purpose. It is using logic and reasoning in dialogue with others. It is directing action and making decisions. It is purposeful sorting out; discriminating among alternatives. Extraverted Thinking asks questions, collects information in an orderly way, and solves problems in a systematic manner.
- **Introverted Thinking:** presumes logical order rules the Universe; illogic is dismissed as just so much mental clutter that needs to be swept out of the mind. Information is taken in and logically organised in clusters of thought, with principles at the foundation. It strives to fit new pieces of information into clusters of thought where it most logically fits. It sorts out and

discriminates that which makes logical sense from that which does not. Like a detective, Introverted Thinking is drawn to seeking clues and root causes - to solve a problem or a riddle.

- **Extraverted Sensing:** is about seizing the moment, becoming immersed in the here and now, and spontaneously interacting with people, things, and situations of interest. It is being aware of, fully tuned into, and energised by the options and impulses of the moment. It is making "work" into play, learning by doing, and enjoying the creative process. It is being attuned to the variety, quality, and sensate appeal of sensory experiences. Extraverted Sensing notices tangible realities and relates to them in a pragmatic fashion.
- **Introverted Sensing**: attends to, enjoys acquiring, and relying upon an internal library of detailed personal knowledge, facts, feelings, sensations and information gleaned from experiences. Information and impressions from present experiences are archived in an orderly way into memory - which is typically a vast internal storehouse of data, details and impressions. The Introverted Sensing mind seeks rhythm, reliability, and order in its internal library and in its relationships with people and the outside world.

These two Jungian functions provide the competence or aptitude lens that we use to unconsciously make sense of the problems we identify and are confronted with, both alone and with others. They are the task focussed and objective 'what is it' of our connection to others. Hence our Thinking Centre provides us with the aptitude for sense-making.

With the caveat mentioned earlier the sense-making function anchored in the Thinking Centre is adept at tasks that involve being better at:

- Language
- Logic
- Critical thinking
- Numbers
- Reasoning

In summary, sense-making is objective. It is about evidence and analysis. It is about the practical application of our knowledge and competence. It is informed by our Thinking Centre and Practical (Sensing) Drive.

It is a process of clarifying and removing ambiguity and uncertainty by searching for and organising similarities and differences from data sources through which intention-directed interpretations for choice-making are established. Therefore, sense-making as a process is the foundation of knowledge creation, where the quality of sense-making affects the quality of knowledge produced, and the outcome of choices based on that knowledge.

It answers the question "What is it?"

Against that background let's look at the connection-making mindset.

CHAPTER 9

The Connection Making Mindset

We could look at what Humpty Dumpty says about connection-making. But this time we will hear from the Cheshire Cat!

"But I don't want to go among mad people." said Alice.

Oh, you can't help that," said the Cat. "We're all mad here. I'm mad. You're mad."

"How do you know I'm mad?" said Alice.

"You must be," said the Cat, "or you wouldn't have come here."

The third mindset of our Reactive Self is connection-making. Connection-making can be challenging and sometimes you are "mad" to go there. Why is it that some people don't understand you, no matter how much you try? In a recent book by Thomas Erikson: Surrounded by Idiots, the first chapter is titled "Communication Happens on the Listeners Terms.". He says:

> *"Everything you say to a person is filtered through (his) frames of reference, biases and preconceived ideas. What remains is ultimately the message that (he) understands"*

It is about recognising that, in your connection-making, there is a difference between your meaning-making and sense-making mindset and the meaning-making and sense-making mindset of others.

With that in mind let's have a look at where the connection-making mindset of our Adaptive Learning Map© is located.

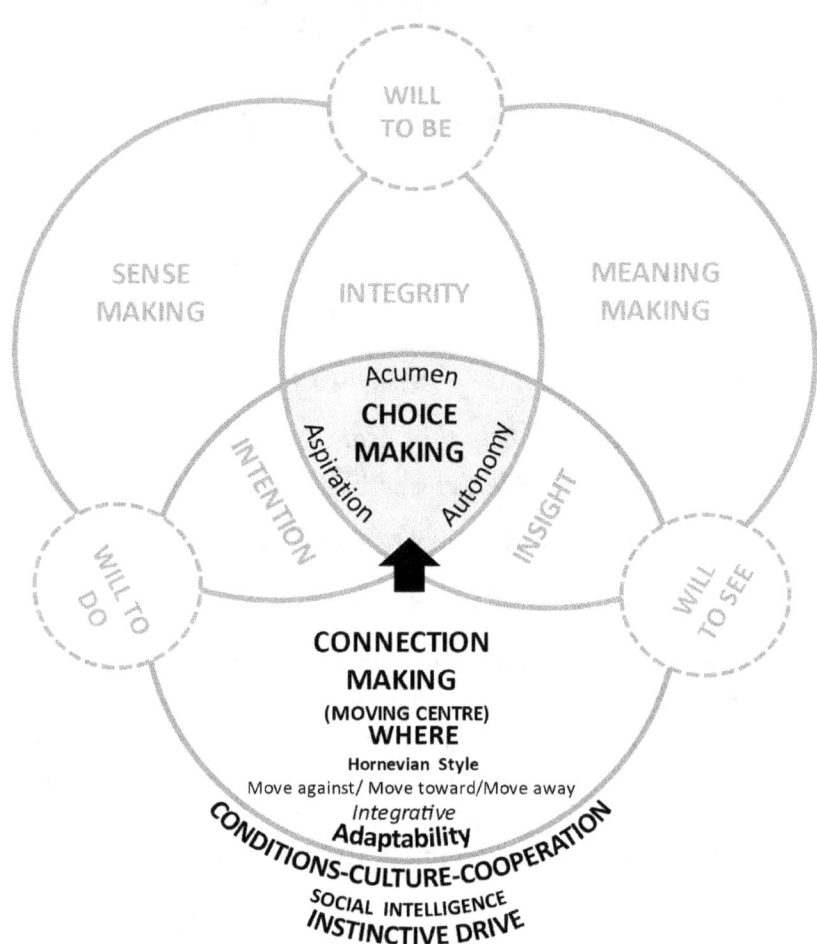

Figure 15: The Connection Making Mindset

The connection-making mindset has several key characteristics. It is:

- about Cooperation, Culture and Life Conditions
- about the development of our Adaptability

- informed by our Instinctive Drive,
- based in our Moving Centre,
- supported by Social Intelligence, and
- develops from our Social Style.

Aristotle took the position that not all connections to others were the same. He identifies three distinct types of connection, in what he calls friendship.

The first is a friendship connection of utility. In this type of connection, the two people are not in it for the sake of any affection for one another, but because each receives a benefit from the relationship. This type of relationship is temporary and due to a shared situation. When the benefit ends so does the connection. An example is a work relationship. You might enjoy the time you spend together, but once the situation changes, so does the nature of your relationship. When you leave the organisation, despite the promises to keep in touch, you more often don't, unless there is ongoing utility.

The second is a friendship connection based on the pleasure of the person's company. Again, it is often a temporary connection. It is fine so long as the two parties gain enjoyment from their connection, but ends when their tastes or lifestyles diverge. It can be seen with an old school friend you meet later who was the life of the party back in the day, but with whom you now find you have nothing in common.

The third type is a friendship connection that is based on mutual appreciation of the character and authenticity of the other person, rather than on transactional value or a shared pleasure. Here it is the qualities of the individuals themselves that bind them together as friends.

To Aristotle, few things came close to the value of such a relationship. As he puts it:

> *"But complete friendship is the relationship of good people similar in virtue; for they wish good in the same way to each other insofar as they are good, and they are good in their own right. Now those who wish good to their friend for the friend's own sake are friends most of all; for they have this attitude because of the friend (himself), not coincidentally. Hence these people's friendship lasts as long as they are good and virtue enduring"*

The depth and intimacy of such connections means that they most likely include the other two kinds of friendship: there is utility and pleasure involved too. It is a connection based on mutual appreciation.

Mutual appreciation-based connection involves:

- **Perspective** – seeing the other person in context and recognising the situational impact on them,
- Potential – both of the people involved see the continuity of the relationship into the future as a given. They don't have to work at it as it comes naturally,
- **Presence -** when we connect with others ensuring we are fully present in the moment of connection and to the shared experience we are having with another,
- **Insight – recognising that mutual appreciation** is based on self-awareness. It doesn't work if we are trying to be something we are not,
- **Intention – being open about what you are trying to achieve and inviting them to share their thoughts and intentions,**
- **Integrity – there is a sense of trust existing between you and the other person based on personal integrity.** This means following your moral or ethical convictions and doing the right thing in all circumstances, even if no one is watching you.

INSIGHT INTENTION AND INTEGRITY

Mutual appreciation is the foundation of cooperation *Cooperation* means working with someone in the sense of enabling them to be more able to do something (typically by providing information or resources they would not otherwise have). Cooperation means working together independently.

It can be distinguished from collaboration. Collaboration means actually working alongside (often for) someone to achieve a common goal. Cooperation, on the other hand, means working together independently on personal goals.

It is best understood by making a distinction between "collectives" that are hierarchy-based and "connectives" that are wirearchy-based.

- Collectives collaborate: Collectives are part of the structure of the organisation hierarchy. They give priority to the group over the individual and encourage members to adopt a joint identity that unites them around their shared goal.
- Connectives cooperate: A connective doesn't give priority to the group or the individual but instead supports and encourages both simultaneously. There's no subordination of identity in a connective because each member is actively pursuing their own goals and supporting those of others.
- Collectives are breeding grounds for politics and power struggles. Even with the best intentions, collaboration often encourages pyramids of power and authority. The higher up the pyramid you are in a collective, the more freedom you have to carve out your own individual identity and direct the group's efforts towards your own goals.
- Connectives are self-organising and self-sustaining. No master architect, conductor, or blueprint is needed. You can join or leave a dance party at any time and the beat goes on with or without you. Dancing was always based on structured steps (usually where the male "leads") but now

days once the music comes on people just move organically with it. They dance to the beat of their own drum.

There are hierarchies embedded in the natural order. But the natural order is also overflowing with self-organising cooperative networks. In a forest there are countless levels of interdependency and cooperation at work, in which self-centred goals intersect to sustain each other and create larger, unpredictable, organic patterns. Collectives are brought into existence by design and operate as closed systems. Connectives emerge from the universally connected digital space and operate adaptively.

A networked knowledge sharing community is a connective that informs the individual in a way that they can cooperate, and at the same time, contribute to organisation goals and plans collaboratively. Knowledge transfer is very difficult to achieve when the goals and plans become a top down driven, straight-jacket that is impervious to ideas and challenge. Collaboration cannot happen without cooperation. Cooperation ("I" focus) is the bedrock of collaboration ("we" focus). We need to recognise cooperation involves engaging each individual based on "who" they are, "what" they need or want and "why" they choose to be engaged. Cooperation is a core element of connection-making.

Cooperation is also underpinned by certain moral duties, for example, to keep promises. It has a future dimension to it that can be undermined by unforeseen events. Connection-making is often informed by natural and organic processes that have continuing cooperation as their foundation. Consequently an intention to cooperate will lead to genuine ways to explain or resolve any moral duties that have been conflicted. Cooperation is underpinned by integrity.

Connection-making is fundamentally a natural and organic processes, although you would not know that by looking at the corporately controlled internet we have today. Today's internet inherited the political and technical baggage of broadcast era networks

INSIGHT INTENTION AND INTEGRITY

whose mechanical and closed system architecture is completely out of tune with the ever-evolving, open systems logic of our connected culture. The future is invariably an extrapolation of the past, with a few exceptions, largely because our connection-making is embedded in our culture and our associated habits and the structures that support them.

Adaptability is the ability to change our behaviour, direction or approach to doing things, in order to suit a new situation. Being adaptable means working without boundaries, and being open to finding diverse and unexpected solutions to problems and challenges. Without limitations on your thinking and feelings, challenges become something not to fear, but to enjoy working through. You will also be willing to engage a variety of people with diverse skills to share knowledge and build relevant networks of highly engaged and capable people. It is the pre-eminent skill for developing connections with others. Adaptability is an essential foundation of the connection-making dimension of emergent leadership.

The connection-making of our Reactive Self is primally organised by our Moving Centre. Our Moving Centre has, as its foundation, our self-preservation, self-renewal and social primal instincts that were discussed in developing your understanding our personality lens. We have these three primal survival instincts in common with our evolutionary ancestry that operate as an automatic response to external stimuli, usually a perceived threat. Remember we are still dealing with our Reactive Self mindset here.

In essence, every person has three primal instinct clusters that are genetic in origin and are supported by automatic energy. Being driven by automatic energy makes primal instincts as unconscious to us as the physical functioning of our body such as breathing and digesting food are.

The following descriptions developed by Katherine Fauvre provide a deeper understanding of each instinct.

The self-preservation instinct cluster *is about our focus on physical safety and comfort, which can translate into concerns about food, money, housing and physical health. This instinct is directed at the physical environment and in a healthy state appears as the ability to take care of basic life necessities – paying bills, maintaining the home, acquiring useful skills, and so forth.* Sometimes people who have a lot of this automatic energy are so grounded that they can seem sombre and serious. When we are using a self-preservation instinct, we tend to be focused on getting our physical and material needs met, and on defending what we have. People with high self-preservation instinct establish and maintain their boundaries, drawing a circle around themselves to say, "Inside this circle is ME and MINE; outside is NOT ME and doesn't belong here." A special person may be included inside the circle but only upon invitation. The driving force is the message, "I have to take care of myself." Other people, who do not have strong a self-preservation instinct, may see them as selfish, aloof, or always surrounded by an invisible wall.

The self-renewal instinct cluster *is about our focus on one-to-one relationships and intimacy, which can translate into a desire for communicating on a one-to-one basis rather than with a larger group. This instinct is directed at the creative drive for renewing life and the attraction to another person. In a healthy state this instinct is directed at the desire for intensity of experience - any activity that will provide a "charge".* People who have a strongly developed self-renewal instinct are subconsciously saying, "I need who you are and what you have in order to be whole." They seem to express a sense of intimacy, a longing for completion, rather than for companionship. They want intense contact in all their interactions. For this reason, other people may misinterpret their cues as being sexually oriented, rather than a desire for one-to-one interaction at a physical, mental or emotional level.

The social instinct cluster is about our focus on group interactions and a sense of value that comes from participation in collective/tribal activities. This instinct is the foundation of survival by enabling the vulnerability of the individual in a hostile environment to be overcome, and by ensuring social cohesion through adherence to cultural or tribal norms, including our "place" within the hierarchical social structure of the group. There is a tendency to believe that people with high social instinct are extraverts, but this is not necessarily true, as the instinct is not toward being an "outgoing person" but rather toward caring about community and one's place within the community. Their instinct is to be aware of other people and to develop a sense of how to interact within the group. They can become people-pleasers, giving themselves away for the sake of the needs of the group – family, club or team - and then often regretting it.

In theoretical terms we have an instinctual stack that operates as an "independent personality" lens that will shape the way our connection-making shows itself. One instinct cluster is dominant in its expression in that it is employed most easily, and invariably unconsciously. Our dominant instinct indicates what we automatically notice (attend to) and prioritize for action. The secondary instinct cluster is our fall-back position, the type of response we use to support our dominant instinct. Finally, there is the least used instinct cluster, the aspect of our lives that we overlook and tend to take for granted. Identifying our dominant, secondary, and least used instincts indicates our "instinctual stack."

In some interesting observations about the role of instincts in connection-making, Chernick Fauvre says:

> "*Self-preserving moves to Self-renewal:* the self-preserving instinct person considers a mate as an essential need to maintain and ensure security. Therefore when in search of a mate the self-preserving person will feel anxiety and suspense until a mate is secured. In order to attract a mate, the self-preserving person will shift to their respective self-renewal instinctual drive to accommodate this fear. Outwardly the self-preserving person will behave like the self-renewal person, pay more attention to their desirability and will be sensual and flirtatious. At first, the self-preserving person will spend more time one on one with the possible mate. Once the mate is secured, the self-preserving person will return to basic routines that would ideally include the mate. An area of pain and disappointment for this person is when they have a mate that is unwilling to pay attention to issues of security and dispute their need for inner calm.
>
> *Social moves to Self-preserving:* the social instinct person will think in terms more indicative of the self-preserving instinct when selecting a mate. This is important to ensure the desired security that rank and social status can provide. The social person seeks a mate with shared social vision and similar values. This is necessary to fulfil the desire for a mate that will

INSIGHT INTENTION AND INTEGRITY

join them in their activities. Therefore a secure social position is attention. Much attention is paid to the potential mate's connections, rank and ability to provide financial security. This person enjoys bringing others together, feeling the "the more the merrier". They are often adept at creating the centre stage and often use their home for social events, gatherings and causes. At first the social person will spend more time one on one with the potential mate. Once the mate is in place, the social person will return to outside interests, groups and/or activities, ideally, this is with their mate. An area of pain and disappointment for this person is when they have a mate that is unwilling to pay attention to their need for people, activities and, causes and is unwilling to share their interest in others.

Self-renewal moves to Social: the self-renewal instinct person will seek the greater world or social arena to find a desired mate. The self-renewal person is normally happy tucked away in a secluded setting with one significant other. However, when alone or in search of a mate, this person will behave much more like the social instinct person. One must be with others to find "the other". Once the mate has been selected, the social activity will be replaced by the dominant drive for time spent in union with the other one to one. At first the self-renewal person may spend time with the potential mate in the company of others. They become a pair even in groups. Then when the passion for deeper connection is ignited the self-renewal person will want to totally bond with their desire other. When the mate is secured, the self-renewal person will return to a one-on-one style of relating. Ideally, this is intense time

173

spent with the desired other or mate. An area of pain for this person is when they have a mate that is unwilling to pay attention to their degree of connection and intimately share their deepest innermost thoughts."

You can understand your instinctual stack by competing the questionnaire in the Tool Kit.

The Moving Centre is also temperament driven and reflects our Jungian orientations of extraversion, introversion, judging and perceiving. The two orientation dimensions (extraversion-introversion and judging-perceiving) are the key to understanding the way that meaning-making (intuition and feeling) and sense-making (sensing and thinking) functions are expressed. Together they are the temperament drivers of the way we engage in connection-making with each other.

Let's revisit the four dimensions of temperament we discussed when developing our personality lens. Temperament is a reflection of the relative strengths of extraversion (outgoing) or introversion (reserved) and judging (structured) or perceiving (flexible) preferences. The resulting temperaments are:

- Extraverted Judgers (Challengers)
- Extraverted Perceivers (Experimenters)
- Introverted Perceivers (Maintainers)
- Introverted Judgers (Organisers)

Extraverted Judgers (Challengers): emphasise acting on external information. As extroverts, they tend to feel that it is up to them to initiate contacts with other people, whether in the context of establishing or maintaining a relationship. They will not necessarily act on that, though, and sometimes wish others would take over this role. They will critically view others who they perceive as having some type of information and not acting on it or applying it. They expect new information to be applied towards a productive purpose and question the capabilities of someone who has valuable information and doesn't use it. Although this criticism can be leveled at any type, it is often directed at Introverted Perceivers – Maintainers, their opposite temperament.

Extraverted Perceivers (Experimenters): place significant value on generating ideas and using their own volition. As such, they tend to view negatively others who appear limited or restricted in either their ability to exercise choice or their ability to accept or even consider other possibilities. Although this criticism can be leveled at any type, the types it is often directed at Introverted Judgers – Organisers, their opposite temperament. As extroverts, they tend to feel that it is up to them to initiate contacts with other people and feel quite natural in that role.

Introverted Perceivers (Mantainers): value the ability to be prepared for one's present and future environment. As introverts, they tend to be relaxed and somewhat passive about initiating relationships with other people, mostly assuming that others will take the initiative. They look down upon others who appear to not be cognisant and adapted to either the present situation and/or impending future possibilities e.g., questioning someone going outside in freezing temperatures without a coat on. Although this criticism can be levelled at any type, it is often directed at Extraverted Judgers – Challengers, their opposite temperament.

Introverted Judgers (Organisers): place great importance on maintaining and consistently following one's own principles and rules. As introverts, they tend to be calm and relaxed about initiating relationships with other people, mostly assuming that others will take the initiative, but will be more inclined to try to make sure a relationship is maintained once established. However, they will judge another person very harshly if they deem that person has not consistently followed their own principles. If they vocalise this criticism, it will often be couched bluntly and unencumbered by diplomacy, as the offender's violation of principle flies in the face of their own principles. A severe enough violation, in their eyes, may cause them to question or even terminate the relationship with the other person. They do not necessarily expect others to share their same values, and they are generally comfortable with others who have opposing viewpoints, as long as they are based on consistent reasoning.

Each of the temperaments see the other temperaments differently in their connection-making context. The key differences are shown in the table below:

Challengers (Extraverted Judging) see:
• **Experimenters** (Extraverted Perceivers) as unpredictable and moody, and therefore a bit irritating, but also as extremely energetic once they do focus on doing something, as well as the source of initiatives that may be worthwhile. • **Maintainers** (Introverted Perceivers) as unpredictable, moody, as well as too passive and unreliable, especially if they are required to show initiative or even reciprocity. • **Organisers** (Introverted Judgers) as solid, reliable, and reassuringly predictable, and usually not inclined towards being the first to take the initiative in taking action.
Experimenters (Extraverted Perceiving) see:
• **Challengers** (Extraverted Judgers) as active but too 'now' focused and inflexible, slightly annoying due to a lack of sense of spontaneity. • **Maintainers** (Introverted Perceivers) as pleasantly flexible and responsive to their initiatives, sometimes too unpredictable but for that very reason never boring. • **Organisers** (Introverted Judgers) as too predictable and boring, too unwilling to do things on the spur of the moment.

> **Maintainers (Introverted Perceiving) see:**
>
> - **Experimenters** (Extraverted Perceivers) as pleasantly energetic in an unpredictable and therefore not boring way, also able to take for granted variations in levels of energy in others.
> - **Challengers** (Extraverted Judgers) as annoyingly pushy and insistent in their initiatives; they may respect their energy levels but also wonder if they don't see that a lot of that energy is spent wastefully to no good purpose.
> - **Organisers** (Introverted Judgers) as boring and too concerned with stability.
>
> **Organisers (Introverted Judging) see:**
>
> - **Experimenters** (Extraverted Perceivers) as unreliable, and too unpredictable in their impulses and initiatives.
> - **Challengers** (Extraverted Judgers) as driven and willing to take the initiative and get things going in a structured, constant way.
> - **Maintainers** (Introverted Perceivers) as unreliable and unwilling to take any initiative, with too low levels of energy.

This leads us to the idea of social intelligence as the culture-based foundation of connection making. Social intelligence is about our learned strategies for interacting with the world and others in it that reflect our beliefs and values maturity level, that are life conditions and culture related.

Social intelligence has the following characteristics:

- The ability to carry on conversations with a wide array of people and verbally communicate with appropriate and tactful words,
- Being **adept at learning how to play different social roles,** and well-versed at the informal social rules that are the foundation of social interaction,
- Being **excellent listeners,**
- Knowing how to **efficiently analyse other people's meaning-making and sense-making drives by paying attention to what they are saying and how they are behaving,**

- Putting their **skills into practice and feeling at ease with many different types of personalities,**
- Taking **care of the impression of themselves they make on other people.** This is the hardest skillset because it requires **getting alignment of intentions using accountability and authenticity by making their meaning-making and sense-making drives visible without imposing them on the other person.**

Robert Kegan's idea of cultural embeddedness is a way of considering the differing social intelligence lenses that people use in connection-making. Kegan says that we develop as human beings between states of individuation and states of cultural embeddedness. He says:

> "There is never just a you; and at this very moment of your own buoyancy or lack of it, your own sense of wholeness or lack of it, is in large part a function of how your own current embeddedness culture is holding you." (the emphasis is mine)

The cultural embeddedness idea is also a significant part of the work of Clare Graves. Graves developed an approach that describes bio-psycho-social systems along an evolutionary continuum. Each level is designated by a colour, e.g. Blue, and two letters, e.g. D-Q. The first letter stands for the life conditions on which the level is based and the second for personal needs drivers used to deal with problems arising from the related life conditions.

INSIGHT INTENTION AND INTEGRITY

COLOUR		PERCEIVED LIFE CONDITIONS		PERSONAL NEEDS DRIVERS
First Tier				
Beige	A	State of nature and biological urges and drives: physical senses dictate the state of being.	N	Survival: as natural instincts and reflexes direct; automatic existence.
Purple	B	Threatening and full of mysterious powers and spirit beings that must be placated and appeased.	O	Tribal: according to tradition and ritual ways of group; tribal; loyal.
Red	C	Like a jungle where the tough and strong prevail, the weak serve; nature is an adversary to be conquered.	P	Power: asserting self for dominance, conquest and power; exploitative.
Blue	D	Controlled by a Higher Power that punishes evil and eventually rewards good works and righteous living.	Q	Obedience: dutiful as higher authority and rules direct; conforming; guilt driven.
Orange	E	Full of resources to develop and opportunities to make things better and bring prosperity.	R	Achievement: pragmatically to achieve results and get ahead; test options; manoeuvre.
Green	F	The habitat wherein humanity can find love and purposes through affiliation and sharing.	S	Humanity: respond to human needs; affiliative; situational; consensual; fluid.

Second Tier				
Yellow	G	A chaotic organism where change is the norm and uncertainty an acceptable state of being.	T	Knowledge: functional; integrative; interdependent; existential; flexible; questioning; accepting.
Turquoise	H	A delicately balanced system of interlocking forces in jeopardy at humanity's hands; chaordic.	U	Global: experiential: transpersonal; collective consciousness; collaborative; interconnected.

A person isn't generally locked at a single level. The letter pairs can shift with respect to each other and, to some extent, be shifted by conditions. For example, it's possible for someone to live in an E-level world but only have access to Q-level means of dealing with life; or to have an S-level personal needs driver while being caught up with overwhelming C-life conditions.

Based on this hierarchy what emerges is a description of values and belief systems/worldview at each level that is an indicator of just how your awareness about life in general may have evolved and the higher levels of maturity that are open to you.

LEVEL/VALUES	BELIEF SYSTEM/WORLDVIEW
	First Tier
1 – Beige: Survival *Instinctive.*	The world is based on the biological imperatives of survival: basic needs for food, shelter, sex and comfort. Relevant to newborn babies but few other people apart from extreme situations or a life-threatening crisis.
2 – Purple: Tribal *Loyalty, Inclusion, Allegiance.*	The world is mysterious, containing good and evil spirits – sacred symbols and totems provide protection from harm. This is seen in its purest form in some tribal cultures. In western society it is seen in more diluted form in clubs (e.g. football supporters), strong family units, cults, and some organisations which are dominated by loyalty to a dominant leader. Our tribe and its chief (and ancestors) are the most important things in life.
3 – Red: **Power** *Immediate gratification, Domination.*	The world is all about strength, aggression, anger, selfishness. Success is about winning respect and avoiding shame. Seen in the 'terrible twos' of childhood, rebellious youth breaking from the tribe and tradition. Macho behaviour often seen inside prisons and in business leaders happy to use punishment, force and bribery to get what they want. Egocentric and exploitative. I do what I want and to hell with everyone else.
4 – Blue: **Obedience** *Authority, Order, Duty, "Truth"*	The world is rational, well-defined into distinct categories and well-ordered. Strong sense of what is right and what is wrong, and requirement to obey authority. Success is about maintaining stability and punishing anyone who rocks the boat. Rewards will come from working hard and keeping ones nose clean. Seen in absolutist organisations like strict religions and the military.

5 – Orange: **Achievement** *Success, Materialism, Status.*	The world is a playground of personal freedom, abundance, achievement, and enjoyment of material rewards. Skilful and ethical use of power in pursuit of popularity, prestige and accomplishment. Creation of wealth through innovation, science and technology. Right at the heart of personal and business drive for success: the cornerstone of entrepreneurial capitalism. The unhealthy aspects are based on greed and selfishness.
6 – Green: **Humanity** *Equality, Fairness, Involvement.*	The world contains a spiritual void that requires the rediscovery of basic human needs like love, inner peace and caring for others. Everyone has a right to be nurtured and respected: people are more important than things. Seen in organisations that tackle prejudice and inequality. The unhealthy aspects will be seen when the desire for endless consultation risks slow decision-making and lack of strong responses to tough issues.
Second Tier	
7 – Yellow: **Understanding** *Learning, Curiosity.*	The world (including humanity itself) is exciting, diverse and curious and needs to be studied, analysed and understood. The world's challenges respond to learning, competence, reason, science and design. Less concerned about ego: willing to take a contrarian position if it fits the analysis.
8 – Turquoise: **Universalism** *Planet as single entity*	The world is in danger of geo-political collapse because of short-termism and short-sighted approaches. In order to eliminate war, poverty, hunger disease and political oppression we need meta-solutions at a higher logical level than current systems. It would require leaders to move beyond local, individual boundaries. Introducing a sense of (non-religious) spirituality into global issues.

Graves approach is based on the idea that as human beings we develop through a series of levels or behavioural states. At each level we learn and act in a way that is consistent with the particular level of cultural embeddedness.

The Gravesian model is not a typology for categorising people into boxes. It is a model which seeks to surface ways of thinking about a quality that resides, in varying proportions, within human beings, not labels for kinds of human being. The question is not how to deal with a person at a given level, but how to understand the life conditions/personal needs drivers of each level *when they are activated* in the person.

Whether at work or in school, we are over-stretched and stressed, or under-employed and bored, because of these misalignments according to Graves. Most of us operate with mixtures and blends of these levels, though one or two are often dominant.

The Gravesian approach means that human development is continuous and never finished. It changes in accord with changes in life conditions of existence, thereby creating new belief systems in which the old belief systems are integrated. When a new system or stage unfolds, we also change our mindset and habits to adapt to these new conditions.

The idea of two interacting forces is central to Graves' theory, and forms the foundation of Spiral Dynamics, developed by Beck and Cowan, which has emerged from his approach. Our innate predisposition and neuronal systems (genes), as well as the social and cultural experiences gained through being alive and conscious (memes), help shape who we are.

The level of deep values is what Spiral Dynamics seeks to make visible, so we can recognise the worldviews and strategies we use to give meaning to our family, work and cultural context (life conditions). Christopher Cowan says:

> *"If surface values are like leaves floating on a stream, the next layer, hidden values, is the core current that carries them bobbing past. A good sense for hidden values sniffs out the reasoning beneath surface values and exposes why long-standing beliefs, attitudes, and traditions exist in organisations ...... Values have momentum like flywheels - hard to stop and difficult to turn. Powerful as hidden values are something deeper shapes them.*
>
> *Spiral dynamics is the bedrock of deep values. Hidden values flow from deep values. Spiral dynamics is the study of the emergence and patterns of deep values that mould strategists' worldviews, form corporate mindsets, structure leader/follower relationships, establish decision structures, and define reality."*

In summary, the Spiral Dynamics approach has the following zones:

ZONES IN THE SPIRAL DYNAMIC CYCLE					
World View	**Purpose**	**Key Goal**	**Strategy**	**Approach**	**Focus**
First Tier					
Beige AN	To survive as a physical being	Just staying alive	Respond as instincts and senses direct to meet biological needs	Instinctive, automatic, and reactive	**Me**

INSIGHT INTENTION AND INTEGRITY

Purple	BO	To find safety and bring honour to family and ancestors	Finding safety/ kinship/ harmony/ reciprocity	Follow ancestral ways and elders, listen to spirit world, form safe tribes	Ritual ways where all share in and follow elders, chief, customs	We
Red	CP	To get power and respect, have a good time, be heroic	Raw individualism/ exerting dominance/ power/ survival	Exploit others, feel no guilt, be courageous, avoid shame, live in the moment	Hands-on, tough work controlled by firm, respected boss	Me
Blue	DQ	To find purpose and ultimate security by living righteously	Meaning in life and death/ stability/ order/ deserve reward	Seek absolute truth, obey rightful higher authority, keep things in order	Linear processing, by-the-book with errors punished, dutiful	We
Orange	ER	To make things better by setting goals and mastering life's game	Autonomy/ success/best options/ material gain/ novelty/ change	Strive to win, make things better now, risk as needed, network, explore options	Competing to gain advantage and come out in control, on top	Me

Green	FS	To find peace in a sharing community by becoming useful	Affiliation/ peace of mind/ balance/ sense of community	Sacrifice for mutual gain, share, cooperate to build consensus, teamwork	Cooperative in joint ventures where all contribute and share	**We**
Second Tier						
Yellow	GT	To be free to explore important things and inter-connections	Knowledge/ freedom to be free/ discovery of what life is about	Learn diverse things, follow personal principles, be flexible, non-competitive	Independent focus on complex systems and functional flow states	**Me**
Turquoise	HU	To become one with all things and thus a responsible being	Viability for all beings in a complex, sustainable world	Explore consciousness, be holistic, exercise global responsibility and interests	Unify and integrate diverse knowledge and ways of being	**We**

Consciousness continues its upward flow. None of the Spiral Dynamics First Tier memes can fully appreciate the value of the other memes. Each believes that its worldview is the only true perspective. However, a qualitative leap in consciousness occurs when a person moves past the Green meme into Second Tier.

INSIGHT INTENTION AND INTEGRITY

Individuals who operate from the Second Tier can fully appreciate the value and necessity of all the memes. They understand that the health of the entire spiral, or all memes, is essential. At the Second Tier, fear and anxiety largely disappear from consciousness. At the Second Tier mental activity consists of joining, linking, and synthesising in pluralistic systems.

The power of Spiral Dynamics is in the transition points between levels that reflect the capacity we have to be open to a higher level of collective contribution.

The transition points are:

Beige/Purple – Awakening of a sense of dependent self in a mysterious and frightening world	Me to We
Purple/Red – Awakening of an egocentric self that is determined to break the shackles of the family or tribe and become independent	We to Me
Red/Blue – Awakening of purposeful self with guilt in search of a meaningful existence and reasons why we live and die	Me to We
Blue/Orange – Awakening of an independence-seeking self who challenges higher authority and tests possibilities	We to Me
Orange/Green – Awakening of a socio-centric self who strives for belonging and acceptance to discover inner harmony	Me to We
Green/Yellow – Awakening of an inquiring, interdependent self who no longer needs approval yet can cooperate	We to Me
Yellow/Turquoise – Awakening of an experiential self who seeks ways of being that use knowledge to restore natural harmony and balance	Me to We

These transitions underpin the development of social adaptability. Social adaptability is about how one or more people can share a current reality based on a common understanding. We view our world from a different street corner than others, but it isn't the street corner we are on that determines what we see, it's the journey of life conditions we experienced in getting there.

The underlying personal attribute of connection-making is in the alignment of our differing instinctive and socialised identities. This is not referring to shared goals. It is referring to aligned behaviours based on mutual understanding of the 'where' of our connection-making: our life conditions and preferred social style in coping with those life conditions. This is the nature of our cultural embeddedness.

Beck and Cowan provide some useful principles that can be used to develop social adaptability in any important connection-making interaction.

- Step outside your own meme (our socialised rather than gene-based self-identity) profile,
- Identify the prevailing life conditions,
- Look and listen for differences between *what* the other person thinks (their sense-making structure) and *why* the other person thinks (their meaning-making structure),
- Recognise these differences create different ways of behaving in the same situation,
- Recognise that our behaviour ebbs and flows as conditions get better or worse.

These principles are useful in enabling us to step back from what is being said to *why* it is being said. This will help in understanding the level of the spiral the other person is operating from and provide the real foundation for flow of meaning or dialogue. Spiral Dynamics describes the increasing levels of complexity created by each level and provides us with our hidden and deep values context.

Lets' now consider *how* it is being said – the tone of our connection-making with another. A useful concept for considering the approach we use to connect with others is called transactional analysis.

INSIGHT INTENTION AND INTEGRITY

As was discussed earlier, Transactional analysis, which was developed by Eric Berne, looks at each interaction between two people through the lens of three ego states, or personas, – parent, adult and child.

- *Parent*: a state in which people behave, feel, and think in response to an unconscious mimicking of how their parents (or other parental figures) acted, or how they interpreted their parent's actions. This is our ingrained voice of authority, absorbed conditioning, learning and attitudes from when we were young. We were conditioned by our parents, teachers, older people, next door neighbours, aunts and uncles, Father Christmas and Easter Bunny. Our Parent is made up of a huge number of hidden and overt recorded playbacks. Typically embodied by phrases and attitudes starting with 'how to', 'always', 'under no circumstances', and 'never forget', 'don't lie, cheat, steal'.
- Our Parent is formed by the impact of external events and influences upon us as we grow through early childhood. The Parent is like a tape recorder. It is a collection of pre-recorded, pre-judged, prejudiced codes for living. For example, a person may shout at someone out of frustration because they learned from an influential figure in childhood the lesson that this seemed to be a way of relating that worked. The Parent decides, without reasoning, how to react to situations, what is good or bad, and how people should live. The Parent judges for or against and can be controlling or supportive. When the Parent is critical it is called the *Controlling Parent* with two states – structural (positive) and critical (negative). When it is supportive it is called the *Nurturing Parent with two states* -supporting (positive) and spoiling (negative).
- *Adult*: a state of the ego which is most like an artificially intelligent system processing information and making predictions about major emotions that could affect its operation. This is the mature ego state that transaction analysis seeks to embody. While a person is in the adult ego state, they are directed towards an objective

- appraisal of reality. When in the Adult ego state the person uses logical thinking to solve problems making sure that their own Child or Parent emotions do not contaminate the process.
- *Child*: a state in which people behave, feel, and think similarly to how they did in childhood. The Child is the source of emotions, creation, recreation, spontaneity, and intimacy. When we are in the Child ego state we act like the child we once were. When anger or despair dominates reason, the Child is in control. For example, a person who receives a poor evaluation at work may respond by looking at the floor and crying or pouting, as when scolded as a child. Conversely, a person who receives a good evaluation may respond with a broad smile and a joyful gesture of thanks. We aren't just putting on an act; we think, feel, see, hear and react as a three or five or eight-year-old child. The ego states are fully experienced states of being, not just roles.
- When the Child is hateful or loving, impulsive, spontaneous or playful it is called the *Natural Child with two states* - spontaneous (positive) and immature (negative). When it is thoughtful, creative or imaginative it is called the *Little Professor*. When it is fearful, guilty or ashamed it is called the *Adapted Child with two states* - co-operative (positive) and compliant/resistant (negative).. The Child has all the feelings; fear, love, anger, joy, sadness, shame and so on. The Child is often blamed for being the source of people's troubles because it is self-centred, emotional, powerful and resists the suppression that comes with growing up.

Berne differentiated his Parent, Adult, and Child ego states from actual adults, parents, and children, by using capital letters when describing them. These ego states may or may not represent the relationships that they act out. For example, in the workplace, an adult supervisor may take on the Parent role, and scold an adult employee as though he were a Child. Or a child, using the Parent ego-state, could scold her actual parent as though the parent were a Child.

Within each of these ego states there are subdivisions. Parental figures tend to be either more nurturing (permission-giving, security-giving) or more criticising (comparing to family traditions and ideals in generally negative ways); Childhood behaviours are either more natural (free) or more adapted (compliant) to others. These subdivisions categorize individuals' patterns of behaviour, feelings, and ways of thinking, which can be functional/productive (*positive*) or dysfunctional/counterproductive (*negative*).

There are multiple transactions that can occur between two people as shown below.

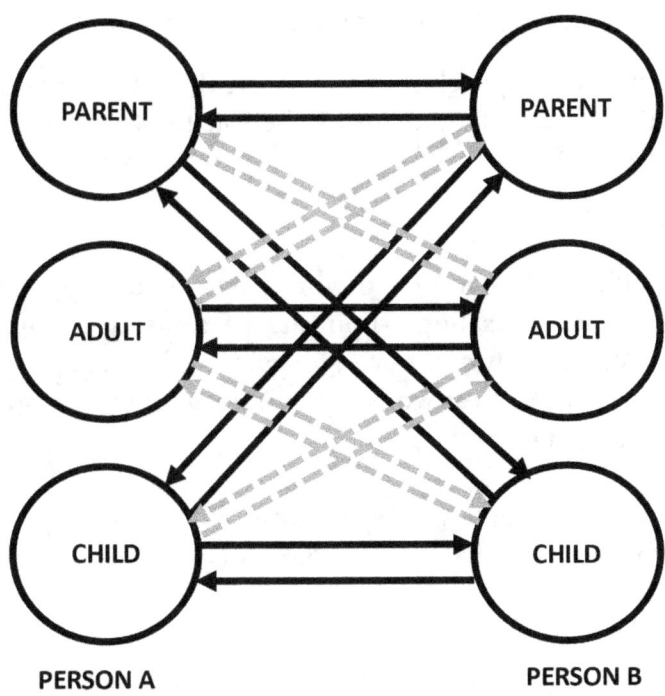

Figure 16: Transactional Analysis Interactions

Transactions occur when any person relates to any other person. Each transaction is made up of a stimulus and a response and transactions can proceed from the Parent, Adult or Child of one person to the Parent, Adult or Child of another person.

A *complimentary* transaction involves the same ego state in each person. In a *crossed* transaction the transactional response is addressed to an ego state different from the one which started the stimulus.

Communication can continue between two people as long as transactions are complementary: crossed transactions are challenging because they disrupt communication.

If a crossed transaction occurs, there is an ineffective communication. Worse still either or both parties will be upset. In order for the relationship to continue smoothly the initiator or the respondent must rescue the situation with a complementary transaction.

There are some simple clues that indicate the ego state of the person sending the signal that you will be able to identify in yourself and others

Parent state

- Physical - angry or impatient body-language and expressions, finger-pointing, patronising gestures
- Verbal - always, never, for once and for all, judgmental words, critical words, patronising language, posturing language.

It is important to be aware of cultural differences in body-language or verbal cues that appear 'Parental'.

Child state

- Physical - emotionally sad expressions, despair, temper tantrums, whining voice, rolling eyes, shrugging shoulders, teasing, delight, laughter, speaking behind hand, raising hand to speak, squirming and giggling.

- Verbal - baby talk, statements such as I wish, I dunno, I want, I'm gonna, I don't care, oh no, not again, things never go right for me, worst day of my life, bigger, biggest, best, many superlatives, words to impress.

Adult state

- Physical - attentive, interested, straight-forward, tilted head, non-threatening and non-threatened.
- Verbal - why, what, how, who, where and when, how much, in what way, comparative expressions, reasoned statements, true, false, probably, possibly, I think, I realise, I see, I believe, in my opinion.

There is no general rule as to the effectiveness of any ego state in any given situation (some people get results by being dictatorial (Parent to Child), or by having temper tantrums, (Child to Parent), but for a balanced approach to life, Adult to Adult is generally recommended. The increase in non-face-to-face communication through email and to some extent video links is raising a whole new potential for miscommunication. And remember, when you are trying to identify ego states: words are only part of the story. To understand connection-making in face-to-face interaction also you need to see and feel what is being said as well.

According to research by Albert Mehrabian, in communicating feelings and attitudes (and without applying it to all communications) people attribute:

- 7% of meaning to the words spoken.
- 38% of meaning to the way that the words are said – the tone of voice.
- 55% to facial expression.

Connection-making is multi-dimensional, and the elements are largely below our consciousness so it may take some time to give meaning to and make sense out of them. Mature connection-making is intuitive and has emergent qualities, so it is more useful to reflect on what you have covered before, during and after your interactions with others.

Let's just reflect for a moment on what has been covered in our approach to understanding blind spots of our Reactive Self in this Part. They are the three mindsets that impact on our Reactive Self choice-making:

- Meaning-making and its foundations in the Feeling Centre, character and emotional intelligence,
- Sense-making and its foundations in the Thinking centre, competence and intellectual (cognitive) intelligence, and
- Connection-making and its foundations in the Moving Centre, life conditions and social intelligence.

These mindsets provide a framework for developing our Practical Drive, exploring our Instinctive Drive and engaging our Creative Drive, so that we can lead with insight, intention and integrity in our real time interconnected world.

Let's now bring the three mindsets of meaning-making, sense-making and connection-making together in the one map so you can see the whole reactive choice-making picture.

INSIGHT INTENTION AND INTEGRITY

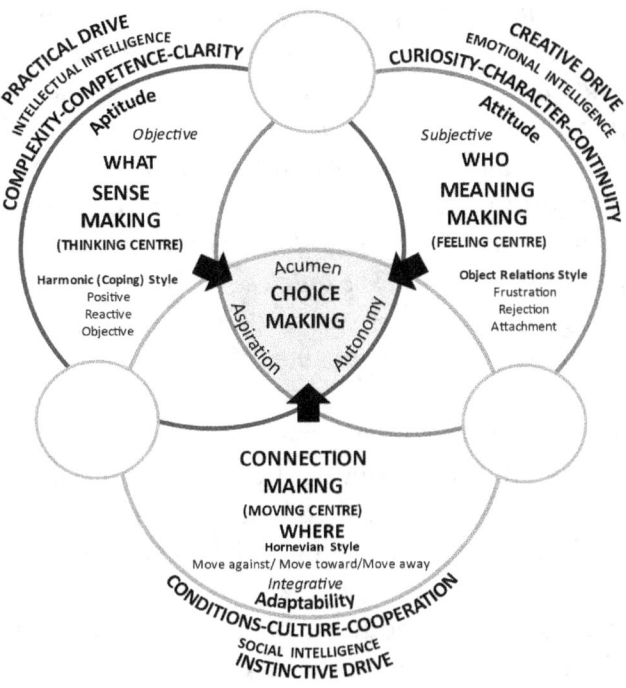

Figure 17: The Three Reactive Self Mindsets

By now you will have an emerging sense of the choice-making limitations of your Reactive Self and the accompanying mindsets of meaning-making, sense-making and connection-making and will begin to ask, "how do I begin to apply all of this?" This is a book that will provide ideas for you to consider not a book of "how to" solutions. That would just reinforce the learning by memorising approach. To get some understanding of why "how to" solutions are not being provided we need to return to how we got to learn what we know.

It began before we were born and reflects our innate "learning by being present" nature – learning by immersion. In his book Supersense, Bruce Hood relates an example of our "learning by being present" nature.

> *"..if you get pregnant mothers in their third trimester to read aloud passages from Dr Seuss's The Cat in the Hat, their unborn babies can hear and remember this experience. When they are born, if you stick a rubber nipple in their mouth to measure their sucking, they will stop when they hear the tape recording of their mother reading the same passages. The only way they could have heard this was from inside the womb. Learning clearly takes place before birth."*

Much of what we learn involves the unfolding of our inbuilt natural mechanisms of human development, from initial grasping of objects to eventually sophisticated discernment of complex phenomena, such as face recognition and language subtleties. Our learning initially progresses by trial and error and as we learn we give up earlier ideas about how the world works. Remember when you believed that the moon followed you on a clear night! Of course, most of us still retain superstitions that have no validity in fact, but we struggle to give them up even in the face of clear evidence to the contrary.

As new ideas emerge in our world of connection-making we assess their meaning based on what we have already experienced, and if they make sense, we adopt them without consciously or fully discarding the old idea.

As Emmanuel Kant said in the Critique of Pure Reason:

> *"All human knowledge begins with intuitions, proceeds thence to concepts, and ends with ideas."*

The ideas presented in this book will induce different sense making, meaning making and connection making responses in each different reader. We are all in unique and ever-changing interactive learning contexts. No universal "how to" is useful in that situation. Once you have absorbed the information in this book

INSIGHT INTENTION AND INTEGRITY

you will only know its "truth" for you by applying the ideas in it to interactions with your environment and others in it.

At this point you may find these ideas are either resonating with you or confronting you intellectually or emotionally. It is important to be aware that you will be either sorting this information in a sensing or intuitive way and deciding whether to act on it in a thinking or feeling driven way. The judging or perceiving aspect of your moving centre will also be at play in a deliberation (in a judging closed-minded right or wrong) or liberation (in a perceiving open-minded exploring) way.

Reserve judgement as the next Part will help you stand back from what has been covered and see it from a fresh perspective.

Now for Part 4 – Sight for Fresh Eyes.

PART 4

SIGHT FOR FRESH 'EYES'

The fourth Part looks at the three 'eyes' of emergent leadership - insight, intention and integrity - as foundations for the conscious development of our personal leadership role in the interconnected world of wirearchy.

They each act as the leadership bridge between the three Reactive Self mindsets:

- Insight is the leadership bridge between meaning-making and connection-making
- Intention is the leadership bridge between sense-making and connection-making, and
- Integrity is the leadership bridge between sense-making and meaning-making.

They give us access to the three unconscious emergent leadership qualities:

- Insight gives us access to our potential and voice,
- Intention gives us access to our priorities and vision, and
- Integrity gives us access to our purpose and values.

CHAPTER 10

Insight - The Pathway to Potential

"Insight cannot be taken back. You cannot return to the moment you were in before."

Hilary Mantel

If our Reactive Self processes of meaning-making, sense-making and connection-making are so dominated by our reactiveness to what is outside of us, what other dimensions of our self might we be able to access if we gave attention to this socialisation of our potential? We may discover that we are actually capable of being more than the sum of our experiences. Would our newfound consciousness lead us to getting in touch with our creative connection to the natural living order?

The challenge we all face, when we begin to recognise we are more than the sum of our experiences, is that of becoming open to explore the instincts, motivations, and defensive strategies that underpin our Reactive Self – our current meaning-making, sense-making and connection-making mindsets. We initially grasp at new techniques and adopt new formulas for success that suggest solutions to our sense of underlying dissatisfaction. We set goals, make new resolutions (especially at New Year) and may go to workshops run by motivational speakers and buy their self-help materials. We view their YouTube sessions and may become followers of 'influencers'. We search for the answer outside of us as we have always done.

Much of this effort is anchored in trying to solve the problem of our underlying dissatisfaction by imposing a new layer of beliefs over our existing Reactive Self. In Part 2 our understanding of the inner constructs (mindsets) of our Reactive Self that influence our meaning-making, sense-making and connection-making, was developed.

You will now be aware of the nature of the habits and mindsets that keep the defensive strategies of your Reactive Self in place. This Part will open your 'eyes' to the three domains of Insight, Intention and Integrity that underpin the next stage of your emergent leadership development journey.

At the outset we need to recognise that our Reactive Self may also be the one that we adopted some time ago to please or placate others. This is the result of "falsifying our type": we adopt a role that we "accept" as our lot in life but it is never fully satisfying and continually drains us. However, our natural Jungian function lead role is where our latent potential lies and we will consider that when we look more closely at our Sensitive Self. Many do not discover their natural lead Centre and suffer from often debilitating fatigue and other states of illness.

The least understood attribute of our Reactive Self is its capacity to falsify our type. Benziger makes the following observations about this universal problem. She says:

"Significantly, the neuro-physiological information identified as validating Jung, combined with observations of (my) own clients, led to making two discoveries of signal importance to those seeking to apply Jung's model to help clients. The discoveries were that:

- Extended falsification of a person's type, or natural dominant function, has unique, powerful, negative neuro-physiological ramifications; and
- When an effort is made to identify the person's natural lead function - using an assessment like the MBTI or an interview/evaluation by a trained therapist, the functions identified as the person's 'natural lead' is very often not

their natural lead, but rather the mode they've chosen to develop and use to survive, fit in or be rewarded. In other words, despite the best intentions of professionals, efforts to apply Jung's model often went off track or were less than effective, inadvertently encouraging the individual to persist in falsifying their type."

And

"To more fully understand Falsification of Type and its significance, it is helpful to: first establish the relationship between falsification from invalidation; then distinguish Falsification of Type from the other kinds of falsification.

Invalidation is any reaction from one's environment or one's self that implies one is not "OK" or of value. It often occurs when an individual is a misfit in some way relative to the majority of persons in his community or group. Thus, a person can be invalidated by his environment because of traits that are innate and non-negotiable (e.g. gender, race, height, natural hair colour, eye colour and natural lead function) as well as traits that are the result of his life experience (e.g. education, socio-economic level, weight and dress). Regardless of the source, invalidation causes internal turmoil and stress. These, in turn can lead an individual to seek to modify or falsify the invalidated trait in order to fit in and/or be rewarded. Not all chronic invalidation leads to falsification, but much does.

The problem is that while certain types of falsification (changing one's pattern of dress and speech, bleaching one's hair, wearing lifts) may have "no negative results" from a neuro-physiological perspective as far as we know, Falsification of Type places highly specific and

> *severe physiological demands on the human organism - as a result of the inappropriate, persistent increase in oxygen uptake by the brain when falsifying, (i.e. using a function that does not enjoy a naturally low level of electrochemical resistance and thereby naturally efficient use of that function). Thus, Falsification of Type compounds the psychological problem rooted in the experience of emotional pain that accompanies chronic invalidation, with a physiological one that weakens the system as a whole and leaves the person less and less able to enjoy life."*

Jung himself observed that the cost of falsification of type in terms of fatigue as well as neuroses was substantial and could only be corrected by the person embracing their natural lead function. Jung sensed that these costs were rooted in neuro-physiology. Benziger's work identifies that neuro-physiology and clarifies why it leads inexorably to exhaustion. Indeed, many also suggest that owning, honouring, and utilising innate gifts may be the most effective method to manage energy and sustain wellness.

Benziger then says that:

> *"over half of the population may be falsifying at some level. No wonder so many individuals are less than successful. No wonder this stress is being expressed in decreased emotional and physical health. Invalidation and joylessness stem directly from rarely, if ever, being honoured and rewarded for one's innate lead function and giftedness, compounded by a building exhaustion from falsifying."*

It is the Reactive Self that falsifies type.

INSIGHT INTENTION AND INTEGRITY

Against that reflection on the power of our Reactive Self let's reflect for a moment on the core definition of 'emergent leadership'.

Emergent refers to a quality that does not depend on its individual parts, but on their reciprocal relationships to one another. It is a non-linear in form and, as a consequence, emergent behaviour cannot be predicted by analysing the individual parts of a system.

Leadership is the spontaneous assumption of responsibility to contribute to the common good. It is an emergent quality arising from the synergy between insight, intention and integrity – the 'eyes' of emergent leadership. These three 'eyes' underpin our voice, vision and values. It is about responding, rather than reacting, in the moment and being responsible for the choices we make ourselves and influencing responsibility in others for the choices they make.

Emergent leadership is person centric and reflects the presence of wirearchy. Wirearchy is **a dynamic two-way flow of power and authority**, based on knowledge, trust, credibility and a focus on results, enabled by interconnected people and technology.

When the three 'eyes' (insight, intention and integrity) are well developed then leadership will occur spontaneously – it will simply emerge in your connected context to share knowledge that contributes to the common good. That is the essence of adaptive learning.

The relationship between these three 'eyes' of emergent leadership are shown in the Adaptive Learning Map© below.

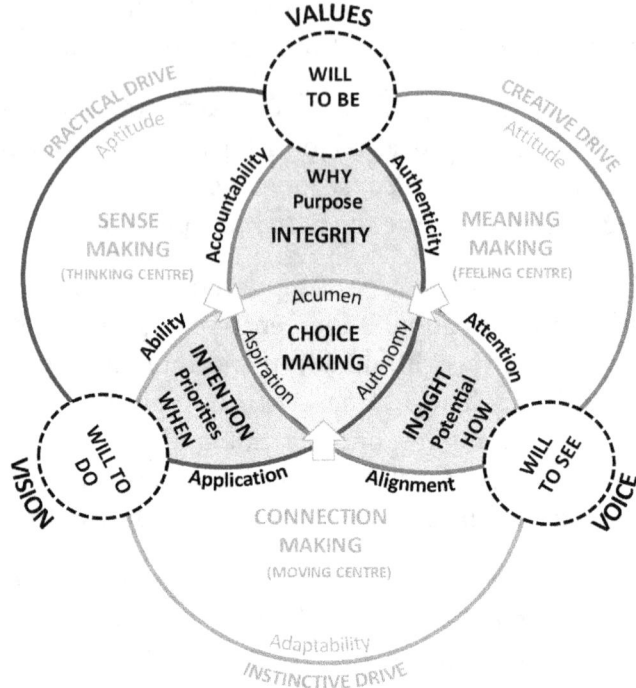

Figure 18: The Three Eyes of Emergent Leadership

The three 'eyes' of emergent leadership act as adaptive learning 'bridges' that sit between the three mindsets (meaning-making, sense-making and connection-making) of our Reactive Self:

- Insight is the learning bridge between meaning-making and connection-making
- Intention is the learning bridge between sense-making and connection-making, and
- Integrity is the learning bridge between meaning-making and sense-making.

They give us access to the three unconscious personal qualities:

- Insight gives us access to our potential and voice,
- Intention gives us access to our priorities and vision, and

INSIGHT INTENTION AND INTEGRITY

- Integrity gives us access to our purpose and values.

Against that higher level overview let's look at the Insight domain and where it sits in our Adaptive Learning Map©.

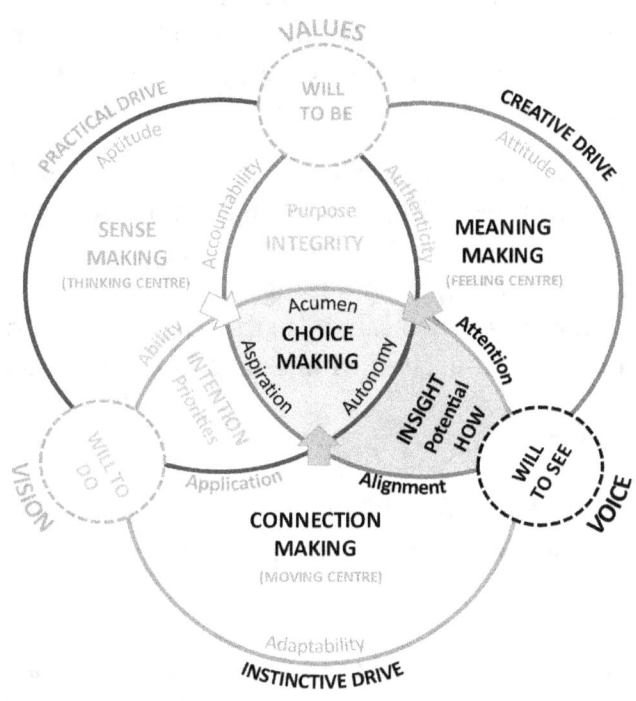

Figure 19: Insight

Insight, as the first "eye" of emergent leadership, is:

- the learning bridge between meaning-making and connection-making,
- about your voice,
- about your self-others relationship,
- about your potential,
- about the mindset interfaces of attention and alignment,
- energised by the 'will to see',

- about exploring the 'how do I behave?' question, and
- the foundation of personal autonomy.

Insight is about understanding that the interaction between our Feeling Centre and Moving Centre shapes what we give attention to and provides alignment of our meaning-making and connection-making mindsets. It is the capacity to get above the Reactive Self 'territory' of our interactions with others (our environment and our cultural context and life conditions) and see them with fresh eyes.

Insight is the capacity to be open to our latent potential and see ourselves as integrated beings in the living natural order. This latent level of potential is activated by an emergent connection to the living natural order through developing our insight rather than just using our intuition - our so called "sixth sense" - and the discovery of new patterns of connection within our self and to others.

Gary Klein says:

> *"Intuition is the use of patterns we have already learned, whereas insight is the discovery of new patterns."*

Insight is an important construct in choice-making, as it is the main influencer of our 'self to other' sense of autonomy, in the meaning-making and connection-making locations of the leadership territory. Insight is initiated by your 'will to see' and its associated sensitive energy which will be discussed in the next Part.

The first step in developing insight is to recognise that our five senses are limited in what they are capable of noticing. Our sight is limited in that we cannot see ultra-violet or infra-red light, we cannot hear ultra sound, and we cannot smell over great distances. There is more in our environment than we sense. Our mind is experientially constrained by the thoughts and feelings emanating from our memory: the synaptic connections and neural pathways of our social experience and our genetic inheritance. There is also more to our mind than we can know. That is why we are often surprised by our own reactions to situations and the reactions we get from others.

It is difficult to see ourselves how others see us. That is why other-based feedback is essential in order to determine how our behavioural patterns affect other people. This, in turn, can help to improve our self-insight, relationship building and personal development. A key to unlocking how we interpret feedback from others is to be found in what we give attention to.

Attention is the behavioural and cognitive process of selectively concentrating on a discrete stimulus while ignoring other perceivable stimuli. The word "attention" comes from the Latin *attendere,* meaning "to reach toward", to the focus on others, which is the foundation of empathy and of an ability to build social relationships, the second and third pillars of emotional intelligence.

Attention can be grouped into three broad buckets - focusing inwardly on *ourselves,* focusing outwardly on *others,* and focusing on *the wider world.* The first two, focussing inwardly and focusing outwardly on others help develop the primary elements of emotional intelligence. The third bucket - deeper understanding of how we focus on, and cope with, the life conditions of the wider world - provides an awareness of our cultural embeddedness and enables us to intelligently question our beliefs, improve our know-how, and apply it creatively to solve complex problems collectively.

What we give attention to is precarious. We can sense this when we have been effortlessly engaged in an activity - when we are said to be "in the zone". Equally when we have been engaged in an activity and nothing seems to work no matter how much we strive. But it is much more difficult to understand what the ingredients are that create that effortless experience or mental block.

We can make a start by understanding the LOLO effect (what our attention "locks on" to and "locks out") as we collect, and sort, the abundance of data and information 'triggers' presented to us through our five physical senses, or through our mind, as thoughts and emotions. Understanding the LOLO effect is basic to understanding why we see the world differently from others.

The key to understanding the LOLO effect is to recognise that only information with "now value" - information we instinctively or habitually focus on, need to focus on, or want to apply in the present moment - gets our attention. The best example is when we look at our watch to get the time. The time has "now value", and so we lock on to it, and lock out all of the other detail on the face of our watch – the shape, the brand name, the hour markings and strokes, dots, roman numerals, arabic numerals, special markings and so on.

Try it sometime by seeing if you can recall all of the detail on the face of your watch (if you have one in this digital age!). You will be amazed at what you do not "see" even though you have looked right at it many times. Perversely if you do focus on the detail, to check your recall, it is unlikely that you noticed the time when you last looked at it! When you translate this experience to your self-other observations, you will begin to appreciate the power of the LOLO effect. We are "selective information attenders" and limited in our capacity to "see" reality as it is.

Our immediate LOLO "lens" of attention is the equivalent of the time on the face of our watch - we attend to what we look for in the outside world without seeing the whole picture. Our "lens" of attention is managed by our Instinctive drive. When we need to know the time it is very useful, however when we need to understand our Instinctive drive, or the subtleties of the context we are in, it is very deceptive.

This is even more disconcerting when we consider the different, often strongly held, views people have of the same person, especially public figures who they have not even met. But even with people we "know well" the differences individuals see in each other are often substantial. Expressing our view about how we see another person also forms the basis for how others see us, yet often bears little resemblance to the way we see our self. Once we have "made our mind up" about someone we "lock on" to information to confirm it, and ignore whatever else might be there.

Our attention provides the meaning-making interface with choice-making. It is about the power of our perception of events and others and how we have learned to respond to them. The world is full of stimuli that can attract our attention through our various senses. As we perceive events, the brain selects, organises and integrates sensory information to construct a memory, based on our unconscious way of organising that sensory information. Our sense of potential is embedded in our memory structures and rules for meaning-making and connection-making. "Letting go of the old", in order to realise our full potential, involves a shift from other-observation to self-observation.

Unearthing our sense of potential requires us to connect to our intrapersonal (internal) and interpersonal (external) contexts and, initially, only provides us with a fragile sense of insight.

Gladwell says:

> *"Insight is not a light bulb that goes off inside our heads. It is a flickering candle that can easily be snuffed out"*

Insight challenges the perception we have of our potential - the alignment between meaning-making and connection-making is what we are focusing on here. Alignment involves changing something so that it matches something else. It is about appreciating differences and finding a pathway that recognises the power of other points of view in solving complex problems.

Insight is the alignment bridge between meaning making and connection making and the biggest challenge we face is to find a way to understand meaning-making in the context of our social interactions. This challenge is best approached at the level of behaviour observation, based on understanding the habit-based attention driven nature of our personality. Each person engaged in any social interaction exchanges information intuitively, through give-and-take, about their meaning-making approach that can be observed and responded to.

The alignment we are looking at here is about discretionary effort based on 'mutual appreciation', referred to by Aristotle, not just 'utility'. It is about both aligned meaning-making and aligned connection-making.

Defining social interactions in terms of patterns of alignment shows that sensitive connection-making can occur in the absence of shared goals. This 'shared patterns of behaviour' approach is the key to fully understanding that meaning-making occurs as part of our real time connection-making. Shared goals may or may not flow from that. Shared meaning-making based on insight is the behavioural foundation of sustainable connection-making.

While we have one primary or dominant style, each individual person can, and likely will, display some of all four behavioural styles depending on the situation.

The table below provides a high-level picture of the mannerisms, key behaviours, approach to planning and expectations of others of each Jungian function pair social style that help identify the dominant intrinsic style of yourself and others. Use the table to identify your own dominant behaviour style.

Behaviour Style	Catalyst NT	Synergist NF	Harmonist SF	Specialist ST
Mannerisms	Speak at a fast rate: use loud volume and low vocal pitch. Respond quickly, often sharply. Sound authoritative, in command.	Speak at a fast rate: use medium volume and a lot of vocal inflection. Respond spontaneously and energetically. Sound informal, casual, lively.	Speak at a slow to moderate rate: use moderate volume and balanced vocal inflection. Respond with a deliberate choice of words. Sound congenial, helpful.	Speak at a slow, measured rate: use medium to low vocal pitch and little vocal inflection. Respond with pauses to emphasise words and ideas. Sound serious, unhurried.
Key Behaviours	Tend to be intense, challenging and impatient. Want authority: initiate changes that make intuitive sense Act quickly, after consideration of a number of options.	Desire things immediately; tend to ignore facts. Give little attention to routine matters. Gravitate toward tasks that use interpersonal skills.	Resort to safe positions when conflict arises. Show willingness to listen. Wait for rather than cause things to happen. Like authoritative leadership.	Seek solitude and concentration. Compete with themselves rather than others. Tend to be overly protective. Strive to be expert in one area.

Planning Approach	Organise self and others into a functioning system. Develop back-up plans.	Improvise instead of preparing in advance. Turn from one new interest to another.	Tend to underestimate themselves. Do what "experts" advise them to do.	Like to make judgements based on facts. Gain success by concentration and follow through.
Expectations of Others	Expect others to listen carefully and respond in a timely fashion. Want information summarised rather than spelled out. Expect several options. Permit only a few to be close to them. Place high demands on associates.	Expect a high energy level from others. Prefer to work with others who show independence. Welcome those who make their life more full and lively. Desire to try out imaginative ideas on friends and associates.	Expect others to have caring respect for past events. Desire others to move with moderation and deliberation. Respect those who have "roots". Expect experts to document facts.	Expect others to be clear and concise in their expression. Desire people to contribute the missing pieces to the grand design they are developing. Want firm and timely decisions to be made by others. Insist on penalties for those who perform poorly.

There are a number of connection-making Do's and Don'ts that provide behaviours that others can use to get your positive and reaffirming attention and not use to avoid getting your negative and aggravating attention.

The Do's reflect the natural style of the function pair and enable them to feel empowered to and exercise their voice. The Don'ts reflect areas of personal development of their influence and feedback seeking skills.

Now that you have identified your own primary behaviour style review the table below to see how it reflects the best way to influence you. You will most likely have a dominant and secondary style but for simplicity let's use your likely dominant style.

NT Style: Catalyst	
Do:	Don't:
• Focus on the immediate future • Be brief and efficient • Listen to the outcomes they want • Get to the bottom line • Speak in terms that support their ideas • Give them options • Let them feel in control • Stress how they will 'win'	• Focus on the past • Give too much detail • Be ambiguous • Beat around the bush • Get too personal • Get into a control contest • Force them to back down, however, unless you believe you are right

NF Style: Synergist	
Do:	Don't:
• Focus on the longer-term future • Illustrate concepts with stories • Seek their ideas, input • Focus on the big picture • Show personal interest and involvement • Stimulate their creative impulse • Compliment them • Stress how they will 'stand out'	• Get straight down to business • Dwell on details • Be impatient with side trips and creativity • 'Nitpick' • Be cool and impersonal • Be too serious • Talk down to them • Put down their enthusiasm

SF Style: Harmonist	
Do:	Don't:
• Focus on the past and tradition • Be practical • Be easy and informal • Be personal and personable • Allow then time to 'feel good' • Emphasise a team approach • Stress how they can 'be safe'	• Push for too much detail • Press hard to change things • Hurry them • Push for immediate commitments • Be cool and impersonal • Confront them • Be dictatorial and autocratic

ST Style: Specialist	
Do:	Don't:
• Focus on the past and present • Talk facts • Focus on detail and accuracy • Be logical and well organised • Tell them exactly what you will do and when • Allow time to ponder • Stress how they can 'be right'	• Be vague, inconsistent or illogical • Be intolerant of details • Overlook the past • Rush things • Be too personal • Be overly casual • Appear to not be serious • Press for immediate action

As the bridge between meaning-making and connection-making, insight provides access to your potential to act spontaneously using your preferred function pair behavioural style. It also enables you to appreciate the preferred different behavioural style of others which provides the foundation of developing your voice and respecting the 'attention' style of others. Interestingly the emphasis on being a 'good listener' needs to be complimented by being a good 'attention getter'. People listen if you have their undivided attention even if they interpret what you are saying differently from what you intended. That's when you open yourself up to the possibility of learning more about yourself and what irritates you in others.

Jung said:

> "Everything that irritates us in others can lead to an understanding of ourselves."

The table below provides a simple framework for surfacing the 'irritators' between the Jungian function pair social styles:

	NT	NF	SF	ST
NT	**NT view of NT** Capable, Decisive	NF view of NT Driven, Demanding	SF view of NT Intimidating, Bossy	ST view of NT Controlling, Arrogant
NF	NT view of NF Unreliable, Casual	**NF view of NF** Fun, Interesting	SF view of NF Defiant, Rebellious	ST view of NF Careless, Disorganised
SF	NT view of SF Slow, Vulnerable	NF view of SF Dependent, Helpless	**SF view of SF** Warm, Caring	ST view of SF Emotional, Chatty
ST	NT view of ST Picky, Inflexible	NF view of ST Uptight, Obsessive	SF view of ST Tedious, Aloof	**ST view of ST** Reliable, Competent

You now have some foundation insight into your preferred way of behaving. Insight, paradoxically, is about hindsight (recognising where I have come from) and foresight (recognising where I am going) and provides the leadership bridge between meaning-making and connection-making.

Let's see how what you have discovered impacts upon your intentions.

CHAPTER 11

Intention – The Pathway to Priorities

"Intention is the core of all conscious life. Conscious intention colours and moves everything."

Hsing Yun

Intention is our pathway to understanding and developing our priorities and embracing our vision.

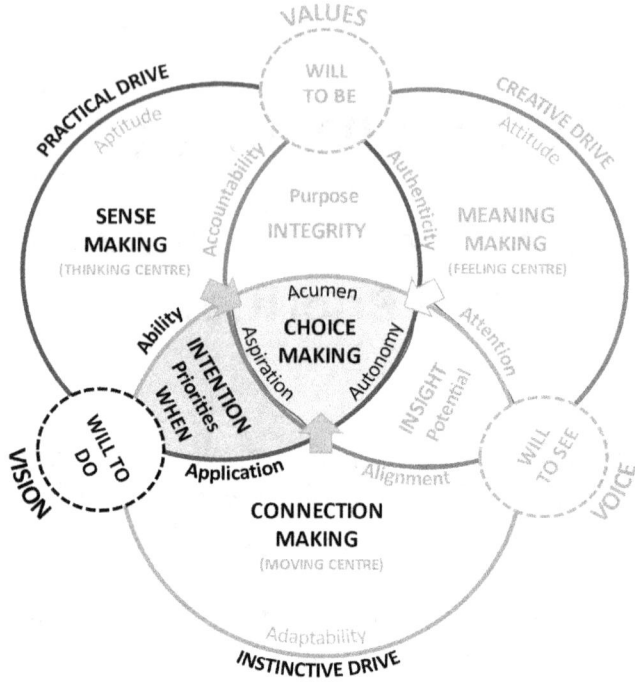

Figure 20: Intention

Intention, as the domain is the second "eye" of emergent leadership, is:

- the learning bridge between sense-making and connection-making,
- about your self-task relationship,
- about your vision,
- about priorities,
- about the mindset interfaces of ability and application,
- energised by the 'will to do',
- about exploring the 'when can I?' question, and
- the foundation of personal aspiration.

INSIGHT INTENTION AND INTEGRITY

An intention is a clear and positive statement of an outcome you want to experience. An intention is a desired future outcome, or vision, that guides your choice-making. Consequently, your intentions influence your actual experiences and behaviour. They guide what information in the environment you give attention and enable you to focus. But be aware of the potential unconscious LOLO (Lock on- lock out) effect that may cause you not to "see" alternative approaches to your choice-making.

Intentions provide a framework for you to set priorities, use your technical competence, and align yourself with the resources you need to achieve your priorities.

When you have a clear and personally compelling intention you will tend to act in ways, respond to situations, create supportive opportunities, and make choices, consistent with your intention. Having clear intentions also helps you to develop new capabilities when change is required.

Intentions can be conscious or unconscious. We never have a purely conscious intention, we also have unconscious intentions. Intention is a mental state. With an intention, you can get yourself to focus on doing this or that. Your intentions allow you to formulate your priorities and plans. It is about the "when" of choice-making.

In a hierarchy the power of "when" is a fundamental means of exercising management control using time as a key measure of performance. Time is a reflection of a wide range of situational and capability variables and yet is the single biggest contributor to the control-order-prescribe focus of hierarchy. In a wirearchy time is a variable that reflects the emergent nature of interactions and the contingent aspects of the relative complexity of the situation you are in.

An appreciation of your own intentions allows you to see time in the emerging situational context and to build contingencies into your "when". Time in a wirearchy respects the organic nature of choice-making. Outside of a crisis, when you are likely to be driven by your instincts, it is important to be gentle with time otherwise it will be your Achilles heel.

Intention is a 'thinking before doing' state. You shape the future by your capacity to respond to new possibilities, and to make them actionable. Intention is what underlies your priorities, and the knowledge-based action you take. It is activated by our 'will to do' and its associated conscious energy that will be discussed in the next Part.

Intention is the active desire to achieve some priority in the future using some specific competency, or mix of competencies. Perceived intentions organise your priorities; they give you a capacity to operate in your connection-making world in terms of outcomes, aims, plans, designs and ends. Intentions are also the active, conscious, future aims we perceive another person to have in our connection-making space.

Clearly, intentions can really be known only to the person holding them. It is only by asking the other person that we get a true picture of their intentions - that is, if they have integrity. Integrity will be discussed in the next chapter. It is sufficient to say here that our faith in their word, gained through our experience of their behaviour in other situations, is the crucial element in accepting their intentions. We trust that they will do what they say they will do and can do what they say they will do.

Because intention directly provides a focus for our choice-making it is useful to distinguish intention setting from goal setting.

Goal setting is a fundamental part of hierarchy but it does not work well in wirearchy where the relationships are about mutual respect and shared commitment that leads to personal growth as one of the outcomes of task completion. This is personal growth as intention. In that sense intentions are not about striving to achieve a goal but about progressively seeing the ways, and finding the means to achieve your potential.,

INSIGHT INTENTION AND INTEGRITY

Goal Setting	Intention Setting
Deals with goals, measures, plans, rewards.	Deals with personal passions, wishes, reflection, and discovery.
Works best when: • you know what the end state looks like and you have control over key variables, • situations of low uncertainty, stable environments, • when top-down directives can get you what you need.	Works best when: • you may not know what the end-state should look like and/or you don't have a lot of control, • dynamic/volatile situations, • when you need to tap into personal passions/commitment to get what you need.
Assumes you can *make* things happen	Assumes you can *shape* things to happen

The intention interfaces between our sense-making and connection-making mindsets are ability and application.

Ability in its normal definition comprises our knowledge and skills that have been acquired through experiential and formal learning that are the foundations of our competence. The development of our intention provides a proactive way of developing our ability that is effortless and integrated with our sense of potential. It is called meta-learning.

It is a level beyond single loop learning (that is focussed on solving problems within an existing structure and technical know-how) and double loop learning (that is focussed on questioning the structure and the assumptions underlying it). Meta-learning is being aware of, and creatively taking control of, your own learning in the context of your choice-making environment.

Meta learning underpins emergent leadership and is impacted by a number of key factors:

- Your self-insight – the awareness of patterns which you notice when triggered (historical ways of relating to others, when you feel safe/anxious, when moving into self-protection mode, noticing aggression triggers) and an awareness of your latent potential,
- Your meaning-making maturity - your level of emotional intelligence and the embeddedness of your blind spots compared to your degree of self-awareness,
- Your sense-making maturity - the assumptions you make about your intellectual intelligence (what are you are able to change/learn, what your depth of know-how is), and
- Your connection-making maturity - your ability to recognise, and respond to, the behaviours in self and others and the ability to notice changes in self and others.

It is a journey of discovery based on self-observation which involves *"separation of oneself from oneself"* as Bennett suggests.

That brings us to the second mindset interface of application. Application is the act of bringing something to fruition and using it for an intended purpose. It usually evokes a strong sense of intention and insight. It typically is accompanied by a commitment to take action that reflects confidence in your choice making.

Commitment is the level of enthusiasm you have towards your tasks. It is the sense of responsibility that you have towards your intentions (priorities and vision) and the intentions of others you are connected to.

There are several reasons commitment is the foundation of application:

- The more committed you are, the more effective you can be in influencing others. If you act with commitment, others will pay attention,
- People who are committed are the ones who don't take discouragement seriously - they apply themselves,

- People cooperate at a higher level when they share commitment. Commitment fosters connection, trust and sharing,
- If people are committed to an effort for a period of time, they will learn what they need to know to be more effective.

The interfaces of application and ability open us to the idea of responsible action – our starting point for conscious choice-making and a key element of emergent leadership.

Responsible action is voluntary. It is, very simply, the ability to consciously choose to engage with others and our environment: to be fully present and intentional. On a deeper level it is the willingness to own our degree of impact in every interaction we have with others, with our intention-based priorities as the catalyst.

It is about owning our unique part in either creating or allowing the overall situation to occur. It is about realising that everyone has impact, and then choosing to authentically respond, not automatically react, to that impact in the most helpful way possible, consistent with our priorities and with the resources available at the time. Responsible action is about facing whatever needs to be faced in the moment. It underpins our contribution to the integrity of the whole living natural order: a unique contribution that is anchored in our latent potential and guided by our life purpose.

In this sense, responsible action means "I own my part in allowing or creating the situation and I am dealing with that situation with a sense of commitment and compassion". It is not about, "I'm not to blame," or "I didn't do it," or "It's not my job."

Even the most well-intentioned and capable among us are invariably bound by our Instinctive Drive and Practical Drive frames of reference, with our vantage point confined to our own street corner of reality.

As an example, when there's a traffic accident, police ask for witnesses to come forward and describe what happened. They like to have as many witness statements as possible so that they can build up enough evidence to give them a broader, more realistic version of events. In a traffic accident, there will be many different perspectives on what happened. The driver of one car will have one view, another driver or a passenger will have yet another view. Each onlooker who witnessed the accident will have a slightly different perspective, depending on where they were, how far they were, how good a view they had, what else was going on, how much danger they felt they were in, how the accident affected them and what the accident meant to them.

Each situation, event, conversation, means something different to all those involved, and also to those not involved. We attribute different intentions to others, that reflect our experience-based belief system, and how we are affected by the event.

We all have our own realities. Our minds are constantly trying to make sense of our world, forming judgements and opinions about every situation, event, interaction. Those judgements and opinions will be affected by our intentions. In describing the accident, the street corner they were standing on is far less important than the journey in life they had in getting there.

Our sense-making ability has evolved to only allow information or 'evidence' which fits with our own experience-based beliefs ("what we know") to enter – the LOLO effect again. Any contradictory evidence or information is rejected, or made to fit, and our beliefs remain unchanged, in spite of apparently contradictory evidence being out there.

When something is disconcerting us, we become part of it and that makes it really hard to stand back from what's happening. It's like using 'Google Earth' to get the detailed picture of a location - we can see the close-up view but we can't see anything else. The more we focus in the more we leave out. Developing our priorities, based on our intentions, requires us to 'zoom out' and see the bigger picture: the context, the "territory".

In summary, there are five important aspects of developing intention.

INSIGHT INTENTION AND INTEGRITY

- The first is realising that everyone involved has unique intentions. No two people prioritise a situation or issue in exactly the same way.
- The second is that a person's intentions give attention to, and organise, what they experience. Change your intentions and you change what you attend to, and the way that you interpret the events in your life. Intentions, furthermore, can create bias. Out of a mass of detailed information, people tend to pick out and focus on those 'facts' that confirm their priorities and to disregard or misinterpret those that call their intentions into question.
- The third is that people can have different intention 'attractors' at different times. As your experiences, assumptions, physiological states, and needs change, your intentions will change. When you are hungry, for example, you notice the food in a room. When you are not hungry, the food tends not to attract your attention.
- Fourth, your intentions largely determine how a message will be interpreted. The same message can mean two entirely different things when it arises from two different sets of intentions.
- Fifth, misunderstandings often occur because we assume that everyone sees things through the same intention lens as we do.

As we engage with others we learn that certain events serve as cues, or signs, revealing information of interest to them. So, words, gestures, and acts on the part of others are signposts conveying information about their intentions. In particular, we learn to attribute "intentionality" to other people on the basis of the cues they provide; that is, their behaviour, as well as their words, contains inferred messages, about their motives and attitudes, whether or not they intend to send such messages.

Every day, we use our senses and observation skills to interact with people. Touch, smell, sight, hearing and taste provide powerful ways for us to understand and navigate daily. We also use our observation skills to make sense of our world in order to know how to perform, act, behave and adjust accordingly.

You identified your 'lead' Social Style (Jungian function pair) in the previous chapter when considering insight. We can also use the function pair to discover the cues and inferred messages that reflect your intentions and motivations.

Let's now look at the key intentions and motivations of each Social Style (Jungian function pair) so that you can develop an understanding of how to observe your own behaviour, how that behaviour is potentially viewed by others and to observe the behaviour of others.

NT Style: Catalyst		
Intention	**As viewed by Self:**	**As viewed by Others:**
(What they want to do)	<ul><li>Seek solutions to problems</li><li>Get immediate results</li><li>Overcome objections</li><li>Accelerate efforts when competing</li><li>Show impatience with status quo</li><li>Take authority</li><li>Provide direction</li></ul>	<ul><li>Change things</li><li>Cause trouble</li><li>Use people</li><li>Respond by posing questions</li><li>Use information to control</li><li>Take risks</li><li>Provide strong leadership</li></ul>
Motivation	**Becomes Self-motivated when given:**	**Motivated by Others who:**
(What they desire for themselves and others)	<ul><li>Independence to act</li><li>Power and authority</li><li>Wide sphere of operation</li><li>Creative tasks</li><li>Freedom from close supervision</li><li>Prestige and challenge</li><li>Opportunity for advancement</li></ul>	<ul><li>Verbalise assertively</li><li>Demonstrate vigorous effort</li><li>Give and take</li><li>Provide direct answers</li><li>Accept criticism</li><li>Seek new challenges</li><li>Work without direction</li></ul>

	NF Style: Synergist	
Intention	**As viewed by Self:**	**As viewed by Others:**
(What they want to do)	• Use tactful communication • Persuade and convince others • Provide tension release with humour • Generate enthusiasm • Contact people • Accept varied opinions • Respond spontaneously	• Promote what is best for themselves • Use outward appearance • Appear excitable • Expect rewards • Overextend themselves • Simplify answers • Desire to assist people
Motivation	**Becomes Self-motivated when given:**	**Motivated by Others who:**
(What they desire for themselves and others)	• Appreciation and positive feedback • New openings and better possibilities • Freedom of expression • Teaching and instructing roles • Connections with higher ups • Opportunities to showcase talents	• Openly express their opinions • Show a good-natured optimistic side • Project personal warmth • Easily grant and request favours • Appear poised and self-confident • Cast off restrictions

SF Style: Harmonist		
Intention	**As viewed by Self:**	**As viewed by Others:**
(What they want to do)	<ul><li>Develop unity with others</li><li>Expect security</li><li>Remain calm and composed</li><li>Build a reserve of strength</li><li>Give attention to details</li><li>Show loyalty</li><li>Stay or sit in one place</li></ul>	<ul><li>Fulfil commitments</li><li>Anxious to please</li><li>Rely upon strengths of others</li><li>Avoid struggle for power</li><li>Show suspicion early in relationship</li><li>Concern for the unexpected</li><li>Assume a participatory role</li></ul>
Motivation	**Becomes Self-motivated when given:**	**Motivated by Others who:**
(What they desire for themselves and others)	<ul><li>Time to achieve methodical outcomes</li><li>Understanding of procedure changes</li><li>Opportunity to structure a plan</li><li>Sincere appreciation</li><li>Identification with team/group</li><li>Credit for successfully completed tasks</li><li>Long term security</li></ul>	<ul><li>Stick to their convictions</li><li>Follow traditional procedures</li><li>Are conscientious and persistent</li><li>Seek help to gain cooperation</li><li>Go directly to the point of an issue</li><li>Attack ideas rather than the person</li><li>Acknowledge anxious feelings</li></ul>

INSIGHT INTENTION AND INTEGRITY

ST Style: Specialist		
Intention	**As viewed by Self:**	**As viewed by Others:**
(What they want to do)	• Adhere to rules and regulations • Show diplomacy and tactfulness • Check for accuracy • Weigh actions against stated goals • Emphasise systematic procedures • Provide order and improved systems • Show concern for practical skills	• Use factual statements as challenges • Assume an investigative approach • Communicate high standards • Criticise performance • Minimise other's emotionality • Put people on the defensive • Comply with authority
Motivation	**Becomes Self-motivated when given:**	**Motivated by Others who:**
(What they desire for themselves and others)	• Task to determine cause of problems • Task of formulating goal or objectives • Expert role in task planning • Reassurance • Sheltered environment • Chance to restore order • Answers about questionable assignments	• Maintain a direct course • Are practical about costs • Show restraint; offer meaningful facts • Demonstrate clear, concise reasoning • Have an ability to plan • Control their time and effort • Reject claims of innocent mistakes

The essence of understanding the intentions of others are our observation skills. Our observation skills can provide us with key information that helps us understand the people we interact with and their intentions. Through careful observation of both verbal and non-verbal cues, we can detect their underlying intentions and motivations. These same observation skills can be used to then create a foundation for authentic connection-making, and for giving and receiving feedback.

The purpose of observation of intentions and motivations is to provide you with the insight to influence others and to share knowledge in the universally connected space that we now operate in and contribute to. In our connection-making context influencing skills are the ability to engage people so that they move beyond the "utility" of the relationship to one of mutual appreciation.

Influencing skills are more than communication; they are more than negotiation; they are arguably more than persuasion. Your personal credibility is key to this, as you need to create a foundation of trust that will underpin your connection-making. It is about gaining wholehearted support and agreement for your ideas or decisions. Understanding the conscious and unconscious expectations of others is both challenging and fragile in the context of the beliefs and assumptions that are the basis of your observations.

The key expectations of each Social Style provided the confirmation of your primary behavioural style that you identified in the previous chapter on insight. Once you have applied these dimensions to yourself you can use that self-observation experience as a foundation for enhancing your observation skills in identifying the range of different behaviours of others when they are faced with the options shown in the table below.

INSIGHT INTENTION AND INTEGRITY

BEHAVIOUR	NT STYLE Catalyst	NF STYLE Synergist	SF STYLE Harmonist	ST STYLE Specialist
Exploring Choices	Desire a number of options	Welcome alternatives	Prefer limited choices	Wish to decide between two choices
Accepting change	Relish the new and different	Enjoy change, want the 'latest'	Stay with what they know	Demand planned change; turn off to the new
Gaining control	Seek control of activities of self and others	Want control only of self	Take responsibility for only their portion	Need only to be in control of their own work
Making decisions	Quick, often impulsive	Commit early; delay full action	Find decision making difficult	Analyse before committing
Accepting information	Dislike detailed information	Scan rather than read content	Request detailed information	Listen and make notes
Revealing direction	Use wide sphere; like things to move quickly	Use wide sphere; like things to flow easily	Use specific focus; move at moderate pace	Use specific focus; hope to avoid mistakes

Requiring organisation	Insist on efficiency and being organised	Show discomfort with too much structure	Reach an organised comfort level	Build a highly structured environment
Willingness to risk	Enjoy high adventure; invest for high return	Join in for excitement and adventure	Need security; use risk taking	Avoid any thought of unstructured risk
Handling details	Delegate non-stressful tasks to others	Delegate 'thing' related details to others	Like the applause for attending to detail	Thrive on detailed work; take pride in being accurate
Time concentration	Want quick answers; has short listening span	Flexible time span; enjoy long conversations	Show high degree of patience	Need uninterrupted thinking time
Time intensity	Demand punctuality; easily angered	Appear lenient, easy going	Speak softly; hold true response within	Weigh and measure response

You must ensure that you regard these dimensions as descriptive rather than prescriptive – they provide you with a compass that can be used to explore rather than define your intentions and those of others. Do not label behaviour as your "isness". Labelling behaviour is the province of the habit-based and past-focused Reactive Self. Making your underlying intentions and motivations visible is the first step in understanding your Conscious Self.

The Conscious Self provides the foundation of your vision – your sense of the present with a focus on the future. Your vision is about long term and presently unrealistic intentions. Your vision enables you to see possibilities that emerge that you would otherwise be blind to. It is not a formula for striving to achieve self-cen-

INSIGHT INTENTION AND INTEGRITY

tred and ego-based outcomes. Striving drives out curiosity and creativity as it relies on what you already know.

You can think of your vision as the picture on the front of the jigsaw box. It guides you and gives you an overall picture of what you are trying to achieve. When it comes to actually putting the pieces together, however, you have to rely on their differing shapes and how they fit together in practice: the picture is too broad to help but guides your piece-by-piece decisions in a somewhat trial and error way.

In other words, your vision needs to give you a broad picture of where you are going: what sort of life you want, how you want to live, what you want to achieve. It guides your intentions and the priorities that flow from those intentions.

Let's now consider the role of integrity as the pathway to your purpose and the 'why' of your sense of self.

CHAPTER 12

Integrity – The Pathway to Purpose

"Integrity is the basis of trust."

Marvin Soskil

The Integrity domain, as the third "eye' of emergent leadership, is:

- the learning bridge between sense-making and meaning-making,
- about our values,
- about our self to self-relationship,
- about purpose,
- about the mindset interfaces of accountability and authenticity,
- energised by the 'will to be',
- about exploring the 'why am I?' question, and
- the foundation of personal acumen.

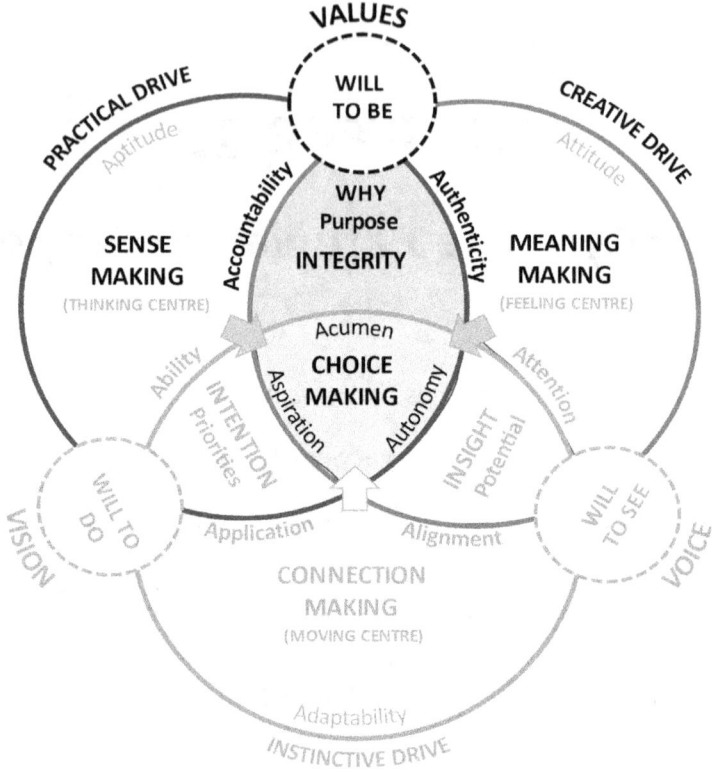

Figure 21: Integrity and the Will to Be

Integrity is one of the most important and oft-cited of virtue terms. When used as a virtue term, integrity refers to a quality of a person's character. Integrity is also attributed to various parts or aspects of a person's life. While integrity includes attributes such as professional, intellectual and artistic integrity, the most important sense of integrity relates to general character – your sense of 'wholeness'.

What is it to be a person *of* integrity? Ordinary discussion about integrity involves two fundamental ideas: first, that integrity is primarily a formal relationship one has to oneself; and second, that integrity is connected in an important way to acting morally.

INSIGHT INTENTION AND INTEGRITY

In other words, there are some accepted cultural constraints on what it is to act with integrity.

These are the five main dimensions of integrity.

- Integrity as wholeness. Integrity consists of a person's values, daily actions, and basic purpose,
- Integrity as consistency between words and actions. A demonstrated consistency within our social behaviour,
- Integrity as consistency in the face of adversity, temptation and challenge,
- Integrity as being true to oneself, by acting according to one's own conscience, and
- Integrity as morality or ethics, by acting in accordance with socially acceptable behaviour, such as honesty, trustworthiness, justice and compassion.

The fundamental thing people find interesting about you is not what you actually do in your job, day in day out, nor your job title or your role, but your authenticity. The question that should occupy the greater part of your reflection on integrity is the contribution based one – why am I here? It is underpinned by your core values and how they relate to the contribution you intend to make for the greater good of others. It is not about goals and ambition but about the sense of values-based purpose that underpins your contribution to the common good.

Purpose is shaped by your values. It guides your life decisions, influences your behaviour, shapes your priorities, offers you a sense of direction, and creates connection between meaning making and sense making. Purpose will be unique for everyone. What you identify as your purpose will be different from others. What's more, your purpose can actually shift and change throughout life in response to the evolving intentions and insights about your own experiences.

Integrity underpins your purpose and is anchored in your values. Each of us holds numerous values with varying degrees of importance in differing situations. A particular value may be very important to one person but unimportant to another.

The values theory of Schwartz, that was discussed earlier when we looked at meaning-making, specifies six main features of values.

- Values are linked inextricably to affect. When values are activated, they become infused with feeling. As an example, people for whom independence is an important value become aroused if their independence is threatened, despair when they are helpless to protect it, and are happy when they can enjoy it,
- Values refer to desirable outcomes that motivate action. As an example, people for whom social order, justice, and helpfulness are important values are motivated to achieve these outcomes,
- Values transcend specific actions and situations. Self-discipline and honesty values, for example, may be relevant in the workplace or school, in business or politics, with friends or strangers. This broader context distinguishes values from norms and attitudes that usually refer to specific actions, objects, or situations,
- Values serve as standards of behaviour. Values guide the selection or evaluation of actions, policies, people, and events. People decide what is good or bad, justified or illegitimate, worth doing or avoiding, based on possible consequences for their held values. But the impact of values in everyday decisions is rarely conscious. Values enter awareness when the choices we are considering have conflicting implications for different values we hold,
- Values are ordered by importance relative to one another. Our values form an ordered system of priorities that characterise us as individuals. Do they attribute more importance to achievement or justice, to novelty or tradition? This hierarchical feature also distinguishes values from cultural norms and attitudes,

INSIGHT INTENTION AND INTEGRITY

- The relative importance of multiple values guides choice and action. Any attitude or behaviour typically has implications for more than one value. The trade-off among relevant, competing values guides attitudes and behaviours. Values influence choice when they are relevant in the context (hence likely to be activated).

The above are features of all values. What distinguishes one from another is the type of intention or motivation that it expresses.

In his book, Pathways to Integrity, Blake Burleson identifies the two core ethical values-based questions in any situation as:

- "What should I do?" and
- "How should I decide?".

He then proposes that there are two main ways to answer the "What should I do?" question that depend upon what kind of conscience we have developed.

- If we have a conscience of principle we will consider the act *alone* where we are seeking to do what is right in the present, using sensing.
- If we have a conscience of potential we will consider the *future* implications of our actions where we are seeking the good for the future, using intuition.

Then says that there are two main ways to answer the "How do I decide?" question that depend upon the head (thinking) or the heart (feeling).

- If we use our sensing function we can then apply our thinking or feeling function to decide if a course of action is the right thing to do in the present moment,
- If we use our intuitive function we can then apply our thinking or feeling function to seek the good for future results.

Consequently, the four Jungian functions of sensing, intuition, thinking and feeling, operating as function pairs, provide an adaptive learning framework for exploring our core values that underpin our sense of purpose and integrity.

The four Jungian function pairs according to Burleson, that form the high-level integrity drivers of our perception, are:

- NT – Intuition and Thinking which is a conscience of potential - focused on seeking the good consistently, known as Justice.
- NF – Intuition and Feeling which is a conscience of potential - focused on seeking the good for others, known as Compassion.
- SF – Sensing and Feeling which is a conscience of principle - focused on doing the right thing by helping others, known as Care.
- ST – Sensing and Thinking which is a conscience of principle - focused on doing the right thing consistently, known as Duty.

We will have a preference for one of these Social Styles (function pairs) as discussed earlier. So in terms of developing a deeper understanding of our true integrity and understanding the potential alternative ways we can reconcile the different values-based perspectives let's look at how Burleson describes each of them in a little more detail.

Justice NT – Intuition and Thinking: is about seeking the good consistently and focusing on broad impersonal concepts and issues and analysing complex situations objectively. The values-based position is grounded in a unifying vision that organises all of life into a comprehensive whole. They bring a global perspective to their ethical judgements. They demand intellectual rigour in formulating their ideas as they seek justice and equity for the larger community. They are the most likely to be the instigators of change and will be quick to criticise an imperfect system.

They are near future focused and impersonal In their approach to issues and concepts.

Compassion NF – Intuition and Feeling: is about seeking the good for others and promoting harmony in complex interpersonal situations and ensuring laws and rules are responsive to people. They are compassionate and idealistic and combine a global vision with a feeling of well-being for people. Their inspiration can be a catalyst for social change. They are tuned into social patterns and focus on possibilities. They seek affirmation and may have a difficult time taking criticism. They are highly tolerant of different moral positions and can suspend their own beliefs to appreciate those of others without having to reconcile any ambiguity. They are longer term future focused and seek to promote peace and harmony.

Care SF – Sensing and Feeling: is about doing the right thing by serving others and attending to the practical needs of individuals. They are typically caring and sensitive people who express their connection to others in immediate and concrete ways. They are extremely loyal and fulfil traditional cultural and social expectations of their community or organisation. The like structured settings in which they can understand the appropriate action to take. They are present and immediate past focused and are very aware of body language and facial expressions to get feedback.

Duty ST – Sensing and Thinking: is about doing the right thing consistently and focusing on minimising of eliminating ambiguity and uncertainty and applying objective rules. The values-based position is grounded in details and facts. The reasoning is linear and their opinions are unbiased, detached, objective and impersonal. They value a correct sequential line of thinking in an almost legalistic style. They are direct and often brutally honest. They believe that there is a right and a wrong in every situation often based on early childhood indoctrination. They are past focused and observe objective rules and standards so that they can do the right thing consistently in the present.

Jung saw these each pair of these four functions as opposites rather than differences and observed that you cannot use both functions, sensing and intuition or thinking and feeling, at the same time. When you use thinking then feeling is put aside and vice versa. They can be engaged alternatively but not together. This results in a dialectic in moral and wider cultural terms. A dialectic is a method of argument that systematically weighs up contradictory facts with a view to the resolution of their real or apparent contradictions. This reconciliation of opposites is the essence of developing wisdom as a reflection of our purpose and integrity.

Jung identifies integrity with wholeness. Morality and wholeness are synonymous: being morally complete cannot be achieved without psychological integration or what Jung calls "individuation": the unique personal development of all four functions of consciousness - sensing, intuition, thinking and feeling. In defining morality in this way we can measure our moral understanding against the nature of our own Social Style (Jungian function pair).

We can then develop an appreciation of the other Social Styles, e.g. the NF type who seeks the good for others (thesis) should also consider the ST perspective of doing the right thing consistently (antithesis) and out of this dialectic comes integration of different perspectives (synthesis). In this way competing opposites can be heard. There is that 'threeness' again. It is the beginning of developing wisdom.

We can also look at these Social Styles in the context of the Schwartz model we discussed in the chapter on meaning-making. The work of Schwartz provides a way that we can consider our purpose from a values perspective. His structure points to also the broad underlying motivations from which he derives a list of ten motivational types of values from three universal requirements:

- needs of individuals as biological organisms (described as "Individual needs"),
- requirements of coordinated social interaction (described as "Social interaction"), and,

- requirements for the smooth functioning and survival of groups (described as "Group needs").

Schwartz claims exhaustiveness of his set of ten basic value types. He says,

> "It is possible to classify virtually all the items found in lists of specific values from different cultures into one of these ten motivational types of values".

The table below shows the motivational goal, the needs source and the specific values that each value identifies with:

Motivational Goal	Needs Source	Specific values
Security: Safety, harmony and stability of society, of relationships and of self.	Individual needs Social interaction Group needs	National security, sense of belonging, reciprocation of favours, clean, social order, family security, healthy
Conformity: Restraint of actions, inclinations and impulses likely to upset or harm others and violate social expectations or norms.	Social interaction Group needs	Obedient, honour elders, politeness, self-discipline

Tradition: Respect, commitment and acceptance of the customs and ideas that traditional culture or religion provide.	Group needs	Accepting my position in life, moderate, devout, detachment, respect for tradition, humble
Benevolence: Preservation and enhancement of the welfare of people we are in frequent contact with.	Individual needs Social interaction Group needs	Honest, forgiving, loyal, spiritual life, helpful, responsible, meaning in life, true friendship, mature love.
Achievement: Personal success through demonstrating competence according to social standards.	Social interaction Group needs	Ambitious, successful, capable, intelligent, influential
Power: Social status and prestige, control or dominance over people and resources.	Social interaction Group needs	Preserving public image, social recognition, authority, wealth, social power
Self-direction: Independent thought and action-choosing, creating, exploring.	Individual needs Social interaction	Self-respect, choosing own goals, creativity, curious, freedom, independent

Universalism: Understanding, appreciation, tolerance and protection for the welfare of all people and for nature.	Individual needs Group needs	Inner harmony, social justice, world at peace, protect environment, equality, broad minded, unity with nature
Stimulation: Excitement, novelty and challenge in life.	Individual needs	Exciting life, varied life, daring
Hedonism: Pleasure and sensuous gratification for oneself.	Individual needs	Pleasure, enjoying life

The Schwartz values dimensions can be arranged in a circular structure, where the closer the values are in either direction around the circle, the more positive the relationship between them; the more distant they are, the more negative their relationship. They are classified on two main dialectic axes: self-transcendence and self-enhancement and seeking stability and openness to change.

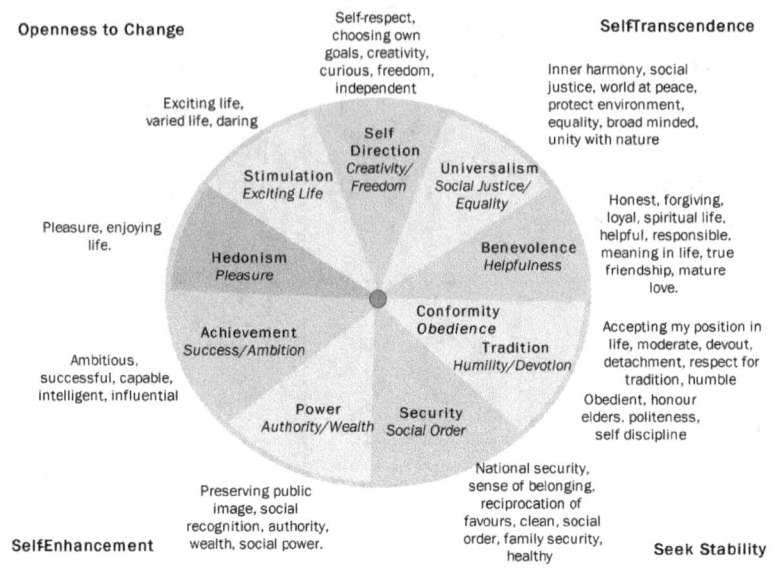

Figure 22: The Schwartz Values Circle

Almost any behaviour has positive implications for expressing, upholding, or attaining some values, but also has negative implications for the values across the structural circle in opposing positions. People tend to behave in ways that balance their opposing values. They choose alternatives that promote higher as against lower priority values. As a result, the order of positive and negative associations between any specific behaviour and the ten values tends to follow the order of the value circle.

Let's now look at the two integrity interfaces between meaning making and sense making mindsets - authenticity and accountability.

If you want to understand the true meaning of authenticity you need to go back to its root. The Latin root of the word "authenticity" is "author", so being "authentic" doesn't mean just being honest about who you are, it's about being your own "author". Authenticity is an active and creative process. It's not about revealing something, it's about building something; and that something is "you".

INSIGHT INTENTION AND INTEGRITY

Authenticity is having presence; living in the moment with conviction and confidence and staying true to yourself. Being authentic means coming from a real place within. It is when our actions and words are congruent with our values. It is being ourselves, not an imitation of what we think we should be, or have been told we should be. There's never any doubt or questioning the integrity of an authentic individual. Their behaviour, in terms of ethics and morals, is predictable. You know what you're going to get. Authenticity is the degree to which an individual's actions are congruent with their values, despite external pressures.

Integrity is authenticity taken up to another level, for in this case one is not only true to our professed ideals, but our professed ideals are now accurate reflections of our deepest values, and commitments. You are true to yourself and others and are not led along by various forces of role playing and self-delusion.

The good news is that if you are fully authentic, you never have to go through the process of revealing who you are. True authenticity doesn't require you to tell anyone else what your values are, because everyone will be able to see your values in the way you live your life. When you are fully authentic you don't reveal your chosen values, you become them - you live them. It is the foundation of your insight and its associated elements of attention and alignment with others.

The other mindset interface, accountability, in a traditional sense is a product of hierarchy. It is a duty to another person, usually a manager, to give an account of tasks completed and results achieved. In a hierarchy the general rule is that accountability cannot be shared. Accountability in many organisations is the basis for allocating blame when something goes wrong and has negative consequences in our unconscious mind.

However accountability that arises from integrity and purpose is about the very nature of the reciprocal relationship you have with others. In a wirearchy it is about being answerable for your commitments to others and their answerability for their commitments to you. It is about both task and relationship behaviour.

Accountability cannot co-exist with any lack of integrity whether it is that of others or your own. In plain language, being accountable is doing what you said you would do. Being true to your word. Following through on your commitments and showing up. For you to be accountable there has to be a consequence. It is about owning both your successes and failures and understanding your part in the successes and failures of others. It can be shared as well as personally owned.

Accountability is more values driven than vision driven. It is about more about behaviour than performance. Performance is an elusive concept that is almost always attributed to the person without regard to the role of processes, technologies, tools and access to information and knowledge, and even more importantly the context, including culture, structure, systems and competitive and regulatory forces. In the context of hierarchy the consequence is that the performance focus of accountability supports the control, order, prescribe mindset and it induces excuse making and blaming others and precludes discretionary effort.

In its true sense accountability is not done to you by others. It is an intrinsic quality the flows from defining your purpose and pursuing it with integrity. It needs to be both inspiring and embrace your identity. It is the foundation for developing your ability and the application of your intentions. Accountability assumes consequences and as such requires more than just conversation. It requires you to account for your contribution after an outcome has been achieved or delivered. At its core accountability results in capability development rather than performance management. It underpins the focus of your sense-making and meaning-making and the development of your task competence and relationship behaviour.

INSIGHT INTENTION AND INTEGRITY

The outcomes of authenticity and accountability provide the interfaces between meaning-making and sense-making as we engage in choice-making.

Integrity enables the choice-making quality of acumen to be the synthesiser of meaning-making and sense-making. As discussed earlier when looking at choice-making, acumen is the intuitive foundation of wisdom. It is keenness and depth of perception. It is about seeing the interdependencies between things and the ability to quickly and accurately understand and make sound judgements about a situation requiring choice.

While it is founded in our technical or intellectual ability it also reflects our intuitive and contextual know how rather than just our technical depth. Personal acumen means clearly seeing the integrated nature, or wholeness, of a situation and this can be difficult because of our blind spots. Blind spots are blinkers that we all have that prevent us from seeing the full picture. Acumen underpins integrity and integrates meaning-making and sense-making.

Now that you have some appreciation of the nature and role of values reflect upon your life purpose by asking:

- Why am I here?
- What are my core values?
- Where do I most belong?
- When am I "in the zone" and feel most fulfilled?
- How do I behave consistent with my purpose?
- What situations challenge me to be authentic?
- What situations demand accountability?

We have now looked at the three 'eyes' of emergent leadership of insight, intention and integrity which leads us to the three higher levels of Self and the elusive concepts of the will to see, the will to do and the will to be and the three energies that underpin them in the next Part.

PART 5

SEEING WITH CLEAR EYES

The fifth Part looks at the nature of our will and the energies that we need to access on our journey of self-development. The Will is described as three separate, but interrelated, higher intelligences. While there is no empirical evidence to support this construct, it serves as a useful way of describing the elusive idea of will in an accessible way. It also sits comfortably with the relationship between the Will and higher life energies.

The three elements of Will and their related energy sources that support them, that will be applied to our self-development, are:

- the 'will to see' and sensitive energy,
- the 'will to do' and conscious energy, and
- the 'will to be' and creative energy.

The three intelligences of our will are the foundation of our three developmental dimensions of Self:

- Our Sensitive Self based on our 'will to see',
- Our Conscious Self based on our 'will to do', and
- Our Creative Self based on our 'will to be'.

CHAPTER 13

Our Sensitive Self - Sensitive Energy and the Will to See

"The most important relationship we can all have is the one you have with yourself, the most important journey you can take is one of self-discovery. To know yourself, you must spend time with yourself, you must not be afraid to be alone. Knowing yourself is the beginning of all wisdom."

— *Aristotle*

The relationship between the three Reactive Self choice-making mindsets - meaning-making, sense-making and connection-making has now been explored together with their three higher level connecting domains of Insight (related to our Potential), Intention (related to our Priorities) and Integrity (related to our Purpose). The three 'eyes' of emergent leadership, Insight, Intention and Integrity that provide us with the foundation stones for getting beyond the habit-based choices of our Reactive Self, are implemented through our day-to-day meaning-making, sense-making and connection-making. Let's now explore the energy sources that underpin the deeper sense of self we need to access in order to realise, rather than just intellectualise, our insight, intentions and integrity. The elusive idea of our Will.

Our early social development evolves by imitation, instruction and indoctrination, the three 'eyes' of our Reactive Self, as we experience the ways others act and operate in our world and learn "to do as we are told". Consequently our categorisation system that turns data into information is one we have adopted by immersion in a cultural, life conditions and family context. We have adopted the "accessible memes" of our environment. This imitation, instruction and indoctrination process is quite inexact and is influenced by both our inherited disposition (our genes) and our socialised disposition (our memes).

As we become aware of phenomena in our external world of others, they acts a 'attention' prompts to our senses. Paradoxically through our unconscious data and information converting processes we develop a conscious sense of separateness from the external world and suppress our inner world to a sub-conscious role that enables us to keep in place an "accepted" and "acceptable" sense of who we are, who others are and why the situation is the way it is – our Reactive Self evolves and dominates both our sense-making and meaning-making.

The saying "where there's a will there's a way" suggests that if we strive, using "will" power, to achieve a more satisfying life, we will find the "way". The very essence of the saying "where there's a will there's a way" implies that the work we have to do (the way) will happen once we have the right level of will power. This idea is at the root of our identity dilemma – our striving is dominated by our existing patterns of "success". Just trying harder is somewhat futile and is often constrained by our work and social roles. Our Reactive Self "knows" that.

We mostly see work as our responsibility to react to those tasks and relationships that come within the scope of our role or job. Invariably again, our role or job is often prescribed for us by significant others' notions of proper behaviour, and is capably and willingly fulfilled by our instincts and habit-based beliefs. We thrive on using our "experience" to fix problems – so much so that we define our Self by the roles we play, or jobs we do, that confirm the competence we have gained from "solving" problems. Our Reactive Self "knows" that.

INSIGHT INTENTION AND INTEGRITY

The culture we grew up in, and now live in, also conspires to keep us in those roles. Ever tried to secure a job without the required "experience"? "But what about my potential?" you splutter. The success we have in the roles we play, which we paradoxically call performance, becomes an obligation to meet the expectations of others. We accept being 'managed'. Our world is a stage and we learn the script so we can play our role on it. Our Will becomes suppressed by our automatic habit patterns of response to our world. Our Reactive Self "knows" that.

Rather than experiencing the joy of realising our latent potential through connection to our life purpose, we take the easy way out and maintain the compliance we give to more powerful others. We, mostly unconsciously, comply with the scripts of the cultural context we are immersed in. We are attached to the underdeveloped role of our Reactive Self and become a one person, one script, one act play. Our Reactive Self, as a belief-based meaning-maker, closes us from getting access to our Will and the energies it provides. We live our life in a state of "have to" rather than "want to".

The Will can be described as three separate, but interrelated, higher intelligences – while there is presently no empirical evidence to support this construct, it serves as a useful way of describing the elusive idea of Will in an accessible way. It also sits comfortably with the relationship between the Will and higher life and infinite energies that were mentioned earlier and will be described more fully shortly.

The three intelligences of Will that support our self-development are:

- the 'will to see' that opens us to sensitive energy and Insight,
- the 'will to do', that opens us to conscious energy and Intention, and
- the 'will to be' that opens us to creative energy and Integrity.

These three intelligences of our will are the foundation of our three unconscious dimensions of Self:

- Our Sensitive Self based on our 'will to see',
- Our Conscious Self based on our 'will to do', and
- Our Creative Self based on our 'will to be',

are shown in their relative place on the Adaptive Leaning Map

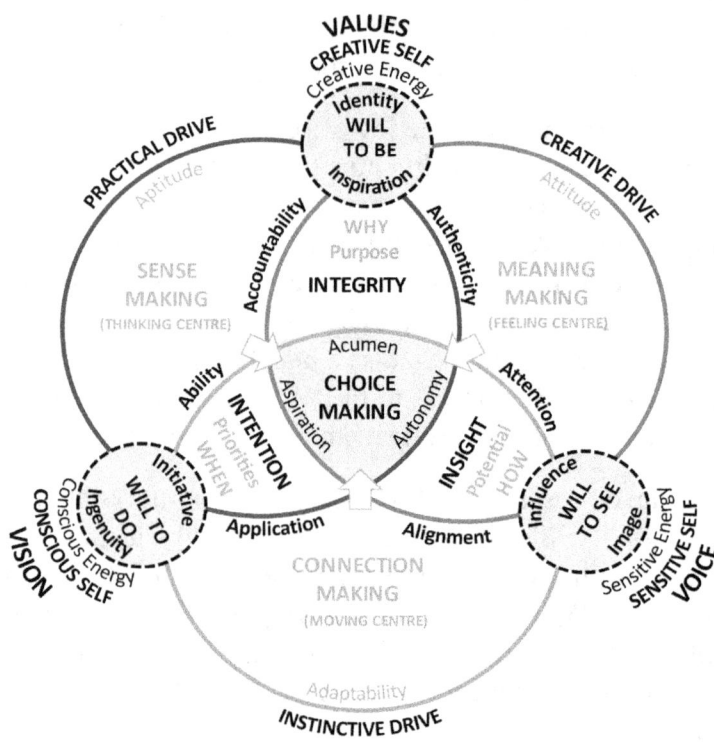

Figure 23: The Three Dimensions of the Higher Self

You will recall that we have already explored the sense we have of ourselves on a day-to-day basis, that emerges from our reactions to the world, and actions of others that we encounter in it, that we have called our Reactive Self. Paradoxically the actions of others are also reactions to their world and actions of others in it. So rather than our sense of Self being about intentional actions and interactions, it is about the continuous self-generated reflexive responses of our various reactions to each other. We wrongly define reactions as actions.

Even when we act 'intentionally', those reactions are anchored in our unconscious scripts, theories and beliefs about the world. Our reactions become a self-fulfilling process that enables us to survive and, in a limited way, succeed in the world. We develop a *Reactive Self*: a self that operates out of habitual inter-reactive patterns of meaning-making, sense-making and connection-making..

Over time we start to recognise that we have to take some responsibility for how our patterns of behaviour impact on the interactions we have with others, and the thoughts and feelings that they generate in us. That may lead us to develop greater self-awareness through learning activities that others send us on, so we can become better managers, better customer representatives, better teachers, etc.

We take some of this in and find that some of it works. We begin to realise that people are different and develop more robust categorisation systems, such as the Jungian-Myers Briggs model, to assist in understanding our personality. We get glimpses of, and are curious about, our *Sensitive Self*: a self that is inquisitive about our interactive patterns and our latent potential.

As we mature, and may recognise that we have unrealised potential, we begin to reflect on the external nature of our sense of who we are. We may stand back from ourselves, and start to develop priorities that are aligned with a new found sense of potential. We may sense that we have a connection to the natural living order, that is constantly evolving as it silently and continuously influences how we experience our Self, and how the others experience us, on a moment-by-moment basis. We may sense that we have a *Conscious Self*: as self that is beyond what we think, feel and do.

In fleeting moments, and sometimes by observing the lives of others, we may recognise another part of our self that suggests there is more to us than we have experienced – a self that can access and shape the natural living order: a self that can experience the natural flow of life: a self that has access to our wholeness. A unique contribution that we are destined to make to the unfolding living natural order we are a part of – a connection to our life purpose. Many search for this sense of self by engaging in various practices and techniques that seek to put them in touch with their "spiritual nature". We sense and feel that we have a *Creative Self*: a self that has access to the flow of life itself.

Each of these faces of Self have three higher intelligences of will and three associated sources of energy:

- Our Sensitive Self with the intelligence of the 'will to see' and its associated sensitive energy,
- Our Conscious Self with the intelligence of the 'will to do' and its associated conscious energy, and
- Our Creative Self with the intelligence of the 'will to be' and its associated creative energy.

To provide some context let's just recap on the energies that were touched on earlier that Bennett identified. His scale of energies provides us with a notional framework for seeing the unseen, and for understanding some of the hidden forces that are at work as we become more self-aware, and eventually at one with life itself. They are shown below.

Level	Description	Type	Category	Awareness
E1	TRANSCENDENT	Energies of the divine	INFINITE (COSMIC)	SUBJECTIVE
E2	UNITIVE			
E3	CREATIVE	Energies of being		
E4	CONSCIOUS			
E5	SENSITIVE	Energies of responding	LIVING	OBJECTIVE
E6	AUTOMATIC			
E7	VITAL	Energies of growth		
E8	CONSTRUCTIVE			
E9	PLASTIC	Energies of form	MATERIAL	
E10	COHESIVE			
E11	DIRECTIVE	Energies of movement		
E12	DISPERSED			

The undeveloped Instinctive drive operates *reflexively* through *automatic* energy – the energy of instinct and habit. Automatic energy is the kind of life energy associated with maintaining our living functions such as breathing, digestion and elimination of waste from our body. It is self-acting energy driven by instinct. As we develop insight and our potential our Instinctive drive learns to operate *responsively* to access *sensitive* energy and see that we are the architects of our own problems in the external world.

The underdeveloped Practical Drive largely operates *reflexively* through the same *automatic* energy as the Instinctive drive by defining problems in linear and closed ways that fail to recognise the complexity of their interdependent nature. As we develop intention and our priorities our Practical Drive begins to operate *reflectively* through accessing *conscious* energy which invites us to engage with our new sense of potential through enhanced observation.

The underdeveloped Creative Drive also largely operates *reflexively* through the same *automatic* energy as the Instinctive drive by giving meaning to things in a pre-determined mechanical way based on confirmation of our past experience. As we develop integrity and purpose our Creative Drive begins to operate *receptively* through accessing *creative* energy which provides values-based purpose that reflects our contribution to the common good.

These three drives are based on our habit-based and genetic intelligence and will persist as the determinants of our future until we access the higher intelligences of our Will. The nature of our Will is such that we initially need to experience it as an idea. Accessing our Will as an idea opens us up to the depth of our potential, enables us to develop our priorities and to realise an expanded sense of our purpose in life. This initial experience of our Will as an idea enables us to venture toward a more profound sense of Self that truly reflects the connectedness we have to the living natural order, and our role in shaping it and being shaped by it, through the unique contribution we make to its evolution, and it to ours.

With that background let's look at the 'will to see' and its related sensitive energy that underpins our Sensitive Self in our Adaptive Learning Map©.

Figure 24: Our Sensitive Self

The initial shift in our awareness generated by our 'will to see' - a force that we cannot readily describe - is initiated when we become aware of the level of energy that underpins our Sensitive Self: sensitive energy. It is based on a shift from other observation to self-observation: a very difficult shift in perspective that involves the transition to a higher energy source. As with all life transitions letting go of the "old" generates a sense of disequilibrium and denial. Consequently we may just develop a better set of excuses for our plight or have more ammunition for classifying the idiosyncrasies of others who aggravate us, and worse, tell them so.

Accessing our 'will to see' enables our Sensitive Self to be fully aware of the sensitive energy available to us. Understanding the nature of sensitive energy is the foundation for developing our Sensitive Self.

In his illuminating book Deeper Man, JG Bennett discusses *sensitive energy* and says:

> *"Sensitive energy enables us to be aware of our thoughts, our feelings, and our bodily states - the associations, reactions, and sensations of our mechanical life. The condition of the man-machine is to exist as thoughts, feelings, and bodily states so that it is a slave to every fleeting impulse. It is only when we are aware of alternatives that we can choose. When we are sensitive we can accept or reject what is before us; but we must be careful not to confuse this possibility with automatic reaction. To avoid this confusion we have to know what it is to hold together opposites. When we like something, it is useful to see how we can dislike it and vice versa. If we find ourselves saying "no" to an idea, it is useful to see ourselves in agreement with it also. It is only when we are able to come under the combined action of "yes" and "no" that we really have the possibility of choice.*
>
> *It is not true to say that with the sensitive energy we are able to initiate an action. **Sensitive operations depend on what has gone before. It enables us to choose within an existing situation but not to change the situation itself. To go beyond what actually exists and to become free from "yes" and "no" we require the cosmic (infinite) energies.**"* (The emphasis is mine.)

INSIGHT INTENTION AND INTEGRITY

When we understand the nature of the 'will to see', we become conscious of sensitive energy. We become aware of "yes" and "no" choices rather than "either-or" choices. This shift in our mindset is the essence of the 'will to see'. We begin to see our limiting beliefs, scripts and theories for what they really are, limiting, and become open to proactively seeking out information from outside of us. We seek out books, teachers and practices to help us begin to appreciate the nature and pattern of our automatic reflexive behaviour. We begin the process of shifting our locus of control from outside of ourselves (blaming and victim oriented) to inside ourselves (responsible and choice oriented). We develop response-ability. This reaching out for new information begins our journey to attain growth as insight.

Unfortunately, we tend not to naturally develop the insight that would open up our awareness of, and give attention to, the ego fixations that underpin our Reactive Self mindsets of meaning-making, sense-making and connection-making. Our "emotive" and "knowing" tendencies combine to ensure our way of seeing things in the world remains firmly in place.

On the one hand our Reactive Self gives us a sense of stability amid continuous change. On the other hand, at this level of emotional intelligence (based on our experience), we can recognise non-satisfying repeating patterns of behaviour in our self and others that gives us a sense that there must be something more and better. This opens us up to the possibility that we are the architect of our own situation and may lead to personal growth as insight - we get to appreciate our own idiosyncrasies and begin to take responsibility for our own behaviour and our impact on others.

The foundations of meaning-making (our Jungian function pair of intuition and feeling) and connection-making (our primal instincts, temperament, social development and life conditions/personal needs level), provide the structural impediments for undertaking the challenges we face in accessing our 'will to see' and in developing true Insight. We need to see them for what they are and how they contribute to our blind spots.

As Henry Thoreau reflected on, from a path that he had worn at Waldon Pond in 1847:

> *"The surface of the earth is soft and impressionable by the feet of men; and so with the paths which the mind travels. How worn and dusty, then, must be the highways of the world, how deep the tradition and conformity."*

We have seen that the Reactive Self represents that "worn and dusty" highway of the mind with its "deep tradition and conformity". However, as we mature, our Reactive Self has the potential to evolve by developing "self" awareness through access to the sensitive energy of our 'will to see'.

Our Sensitive Self is initially about understanding the deep structure of our Reactive Self. We can then begin to comprehend the three intelligences of the Will. The Sensitive Self is the reconciling force between the Reactive and Conscious Self.

Our first sense of a Sensitive Self emerges when we begin to ask "is this all there is" as a consequence of our dissatisfaction with our mechanical life – we feel separate and alone, causing us to wonder about where we belong in the larger scheme of things. We feel that we have unconscious priorities or life purpose that reflect our dormant creativity, and a desire to connect to something larger than ourselves. It is more than our primal instincts, temperament or life conditions.

We feel that we are not integrated with our emerging sense of wholeness. Again this is intuitive rather than instinctive and is evidence of our fleeting access to a higher energy source. It is our intuitive feeling of potential that provides context for developing our priorities and the Sensitive Self that provides the initial entry point for the adaptive learning pathway to our purpose. It is our intuition that gives us natural access to sensitive energy.

Without awareness of our potential, that is more than just surviving by problem solving, our Reactive Self resists intuition as an irrational response (coincidentally, Jung describes the information gathering function of intuition, along with sensation, as 'irrational' functions). Consequently we remain stuck in the patterns of our limiting beliefs. Our Reactive Self does not understand our intuitive potential – in fact, it denies it, or uses its "cleverness" to solve problems, but gives it little credit.

The challenging part of our next level of self-development is to bring information to our Reactive Self mindsets of meaning-making, sense-making and connection-making from outside. That will then enable us to understand the deeper motivations and fixations that we need to recognise and reflect upon. We have already considered a basic level of insight into these deeper motivations using the Jungian model, and the temperament framework, when we looked at our blind spots. These deeper motivations also contain the seeds of our potential. We developed a deeper understanding of the underlying pattern dynamics of our three Reactive Self mindsets. It allowed us to understand where our attention automatically goes in our reactive Self-Other interactions.

Our Sensitive Self opens up our Self-Other meaning-making and connection-making mindsets by giving us access to the energising qualities of influence and image of the "will to see".

Influence is the sense of authority, the right, or the capacity to influence people and get them to do what you want and need them to do, consistent with their own purpose and priorities. There are several types of authority that can be accessed.

- Positional – the ability to influence others based on your official authority and position, which includes:
- Reward – the ability to influence others by giving or withholding rewards,

- Punishment – the ability to influence others by imposing a penalty for fault, offense or violation,
- Knowledge – the ability to influence others based on your knowledge and expertise, and
- Behavioural – the ability to influence others using your behaviour, manner and approach.

Authority is about the legitimate exercise of power in day-to-day choice-making and it often evident in a crisis. Power and authority are separate but related concepts. Power is the possession of authority, control, or personal appeal that a person uses to influence the actions of others. A prime source of power in the universally connected world is the possession of knowledge.

Influence is the power to have an important effect on someone or something. The word Influence has an enlightening root meaning. It literally means "to flow into". When we influence people, our thoughts, ideas, and recommendations "flow into" them to such an extent that they adopt them as their own.

Influence is therefore a way to have impact on other people, and to shape the world around us. Influence relies on persuasive power. It does not contemplate coercive power or control.

In a universe in which everything is mutually interdependent, none of us has absolute control over anything including, much of the time, ourselves. Rather, what we all have in abundance is influence, the power of which seems to function based on proximity: the closer personally and physically others are to us, the greater our influence over them, and vice versa.

Even more interestingly, unlike our attempts to control, our attempts to influence don't require our conscious intent. This is why our ability to influence others is so much more important than our ability to control them; we're always exerting influence simply by being who we are, saying what we say, and doing what we do. The only real choice we have in the matter is whether or not the influence we exert is good or bad.

You can assess the effectiveness of your influencing approaches by distinguishing among the three different outcomes of influence: the acceptance, acquiescence, or avoidance of those you are seeking to influence:

- Acceptance is when the person you seek to influence agrees internally with an action or a decision. The person is committed to it, enthusiastic about it and is likely to exercise initiative and demonstrate unusual effort and persistence in order to carry out the request successfully, even when faced with resistance or setbacks,
- Acquiescence is when the person you seek to influence carries out the requested action, but is apathetic about it, rather than enthusiastic. This person makes only a minimal or average effort, does not show any initiative, and is likely to give up if confronted with resistance or setbacks, and
- Avoidance is when the person you seek to influence opposes the requested action and tries to avoid doing it by refusing, arguing, delaying, or seeking to have the request negated.

The role of personal influence depends on the connection-making mindsets of the individuals who are connecting with one another, and the desired outcomes of that connection. It is about the quality of the relationship between them and depends on:

- Mutuality of control - which is the degree to which the people involved in a relationship are satisfied with the amount of control they have over a relationship,
- Trust - which is the level of confidence that the people involved have in each other and their willingness to open themselves to the other person,

- Commitment - which is the extent to which the people involved believe and feel that the relationship is worth spending energy on to maintain and promote, and
- Satisfaction - which is the extent to which the people involved feel favourably about each other because positive expectations about the relationship are reinforced.

Influence therefore is the power to have an important effect on someone or something. It underpins emergent leadership.

The second energising quality of the 'will to see' is image. Image is short for self-image. A self-image is in its most basic form is an internalised mental picture/idea you have of yourself. It's how you think and feel about yourself, based on your attitude, competence and relationships, that consistently impact your outlook on life as well as your level of happiness and fulfillment.

Your self-image is the impression you have of yourself that forms a collective representation of your strengths and weaknesses. These strengths and weaknesses often are evident through the labels you give yourself that describe your qualities and characteristics. For instance, you might say:

> **I am intelligent...** *therefore I can...*
>
> **I am loser...** *therefore I can't...*
>
> **I am outgoing...** *therefore I am able to...*
>
> **I am shy...** *therefore I am unable to...*

These are just some of the examples of the many labels you potentially give yourself and the inevitable conclusions you may reach. And it is these conclusions you make about yourself that either form the foundations of a healthy self-image or an unhealthy self-image. Moreover, these labels form the foundations of your beliefs.

Your self-image is built upon your perception of reality, and that is influenced by how you believe you are being viewed by society and other people. Your self-image is something that gradually develops over a lifetime of experience through learning and social influence. It is something that is constantly changing over time as you gain more life experience, as you think and reflect, as you learn, and as you interact with other people.

The three elements of your self-image are:

- the way you perceive or think of yourself,
- the way you interpret others' perceptions (or what you think others think) of you,
- the way you would like to be (your ideal self).

The underlying role of our Sensitive Self is to open us up to a positive self-image and unearthing of our potential. Potential is defined as having or showing the capacity to develop into something in the future and the latent qualities or abilities that may be developed and lead to future success or usefulness. It is therefore about your development to a future state. It generally refers to a currently unrealised ability. In the context of our new digital environment, Steve Ballmer says:

> "The number one benefit of information technology is that it empowers people to do what they want to do. It lets people be creative. It lets people be productive. It lets people learn things they didn't think they could learn before, and so in a sense, it is all about potential".

A glimpse of your potential may have been unearthed when you used the Jungian function pair framework to provide some understanding of your insight. The alignment of our way of seeing yourself with the way you see others, underpins the relationship you have between your meaning-making mindset, and that of others, in your social interactions with them.

The alignment of behaviours, which emerge in social interactions, involves individuals experiencing their meaning making mindsets in a progressive and dynamic (real time) manner. As the process of alignment unfolds, each individual openly exchanges information about each other's behaviour and therefore act cooperatively, whether or not a common goal is in place.

It is this alignment of individual meaning-making mindsets with individual connection-making mindsets that then supports the sense-making activities of knowledge sharing, and establishing personal and common goals and intentions cooperatively. As mentioned, cooperation is the foundation of collaboration and is anchored in shared meaning-making. It leads to discretionary effort.

Our Sensitive Self provides the first step in understanding the foundations of our emergent leadership potential in the universally connected world of wirearchy.

Let's revisit the idea of wirearchy to provide some further context.

As Husband explained:

> *"Wirearchy is an emergent organising principle that informs the ways that purposeful human activities, and the structures in which they are contained, is evolving from hierarchy's* command-and-control *(top-down direction and supervision) to* champion-and-channel ... *championing ideas and innovation, and channeling time, energy, authority and resources into testing those ideas and the possibilities for innovation carried in those ideas."*

And as such emergent leadership in a wirearchy is a *"a dynamic two-way flow of power and authority, based on knowledge, trust, credibility and a focus on results, enabled by interconnected people and technology"*.

In a universally connected world the role of emergent leadership is embedded in the capacity to make personal choices and respect

INSIGHT INTENTION AND INTEGRITY

the choices of others, in a way that mutually reflects individual potential, priorities and purpose, in order to enhance the common good. It is anchored in insight, intention and integrity – the three "eyes" of emergent leadership.

Your Sensitive Self enhances the mindset interface processes of attention and alignment that change how we engage in meaning-making and connection-making as a key part of our emergent leadership role in the universally connected digital space of wirearchy. "That's just who I am!" is now no longer good enough when that response is embedded in your Reactive Self that denies your potential.

Your inner voice is embedded in your insight and is about the attention getting nature of your connection-making. If you have another person's undivided attention they will listen to you and with the appropriately focused tone of voice they will understand you.

The definition of "tone of voice" is actually "the way a person is speaking to someone." In essence, it's how you sound when you say words out loud.

Your 'tone' of your voice can have several dimensions including:

- serious vs. emotional – being traditional and straightforward or using strong emotion,
- formal vs. casual – applying cultural protocols or taking a relaxed more easy-going approach
- respectful vs. playful – recognising the power structure or being friendly and humorous
- matter-of-fact vs. enthusiastic.– being down to earth and analytical or being optimistic and imaginative.

Your Sensitive Self provides the sensitive energy that gives you perspective and enables you to see the "yes and no" dimensions of using your inner voice.

Against that understanding of your Sensitive Self let's consider the nature of your Conscious Self.

CHAPTER 14

Our Conscious Self - Conscious Energy and the Will to Do

"The energy of the mind is the essence of life."

Aristotle

There is a relationship between Insight and Intention through the way that our 'will to see' opens up our attention to the nature and role of conscious energy and our 'will to do'.

Let's look at our Adaptive Learning Map© to get our bearings.

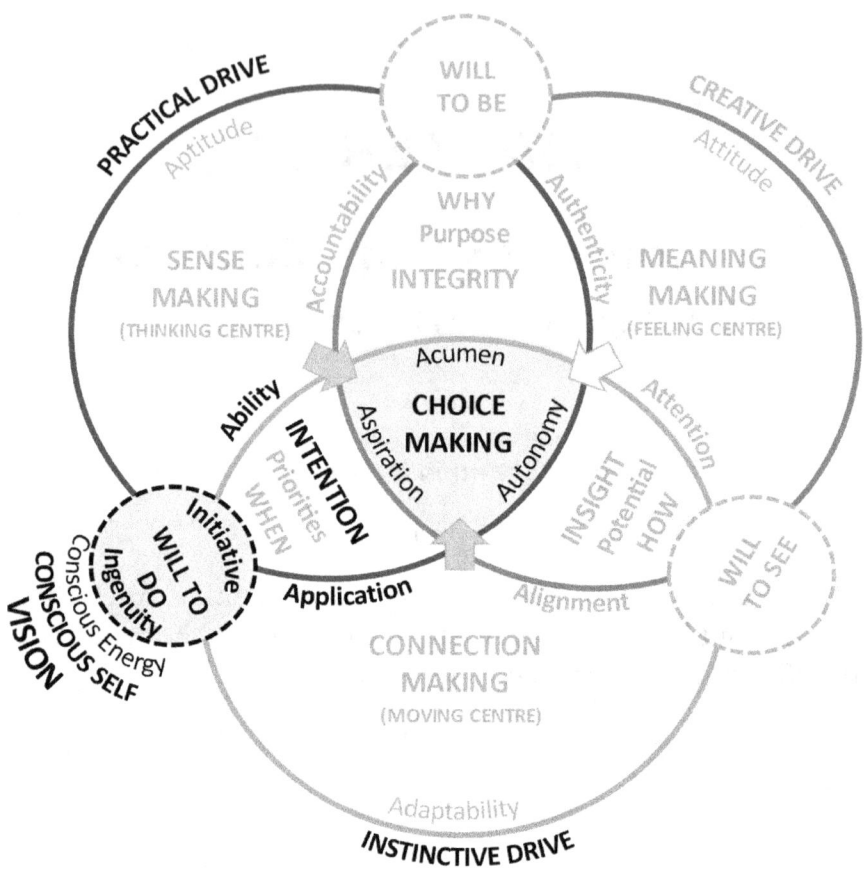

Figure 25: Our Conscious Self

The Conscious Self is supported by the intelligence of the 'will to do' and its associated conscious energy. It is about the application of initiative and ingenuity to our intentions. It is about becoming conscious and recognising the limiting power our Reactive Self, and our newly discovered Sensitive Self, have over our everyday choice-making.

Becoming sensitive involves discriminating between opposites. Since the basic opposites are consciousness and the unconscious, the first challenge is to acknowledge that there are some things about ourselves we are not aware of. When we can 'see' another side of ourselves, there is then the demanding task of discriminating between a whole range of other opposites, most importantly the crucial difference between our inner and outer self and that of others.

Jung describes two distinct ways in which consciousness is enlarged. One is during a moment of high emotional tension involving a situation in the outer world. We feel uneasy for no obvious reason, and, without thinking, suddenly we understand what's going on. The other way is what happens in a state of quiet contemplation, where ideas pass before the mind as separate images. Suddenly there is a flash of association between two apparently disconnected and widely separated thoughts. In each case it is the discharge of a conscious energy-tension that produces consciousness.

In Jung's model of the Self, consciousness is a high-level structure based on the unconscious and arising out of it. He says:

> *"Consciousness does not create itself - it wells up from unknown depths. In childhood it awakens gradually, and all through life it wakes each morning out of the depths of sleep from an unconscious condition. It is like a child that is born daily out of the primordial womb of the unconscious. ... It is not only influenced by the unconscious but continually emerges out of it in the form of spontaneous ideas and sudden flashes of thought."*

Mature consciousness is dependent on the dynamic relationship between a flexible Reactive Self, a developed Sensitive Self and an accessible Conscious Self. For that to happen we have to acknowledge that the Reactive Self and Sensitive Self are not in charge. This is not a natural process; it is a major shift in beliefs and assumptions, like the difference between believing the earth is the centre of the solar system and then learning that the sun is. This generally doesn't happen until you develop the intention to reflect on your experience, and its associated "knowledge" and realise there was more going on than you knew. You begin to develop intention based on your 'will to do'. You develop priorities consistent with your newly discovered potential.

Becoming conscious, then, is above all not a one-time thing. It is a continuous process of assimilating what was previously unknown about our self. It involves a progressive understanding of why we do what we do. And a major step is to become aware of the many ways we're influenced by unconscious aspects of ourselves, which is to say, by our Reactive Self mindsets of meaning-making, sense-making and connection-making.

Jung says:

> *"Everything of which I know, but of which I am not at the moment thinking; everything of which I was once conscious but have now forgotten; everything perceived by my senses, but not noted by my conscious mind; everything which, involuntarily and without paying attention to it, I feel, think, remember, want, and do; all the future things that are taking shape in me and will sometime come to consciousness: all this is the content of the unconscious."*

The 'will to do' is a higher intelligence that we need to develop and that involves accessing conscious energy. This idea is not easy to grasp as it requires a paradigm shift of "doing" from a "machine" view of the world to a "living systems" view of the world. A shift to a view that understands doing as a natural living process of transformation. What we already know and believe about the world does not allow us to "see" this transformation from the vantage point of our Reactive Self. We either get it or we don't - there is no gradualism in this.

INSIGHT INTENTION AND INTEGRITY

Conscious energy is the first level of the infinite energies and enables us to engage our 'will to do': our conscious intention to develop and apply our latent potential and act instantaneously on the possibilities that arise in our context.

Bennett says of *conscious energy:*

> "In ordinary speech, "consciousness" means the state of being aware of things going on, produced by the sensitive energy. What we mean by consciousness is something of a higher order that can be described crudely as an "awareness of our ordinary awareness." If we want to understand transformation in humans, it is necessary to understand the distinction between sensitivity and consciousness. It is easy to believe that we can "observe ourselves." Most people even take it for granted that they know what is going on in themselves and what their states are; but most so-called self-observation is simply the observation by one centre of another. For example, we can think of our body and the way in which it is moving or feel the thoughts that are coursing through our minds."

> "Real self-observation requires what is called the "separation of oneself from oneself". This means a separation from all the functioning of thought, feeling, and body. Our functioning is then still part of "us" but "we" are no longer just a part of it. Once we have had this experience, the taste is unmistakable when it comes to us again. But when it is not there, we can very easily deceive ourselves that it is.

> ***It is because conscious energy is a cosmic (infinite) energy that we cannot "make" ourselves***

conscious. It does not come directly from efforts, as sensitivity does." (The emphasis is mine).

It is not an outcome of applying our Thinking Centre, Feeling Centre or Moving Centre to an observable personal characteristic or quality – one centre observing another as Bennett puts it. It is a shift from the highest level of life energy to the lowest level of infinite energy. It needs to be seen as a pathway to opening ourselves up to the creative energy that supports the development of our purpose – we free ourselves from "having to do something" to developing abilities and connections in a way that is in harmony with the interdependencies the are embedded in the natural living order. We have an "awareness of our ordinary awareness".

It is in this space that we have the possibility of becoming free. Infinite energies are the energies beyond the physical, emotional and mental realms of life. With them our identity goes beyond that of a living (doing, feeling, thinking) body. When we "get it" we are we are able to be consciously engaged with our Conscious Self.

We become open to developing a living, presence focussed, sense of who we are, rather than mechanical, socialised person we had become. We stop playing other-directed roles with their associated unfulfilling behaviours. We don't abandon our experience - that is always useful in our day-to-day choice-making. We see it for what it is: habit-based and limiting. We are on the pathway to becoming intentional with our new found insight.

Intention without insight leads to futile goal setting, identifying with so called self-help gurus and wishful thinking using affirmations - developing a false identity and role playing, both of which are very draining. Intention needs to be energised by conscious energy, an energy of responding rather than reacting. That is why insight and belief in our potential comes first.

This conscious work on our ability and application interacts with our intention and provides the foundation for initiative that is generated by the conscious energy of our 'will to do'. Initiative can be defined as a behaviour that results in an individual taking a self-starting approach to intentions and associated tasks and finding ways and means of achieving them.

Self-starting implies that the priorities are not given or assigned by someone else, but that the person themself takes the initiative to develop their own priorities. A self-starting action is one that exceeds our work or social role and involves discretionary effort.

Personal initiative is based on the fundamental idea that human beings are not only influenced by their environment but also influence themselves. It is seen as behaviour that results in an individual taking an active and self-starting approach to priorities and associated tasks. These individuals are persistent in overcoming barriers/setbacks. Showing initiative involves acting openly on ideas that come up or that may have been neglected by others within your connected community. It is the essence of emergent leadership.

Taking initiative means the ability to see something that needs to be done and choosing to do it out of your own free will without someone else telling you to do it. Doing something that needs to be done out of your own desire to make things better than they were before. It is about intention and priorities.

The other quality of our Conscious Self is ingenuity. Ingenuity is the quality of being clever, original, and imaginative, often in the process of applying ideas to solve problems or meet challenges. Ingenuity involves the most conscious human sense-making and meaning-making processes, bringing together our 'will to see' and our 'will to do' to develop intention and priorities that engage us in connecting with others. Ingenuity involves using imagination to solve complex problems with others as connection-making.

Imagination is an elusive idea. While we can use imagination to solve problems imagination is fully released by engaging with your life purpose. Ingenuity, as applied imagination, is the pathway to our Creative Self and our purpose which is discussed in the next chapter.

Imagination is one of those words that inspire us. It reminds us of children playing .

Einstein said

> "Imagination is more important than knowledge. For knowledge is limited, whereas imagination embraces the entire world, stimulating progress, giving birth to evolution."

and

> "Logic will get you from A to B. Imagination will take you everywhere."

The word gets used in a lot of ways, but for the most part, we mean one of two things.

- First, we use the word to refer to creativity in general - saying that someone has a great imagination or no imagination at all.
- Second, we use the word to refer to mental capacity of some kind - either picturing something in your head, like how your childhood bedroom looked, or hearing a song in your head to try to recall lyrics.

It is perhaps about acting with innocence - not knowing you don't know. As children we did not know the difference between being logical and illogical. This gave us mind boggling extent of freedom which we used to our advantage. As adults, we tend to think logically to prove our intelligence, or so we do not get left out. This pressures us to use the knowledge of our thinking centre, imposing unconscious control over our imagining abilities.

We fail to understand that, while logic makes us travel from one point to another in a sequential manner, imagination has no bounds. Imagination takes us anywhere we choose to go and out of the same day to day problems. It relies on seeing connections between unlike things.

Gaining knowledge empowers our minds and broadens its range. Reading broadens our imagination by stimulating the right side of our brain. It literally opens our minds to new possibilities and new ideas helping us experience the world through our connection-making.

The notion of ingenuity is anchored in an understanding of our 'will to do' as "awakened doing" and the implications that has for our purpose, as a personal values-driven construct that evokes a positive and creative emotional state. Eckhardt Tolle talks about the three modalities of "awakened doing" that flow into what we do, and connects us to the awakened consciousness that is necessary for the subsequent development of our Creative Self.

The three modalities of 'awaked doing' that he identifies are acceptance, enjoyment and enthusiasm. Because Tolle's descriptions are fully complementary to our approach to consciousness and the role of "awakened doing" we will quote the essence of what he has said about each modality.

About **acceptance**, Tolle says:

> *"Whatever you cannot enjoy doing you can at least accept that this is what you have to do. Acceptance means: For now, this is what this situation, this moment, requires me to do, and I do so willingly.... Performing an action in the state of acceptance means you are at peace while you do it. That peace is a subtle energy vibration which flows into what you do. On the surface acceptance looks like a passive state, but in reality it is active and creative because it brings something entirely new into this world. That peace, that energy vibration, is consciousness,*

and one of the ways it enters this world is through surrendered action, one aspect of which is acceptance.

If you can neither enjoy nor bring acceptance to what you do – stop. Otherwise you are not talking responsibility for the only thing you can take responsibility for, which also happens to be the one thing that really matters: your state of consciousness."

About **enjoyment** Tolle says:

"Expansion and positive change on the outer level is much more likely to come into your life if you can enjoy what you are already doing, instead of waiting for some change so that you can start enjoying what you do. Don't ask your mind for permission to enjoy what you do. All you will get is plenty of reasons why you can't enjoy it. "not now" the mind will say. "Can't you see I'm busy? There's no time. Maybe tomorrow you can start enjoying..." That tomorrow will never come unless you begin enjoying what you are doing now.

When you say, I enjoy doing this or that, it is really a misperception. It makes it appear that joy comes from what you do, but this is not the case. Joy does not come from what you do, it flows into what you do and thus from a world deep within you....Then what is the relationship between something that you do and a state of joy? You will enjoy any activity in which you are fully present, any activity that is not just a means to an end. It isn't the action you perform that you really enjoy, but the deep sense of

> *aliveness that flows into it. That aliveness is one with who you are....That is why anything you enjoy connects you with the power behind all creation."*

About **enthusiasm**, Tolle says:

> *"Enthusiasm means there is deep enjoyment in what you do plus the added element of a goal or vision that you work toward. When you add a goal to the enjoyment of what you do the energy-field or vibrational frequency changes. A certain degree of what we might call structural tension is now added to enjoyment, and so it turns into enthusiasm. At the height of creative activity fuelled by enthusiasm, there will be enormous intensity and energy behind what you do.... Unlike egoic wanting, which creates opposition in direct proportion to its wanting, enthusiasm never opposes. It is non-confrontational. Its activity does not create winners and losers. It is based on inclusion, not exclusion, of others. It does not need to use and manipulate people, because it is the power of creation itself, and does not need to take energy from some secondary source. The ego's wanting always tries to take from something or someone, enthusiasm gives out of its own abundance.... Enthusiasm knows where it is going, but at the same time, it is deeply at one with the present moment, the source of its aliveness, its joy, and its power."*

These three modalities provide us with the capacity we need to develop to make a shift from an active/reactive approach to a receptive/creative approach in accessing our emerging sense of purpose.

Our 'will to do' also provides us with ways to see the world as others see it. It enables us to appreciate the intentions, potential, blind spots and mindsets of others - what they value and what they do not, and how they think, feel and act the way they do. When we are aware of the meaning-making, sense-making and connection-making patterns of the people in our life, we can respond with empathy and flexibility to their underlying pattern of motivation, instead of getting caught up in our reactions to their problem defining behaviour. It opens us up to our Conscious Self by being receptive to conscious energy. We move towards consciousness and "awakened doing".

We can then nurture their latent talents and strengths, and know in what situations they are likely to be defensive. We can respond, rather than react, in a way that can be "attended to" by them: we can become responsible for getting others attention rather than blaming others for not listening. We can move our own sense of the continuously evolving, living situation we are in from blame to responsibility. This is a truly empowering intention once it has been grasped.

Be aware, however, that once another person has labelled your behaviour they will seek to reinforce that label whatever protestations you may make to the contrary. While this is frustrating it is necessary to understand that you are not responsible for other people's labelling systems or their choices for self-development. Be conscious of your own actions and they will ultimately be your voice.

By developing our Conscious Self, and becoming personally intentional, and by accessing the conscious energy of our 'will to do', we develop our capacity to act with purpose in our context. This is a higher level of sense-making that underpins conscious action.

The development of our Conscious Self is the building block for developing our Creative Self. This journey could have started with defining our Creative Self, and the role of our purpose, however, it would not have been based on any understanding of the complex foundations of our Creative Self. We would have just added another unattached layer to our Reactive Self and it would have hijacked it. It would have become just another source of tension in our life.

By developing a deeper understanding of our Reactive Self, Sensitive Self and Conscious Self we become open and receptive to our Creative Self, through integration with the natural order of things by accessing the creative energy of our 'will to be'. We achieve a sense of oneness with the living natural order - a capacity to be truly present in the moment.

This leads us to our Creative Self and the 'will to be'.

CHAPTER 15

Our Creative Self - Creative Energy and the Will to Be

"At the intersection where your gifts, talents and abilities meet a human need; therein you will discover your purpose"

Aristotle

Our 'will to be' introduces us to a more eternal sense of self - a sense of self that is creative and informed by our latent potential, our priorities and their connection to our life purpose. A self that we occasionally get glimpses of in those fleeting moments when we are at one with nature, or when we connect intuitively, one heart to another. We sense that we have a creative connection to the greater scheme of things. A unique contribution that we are destined to make to the unfolding living natural order we are a part of – a connection to our inner source of happiness.

The living natural order is all things in our living universe: a universe that is constantly evolving. It silently and continuously influences how we experience our Self, and how the others experience us, on a moment by moment basis. We have a fleeting sense of the Self as boundary-less and that we can be more than just our feeling, thinking and moving Reactive Self. *We get glimpses of our Creative Self* that suggests we have a purpose that is part of our natural connection to life itself.

The Creative Self is the self that reveals your purpose and connects you to your potential and priorities and enables you to see, some would say attract, possibilities as they emerge in the ever-changing world around you. It involves being open to receiving creative energy that is the essence of the interdependent relationship that all things have to each other.

Let's look at our Adaptive Learning Map© to understand the core elements of the Creative Self.

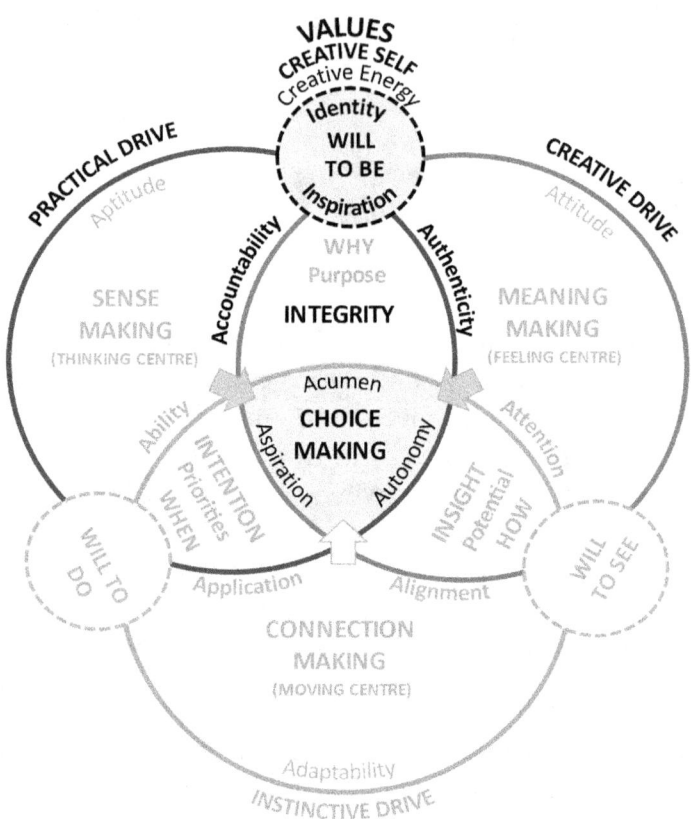

Figure 26: Our Creative Self

Our Creative Self is activated by our 'will to be', as a higher intelligence, through its access to creative energy, the second level of infinite energies. We begin to have natural access to our Creative Self as we interact with the transformative power of the creative energy.

Bennett describes *creative energy* as:

> *"...the energy which gives us freedom and enables us to create ourselves. It is the energy through which we are able to exercise voluntary attention. When we try to attend, we find we have very little power to do it. It all slips away; no matter how hard we try. This gives us a measure of our effective freedom. The creative energy is the energy of "I", and it is only when the will and this energy are united that we have power. A person is only a free individual when they can have the working of the creative energy united with their everyday life.*
>
> *Creative energy is released in the transformation of our consciousness. This transformation we can know in terms of the diminishing power that "negative emotions" have over us and the increasing power that "positive emotions" have in us. The "negative emotions" are the ordinary emotions which are under the law that they must produce their opposites, so that pity turns to disgust and love to hate. The "positive emotions" have no opposites, though they may have the same names as negative ones, such as "joy", "hope", or "love". The positive emotions are not reactions but something evoked in our consciousness by the creative energy."*
>
> *"It is said that to 'do' we must give up the **illusion of doing**."* The emphasis is mine.

Consequently, the 'will to be' enables us to make a paradigm shift – a shift from the experience we have of doing as striving, driven achievement to seeing the potential we have of doing as effortless, creative contribution: a pathway to just being. We move to a state where choice begins with a conscious balancing of our meaning-making, sense-making and connection-making mindsets as we interact with our world – engaging our Creative Self.

It is a state where choice is about being receptive to our latent potential and being truly purposeful in our unique context. This shift enables us to receive the possibilities that emerge from the living environment, by bringing our Practical Drive and our Creative Drive into alignment. We can engage our inspiration in solving problems and generating entirely new ideas. It is about purpose driven inspiration and the discovery of our true identity that underpins our integrity.

Inspiration is a much-used, indeterminate and over hyped word for what is actually a change implying, culture challenging and values engaging phenomenon. So what exactly is inspiration? What are we talking about when we use that term?

Well, moments of inspiration don't quite make sense by normal logic. They feel transcendent, uncontrollable and irresistible. When one is inspired, time disappears or alters its pace. The senses are amplified. There may be shivers down the spine, or a sense of being overawed by something beautiful. Inspiration is when you feel a deep-rooted passion and motivation to do something. There's a thrilling feeling of elevation, a burst of energy, an awareness of enlarged possibilities. The person in the grip of inspiration has received, as if by magic, some new perception, some holistic understanding of the natural order, along with the feeling that they are capable of more than they thought.

Inspiration is not something you can control. People who are inspired often feel that something is working through them, some power greater than themselves. The Greeks said it was the Muses – the inspirational goddesses of literature, the sciences and the arts. Others might say it is something mysterious bursting forth deep in the unconscious, a new way of seeing. Inspiration is not permanent and solid. It's powerful but ephemeral, which is why so many people compare it to a gust of wind. And when it is gone people long for its return.

The poet Christian Winman wrote that inspiration is:

> "intrusive, transcendent, transformative, but also evanescent and, all too often, anomalous. A poem can leave its maker at once more deeply seized by existence and, in a profound way, alienated from it, for as the act of making ends, as the world that seemed to overbrim its boundaries becomes, once more, merely the world, it can be very difficult to retain any faith at all in that original moment of inspiration. That memory of that momentary blaze, in fact, and the art that issued from it, can become a kind of reproach to the fireless life in which you find yourself most of the time."

Most important, inspiration demands a certain integrity, the sort of integrity people feel when they are overawed by something large and mysterious. They are both humbled and self-confident, surrendering and also powerful. When people are inspired they are willing to take a daring leap toward something truly great. They are brave enough to take on the prevailing truth and to try to express it in some new way.

In a way inspiration is also about identity, the other dimension of the 'will to be'. Identity is largely concerned with the question: "Why am I?" Identity relates to our basic values that dictate the choices we make. These choices reflect why we are and what we value. However, few people choose their identities. Instead, they simply internalise the values of their parents or the dominant cultures, such as the pursuit of materialism, power, and appearance.

Sadly, these values may not be aligned with our real identity and create an unfulfilling life. In contrast, fulfilled people are able to live a life true to their values and pursue a meaningful purpose.

Three things are required for identity development.

- Firstly, and this has been discussed already, is discovering and developing our personal potential. This requires exposure to a wide array of activities, some of which we become able to do relatively well.
- Secondly, identity is enhanced by the feedback we receive from others and our own positive feelings about those activities. These activities simply "feel right" to us, and these feelings are useful clues. We are intrinsically motivated to do these activities. They resonate with our values.
- Thirdly, identity is about discovering one's purpose in life. Purpose is about our values rather than our vision, although they are related of course. It is necessary to choose what we are seeking to contribute in our lives to the lives of others. To choose a purpose not compatible with our values is a recipe for frustration and disappointment.

Let's now look at the idea of Creative Self as your present 'cultural embedded' disposition toward creativity.

The ways in which societies have seen creativity have changed over the years and were to great extent determined by the sense of independence and freedom that individuals had in society. Because of the impact of Christianity, which defined creation as God's act of "creation from nothing" there was a long-standing reluctance to accept the idea of human creativity. By the end of the 18th Century and the Age of Enlightenment the concept was being seen more and more in the world of the creative arts and was being linked to imagination: art was synonymous with creativity. In the Eastern context creativity was a kind of discovery and had nothing to do with "creation from nothing".

Until recently creativity has been generally attributed to a certain class of people who are highly competent in the arts, music and literature and so on and often reflects a lifestyle that is somewhat unusual and not part of mainstream society except perhaps when they are successful and acquire celebrity status – because their work becomes an object with material value, or their lifestyle is at the fringe of social norms that become fashionable. Object consciousness of the audience supplants the inspired consciousness of the creator!

The Creative Self reflects the innate innocence that is with us from birth, and is moulded and disenfranchised by life experiences. It is a child-like quality but not a childish one. Some have called this essence, and seek to develop the notion that we need to return to our essence as some sort of qualities that existed before our nature encountered nurture and navigation. What we know is that as a child we emerged from being helpless to learning to be self-sufficient. Our learning is as much a part of our essence as our genetic inheritance is. We are born to learn. Without the capacity to learn we would not survive. It is also clear that some responses to our environment are genetic responses to environmental signals. Bird migration is an example of that.

However we are born with innocence and that is the essence of creativity. Creativity flourishes when we recognise we don't have to know in the present moment and we retain our curiosity. Curiosity is the continuous search for knowledge as futile as that is at times. Paradoxically, curiosity is often killed by knowledge. We experience the curiosity of childhood when we observe the innocence of children, as they explore the world around them, using their natural instincts.

Let's consider this innocence of children for a moment so we can better understand the impact of 'knowledge' on our evolution into adulthood. I came across this very illuminating anecdote on a blog site in my internet travels that put the creativity of innocence into perspective for me. It reflects amazing insightfulness and a delightful creative story-telling approach. It goes:

> *"From the moment we could move, make a sound, bang a drum, splash paint, dig sand, throw food and hold a crayon, we were creating something. It was who we were. What we did. We didn't really understand the world, so we created our own story. Perhaps it was through a song. Or a work of art. A musical masterpiece with our very excellent guitar. It might have been a sandcastle. A cubby house. A tent in the living room. Or should I say, a fortress. An impenetrable fortress. A monster-free zone. You remember monsters right?*
>
> *And sometimes, the only thing our boring, sensible, uncreative parents could see was a mess. A problem. Something else to clean up. Pity.*
>
> *There was a phase of our existence when we hadn't yet learned about concepts like talent, judgment, criticism, approval and rejection. At that stage of our journey, embarrassment was something we were still to learn. Neither had we learned to over-think things. In fact, we didn't think much at all. We just did because doing was such fun.*
>
> *So we created. And we created. For fun. We danced, sang, painted and explored our way through life. We were happy. Ever seen a dancing, singing, painting, creating kid who's miserable? Me either.*
>
> *We didn't wonder if our creative output was good enough. Or how it compared. Ever.*

Then sadly, one day we began to learn about the importance of things like artistic ability. And comparisons. Apparently, there's good and bad art. Who knew? And we learn about singing in tune. What's tune? We learn about dancing in time and knowing the right steps – apparently freestyle is now out. Pity: that was my specialty. And apparently, there are wrong *steps? The grown-ups begin to judge our work and now we get rewarded for colouring inside the lines. There are lines? We learn that some colours just don't go together (but I love the blue-green combo) and we also learn that creating purely for enjoyment, is only for the little kids. Now I have to be creative for a reason. A reason other than fun. And if I'm going to express myself creatively, then I need to work at 'getting better'. To improve my skills. Now I'm confused.*

Maybe it's because I'm six.

Along the way, we are taught (consciously or not, intentionally or not) that spelling, mathematics and science are more important than the creative stuff. Most education systems teach us this 'truth'. Not all, but most. Obviously, we're never gonna get anywhere dancing, painting, singing and writing. Of course.

Then one day we wake up and we wonder: What ever happened to the singer? The dancer? The poet? The painter? The storyteller? The builder of sandcastles? The happy kid who allowed herself to create purely because it made her happy? The kid who didn't need approval, permission or a trophy? The kid who just needed some crayons?

Just reading that alerts us to our lost inner creative space. We have all been there and done that. Once we eliminate the blocks and inhibitions of our Reactive Self that hold us captive, creativity will naturally unfold. We know about this because it is embedded in the synaptic pathways of our brain just waiting to be resuscitated. It gives CPR a new meaning – Creative Purpose Release!

Creativity is the essence of the ever-evolving natural order. It is universal. The coming into existence of the new is a product of the interdependent interactions that occur at every moment, much of which we are oblivious to. The nature of emergence, the idea that when things interact qualities emerge that cannot be found in the interacting parts, has already been discussed. Creativity will happen just because we are there. However with purpose and presence we can see possibilities for our creativity and align them with our priorities and purpose. When we intentionally intervene in our environment we create a state of disequilibrium that generates opportunities as the environment seeks to attain a new state of equilibrium. The search for equilibrium is the essence of disequilibrium: it is called life.

Our purpose, being values based, enables us to see personal meaning in some of the opportunities that emerge. If we understand our potential we can grasp those meaningful opportunities and achieve our priorities. Objective success is always transient. Values based purpose is always accessible. Because the Creative Self is anchored in our purpose it gives us integrity - an integrity that is receptively in tune with the creative energy of the natural living order, rather than just a mechanical adoption of the materialistic imperatives of our social order.

Finally, we need to find opportunities to implement our potential and purpose. This engages our 'will to be' and its associated creative energy. We need to recognise that creativity is an act of receiving energy rather than striving to achieve some illusory goal.

Our Creative Self is an open system. The living natural order is an open system where everything is connected to everything else.

INSIGHT INTENTION AND INTEGRITY

This living connection is non-linear – it is about multiple causes and effects rather than a sequence of cause and effect. We get to realise that things get their identity from their interactions rather than their actions. Creativity is not for others to appreciate or denigrate, it is your connection to the joy of being. It is the joy of being that that flows from your inner self orientation that will be evident to others, rather than the object orientation of some masterpiece you may have created. The distinction will not easily be made if your masterpiece is acclaimed and the applause ignites your Reactive Self. You could become a "one hit wonder".

The three centres that underpin our Reactive Self mindsets provide the foundation for creatively developing our purpose and recognising our potential so let's now return to these centres and look at their hierarchy of potential now that we have explored the three 'eyes' of emergent leadership and their associated intelligence of will and their energy sources.

We already know our three centres are the:

- Feeling Centre that underpins meaning-making mindset
- Thinking Centre that underpins sense-making mindset
- Moving Centre that underpins connection-making mindset

Each centre has a *hierarchy of potential* that reflects a natural pathway of development from Destructive to Reactive to Sensitive to Conscious to Creative Self. These levels of function development and their respective mindsets are shown below. As you read each level seek to identify the one that you normally operate at. The natural centre you have already identified should be the main focus of your "in the zone" potential where you act effortlessly.

Level	Feeling Centre
	Meaning Making
Destructive Self	At this level feelings are typically repressed. Individuals may even deny the very existence of 'feeling'. When feeling is experienced, individuals are overwhelmed by it, in sudden outbursts of extreme emotion - anger, lust, jealousy, etc. When individuals with underdeveloped feeling do feel, their feelings can be comparatively crass - thus there is a tendency toward being 'sentimental'.
Reactive Self	At the second level of development of the feeling centre, the individual begins to accept their feelings, and finds a positive use for them. They begin to discern a wider variety of 'emotions', subtler in nature, less threatening. They realise that feelings help to orient them with respect to objects in the outside world - giving them a reading on their 'likes' and 'dislikes'. It performs a useful, though still often painful, evaluating function
Sensitive Self	At the third level of development of the feeling centre, feeling is experienced as a continuous, ongoing 'process'. The individual begins to recognise the presence of an 'underlying feeling state' in the background of consciousness, manifesting as subtly changing 'moods' that orient one in respect to the world, guiding the selective attention process. By virtue of the constant presence of this subtly shifting background field, consciousness 'self-organises'.
Conscious Self	At the fourth level of development of the feeling centre, the individual begins to experience the 'underlying feeling field' that is constantly present in consciousness as inter-personal in nature. As the individual begins to appreciate the essentially inter-subjective nature of personal experience, relationship plays a more prominent role in the individual's value system. Our skill in empathising with others (literally 'feeling into' their experience) is honed; we have learned how to resonate with them, through a confluence of individual personal 'process'.

Creative Self	At the fifth level of development of the feeling centre, the individual begins to experience what is called 'inter-being'. At this level it is recognised that in some basic transcendental sense, we are 'one' with each other. The 'individual' is a 'singularity' in the inter-subjective field, a construct. We become essentially social beings, in the most profound sense of the word. Our beliefs become a nostalgic part of our sense of self and we engage with others with a sense of joy and generosity of spirit.

Level	Thinking Centre
	Sense Making
Destructive Self	The individual who has thinking as this level is likely to speak in 'platitudes' or be overly 'critical''. Thoughts are experienced as mere random ideas or, unrelated mental images as opposed to hypothesis ('if a, then b) capable of identifying complex cause and effect relationships. The 'laws' revealed by more advanced forms of thinking are likely to be perceived as a threat to the freedom of the individual, associated with 'conditioning', and experienced as constraining and controlling.
Reactive Self	At the second level of development of the thinking centre, the individual begins to appreciate cause-effect relationships and hypothesis ('if a, then b'). We begin to explore how knowledge of the causal laws, that can be expressed using these forms of thought, render control over the data that these laws govern. Rational decision-making, logical argument and systematic operational planning are valued.

Sensitive Self	At the third level of development of the thinking centre, thinking is experienced as 'critical reason', and there is a growing capacity for building complex conceptual systems for the purpose of analytical analysis and for strategic planning. There is a glimmer of appreciation for the 'context-specific' nature of knowledge - for how language and concepts are layered into deep and surface structures.
Conscious Self	At the fourth level of development of the thinking centre, there is insight into the how ways of thinking form, operate, and change - how they *frame* conclusions, but cannot validate their own premises. There is a deepening interest in how thought itself develops including the processes that thinking progresses through, from thesis and antithesis toward synthesis - and how the mind imposes conceptual structures on the realities it seeks to understand.
Creative Self	At the fifth level of development of the thinking centre, thought comprehends its own nature, conceiving itself. It gives birth to acting on one's self by simultaneously, becoming both the container and contained - reflectively unfolding itself out into an infinite series of nested Russian dolls that wrap back around on itself. This capacity to 'act upon one's self' is the evolutionary core around which 'will' and 'intentionality' comes into being, and influence over the outside world becomes possible.

Level	Moving Centre
	Connection Making
Destructive Self	The individual who has moving at this level is likely to be highly image conscious to the extent that they will spend hours on personal grooming, physical conditioning, choosing the "in" fashion labels and be highly agitated and miffed if they do not attract instant compliments and praise for their appearance. They will be totally absorbed with their own success, especially material success, and anything that provides cultural or familial status. They will be self-promoting and expedient in relationships and may engage in self and other deception. They will have a superficiality about them that they are oblivious to.
Reactive Self	At the second level of development of the moving centre, the individual begins to identify with the trappings of their success and will be highly committed to ensuring that their personal performance is rewarded. They become very competitive and highly presentable in the business, sporting or professional niche that they are in. They are career oriented and status conscious. They have a pragmatic understanding of the qualities that make them successful and seek material recognition of those qualities.
Sensitive Self	At the third level of development of the moving centre, moving is experienced as goal orientation and becomes more about self-improvement. They are ambitious and confident about their own abilities. There is an industriousness and persistence about their approach to developing themselves. They are more diplomatic and effective in their interpersonal relationships. There is a singular focus about getting things done and they encourage others to develop personal goals.

Conscious Self	At the fourth level of development of the moving centre, there is insight into their attachment to the trappings of success and they become more other directed in their activities. They develop and adaptability and self-assuredness that is admired by others. They are realistic and recognise their connectedness to the outside world. They sense that they and others have unlimited potential and work to develop that motivation in others. They are purposeful, charitable and poised.
Creative Self	At the fifth level of development of the moving centre, moving comprehends its own nature, conceiving itself. There is an awareness of the inner-directed nature of their well-being and they no longer need to impress others. They become authentic, self-deprecating and modest. They let go of the image that their value is dependent on the positive regard of others. There is a sense of communion with life itself that embodies self-acceptance and genuine embodiment of contribution to the greater good.

We now have a sense of the pathway to an emergent identity at a much higher level of intelligence than we embarked from when we considered meaning-making, sense-making and connection-making earlier. It is not a series of behaviours we need to master but an awakened choice of who we can become based on our purpose. This is an awareness that is about growth as integrity - a sense of values-based one-ness with the those we connect with. It is our Creative Self energised by creative energy.

As Bennett says:

> *"The creative energy is the energy of "I", and it is only when the will and this energy are united that we have power".*

INSIGHT INTENTION AND INTEGRITY

Personal creative power, based on purpose and underpinned by our expanded sense of identity, is the foundation of emergent leadership in an interconnected, and largely boundaryless, world. This power source is generated by our 'will to be' - the realisation of our life purpose, and an awareness of the creative energy of integration with the living natural order, providing us with our sense of Being. Our identity.

Eckhart Tolle describes Being this way:

> *"There is an eternal, ever-present One Life beyond the myriad forms of life that are subject to birth and death. Many people use the word God to describe it; I often call it Being. The word Being explains nothing, but nor does God. Being, however, has the advantage that it is an open concept. It does not reduce the infinite invisible to a finite entity. It is impossible to form a mental image of it. Nobody can claim the exclusive possession of Being. It is your very presence, and it is immediately accessible to you as the feeling of your own presence. So it is only a small step from the word Being to the experience of Being".*

There is a further paradigm shift that must be engaged with at this higher level of awareness that Being is. Being is only able to be experienced when the mind is still – a state of no mind. It cannot be understood mentally. Being is a state of connectedness with something that is essentially you but is greater than you. It is finding our true nature beyond our existing sense of "I". The incessant chatter of our mind is what stops us from finding this sense of inner calm and stillness. Being is about our oneness with everything else rather than our separateness from everything else.

It is naïve to expect that we can survive in our environment by reaching some higher state that enables us to abandon our natural Jungian lead role, and the associated competencies we have developed. Transformation is a complementary process that enhances our natural Jungian lead role and associated competencies by taking them to a higher plane. We will continue to live and interact in a world largely driven by the unconscious automatic actions of others and will be shaped by the way that information is presented to us.

The deeper understanding of our Creative Self leads us to wisdom: the capacity to be open to our full potential as integrated beings in the natural living order. Wisdom is the capacity to get above one's interactions with others, our environment and our cultural context and life conditions. It is the highest level of our sense-making competencies that we discussed earlier.

Wisdom is the essence of integrating sense-making and meaning-making based on your purpose. It is the highest level of our competence hierarchy. Let's just refresh our understanding of the characteristics of wisdom.

WISDOM
Aim: Integrity - Finding or reconnecting to one's purpose: defining or reconnecting with values, vision and mission. Understanding purpose and deep awareness of ecology, community, and ethical action.
Learning mode: Generative learning - values driven: learning for the joy of learning in open interaction with the environment. It involves creative processes, open-ended explorations and profound self-questioning.
Attention: Very long term (distant past, to distant future)
Energy: Creative (Purposeful)

Wisdom is an evolving, open ended and uncertain process. It calls upon all the previous levels of consciousness, and specifically upon special types of human intelligence (moral, ethical codes, etc.). It seeks to give us understanding about which there has previously been no understanding, and in doing so, goes far beyond understanding itself. It is the essence of philosophical probing. Wisdom is the process by which we discern, or judge, between right and wrong, good and bad. Wisdom is a uniquely human state.

Wisdom is about the integration of our insight, intention and integrity, and is anchored in:

- deep understanding gained from experiences,
- curiosity that reflects insightfulness,
- diverse competence grounded in education and intellectual (cognitive) intelligence,
- interpersonal skills supported by emotional intelligence, and
- social intelligence such as non-judgmental attitude.

This higher level of intelligence is activated by the presence of an inner connection to higher energy states in this more evolved state of being – by accessing the natural living order through our "sixth sense" of consciousness (rather than our five physical senses of connection). It is a meta learning level of personal development.

The three meta development levels of wisdom are said to be:

- life-span experience - knowledge that respects people as both the result of, and creators of, their own development, interacting throughout life with family, peers, and other social groups and institutions,
- contextual understanding – knowing that knowledge, truth, and morality exist in relation to culture, society, or historical context, and are not absolute, and
- emergence - acceptance of unpredictability and absence of logical causation.

Wisdom lies in the successful utilisation of intelligence and creativity or what is called "tacit knowledge". This success is created by balancing intra-personal, inter-personal and extra-personal (whole of community work) interests through shared value systems to achieve common good. Wisdom is the elusive building block of our Creative Self.

Our integrity based Creative Self is our metaphor for the evolutionary process that enables us to build upon our insight-based Sensitive Self and our intention-based Conscious Self, and engage in emergent leadership. It is perhaps best mentally understood as oneness with the rhythm of life and is best illustrated by our breathing. Being is embedded in our purpose. It is the essence of an Integrated Self. It is the source of our wisdom. It is about being as a source of connection and contribution to others.

Our Integrated Self is the balance we achieve between our 'will to see', our 'will to do' and our 'will to be' and the related energy sources that enhance our day-to-day meaning-making, sense-making and connection-making. It brings together the core emergent leadership qualities of insight, intention and integrity in a way that reflects our potential, priorities and purpose as illustrated below.

Will Element	Energy Source	Core Quality	Focus	Related Corollaries
Will to Be	Creative	Integrity	Purpose	Inspiration and Identity
Will to Do	Conscious	Intention	Priorities	Initiative and Ingenuity
Will to See	Sensitive	Insight	Potential	Influence and Image

In summary, our Integrated Self comprises the three wills – "to see" (receptive to sensitive energy), "to do" (receptive to conscious energy) and "to be" (receptive to creative energy) – that together open us to our latent potential, our core priorities and life purpose.

The full Adaptive Learning Map© provides a comprehensive structure for seeing the relationships between our blind spots (meaning-making, sense-making and connection-making), and our higher order intelligences ('will to see', 'will to do' and 'will to be'), that support the development of the three "eyes" of emergent leadership in the universally connected world (insight, intention and integrity).

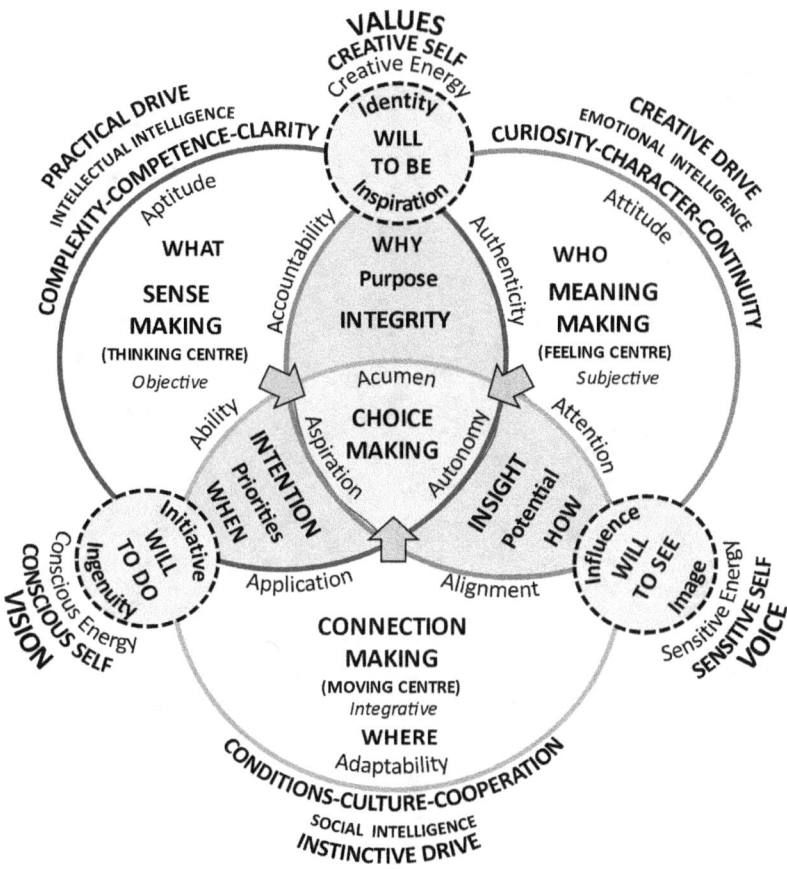

Figure 27: *The Full Adaptive Learning Map*©

All of the jigsaw puzzle pieces and the lid of the jigsaw puzzle box have now been provided for you to contemplate. There is no particular order that you need to put the pieces together – just understand the shape and nature of each piece at the level that your three centres are presently operating. We will now head back to the idea of person-centred emergent leadership so you can see what we have covered means in that context. If the idea of being in a leadership role is too challenging then you can apply the map as a framework for improving your sense of well-being in whatever role that you choose to engage in.

EPILOGUE:

THE EMERGENT LEADERSHIP PARADIGM SHIFT

The Epilogue looks at the role of emergent leadership as the influencer of choice driven behaviour, and is about the central role of the three "I's" – insight, intention and integrity. Adaptive learning is the new leadership mindset and there are no boundaries to our interpersonal connections and knowledge flows. Even though many still live in the earlier serial world of hierarchical power of position, the emerging new source of power is personal and collective knowledge creation and sharing.

EPILOGUE

The Emergent Leadership Paradigm Shift

> *"That is what learning is. You suddenly understand something you've understood all of your life, but in a new way."*
>
> *- Doris Lessing*

The epilogue is about the relationship between leadership and learning in a wirearchy that is captured in the Adaptive Learning Map© framework. John F Kennedy said: "Leadership and learning are indispensable to each other".

Leadership and learning are underpinned by our choice-making and that of others. When we act upon choices we create the context for emergent leadership to occur as we learn to connect to others in mutually beneficial ways that contribute to the common good. Learning begins by reflecting on what has gone before – developing insight about our past choice-making behaviour.

As we have discussed in earlier chapters the Adaptive Learning Map© has three learning loops that integrate the three mindsets (meaning-making, sense-making and connection-making), with the three 'eyes' of emergent leadership (insight, intention and integrity), that are shown below.

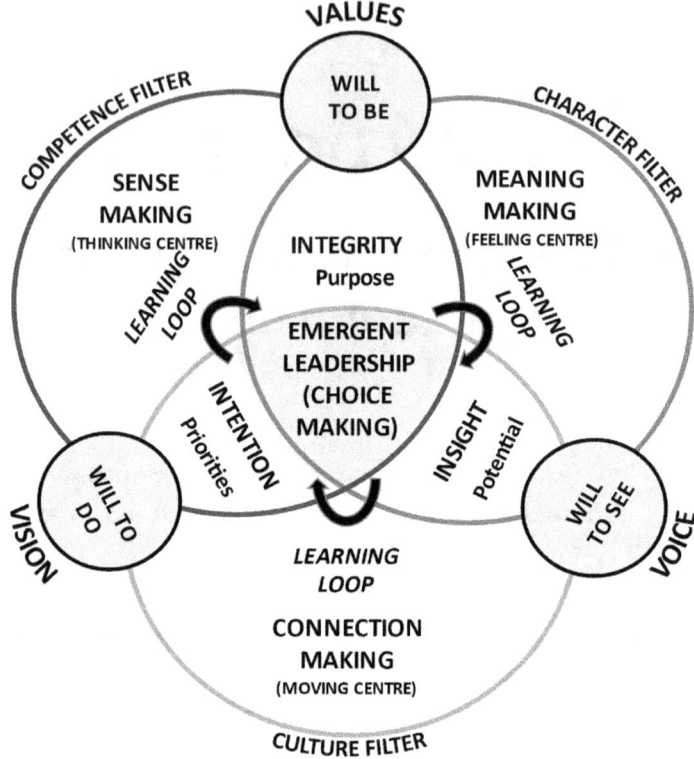

Figure 28: The Adaptive Learning Map© Learning Loops

Let's reflect on where we started with the Humpty Dumpty analogy when he made the choice to sit on a wall!

> Humpty Dumpty sat on the wall,
>
> Humpty Dumpty had a great fall,
>
> All the King's horses and all the King's men,
>
> Couldn't put Humpty together again."

The wall is an analogy for a tipping point.

INSIGHT INTENTION AND INTEGRITY

The emerging global context reflects a tipping point in our history as a consequence of the impact of universal connectedness on the historical model of leadership based on hierarchy. Technology has always shaped culture (how we behave collectively) – think of the impact of the wheel, the printing press, the steam engine, the radio, the telephone, the motor car, the aeroplane and television, to name a few. The evolution of the internet, mobile devices and digital technology and the emergence of artificial intelligence is no different. However, we now live in a wirearchy where connection to each other and to information sources is pervasive. We have moved from passive viewers to active broadcasters to creative, co-responsible contributors to the health of the natural living system. Our capacity to navigate is now just as important as nature and nurture in our evolution as a species.

Just like Humpty Dumpty, hierarchical leadership is "at a tipping point" and we need to find a way to prevent its inevitable fall in a way that respects the interdependent choice-making connections of the context we are in – the emergence of wirearchy.

Let's just reflect on how we defined leadership, emergence and wirearchy in the glossary:

> *Leadership is the **spontaneous** assumption of responsibility to contribute to the common good. An **emergent** quality arising from the synergy between insight, intention and integrity – the 'eyes' of emergent leadership. These three 'eyes' underpin voice, vision and values. It is about **responding**, rather than reacting, in the moment and being responsible for the **choices** we make ourselves and influencing responsibility in others for the **choices** they make.*
>
> *Emergence is a quality that does not depend on its individual parts, but on their **reciprocal relationships** to one another. It is **non-linear***

> *in form and, as a consequence, emergent behaviour cannot be predicted by analysing the individual parts of a system.*
>
> *Wirearchy:* **a *dynamic* two-way *flow* of power and authority,** *based on knowledge, trust, credibility with a focus on behaviours and outcomes, enabled by* **interconnected people** *and technology.*

Leadership has an emergent quality that demands personal insight, intention and integrity as the foundations of cooperative knowledge creation and sharing in our new universally connected choice-making territory. We are used to managing in place-based locations and we are now required to lead in a space-based territory. We now operate in 'space' without having left the planet!

This 'space' induced tipping point will require us to embrace the three 'eyes' of emergent leadership of insight, intention and integrity. They are the three "I's" that we must develop to complement our leadership role anchored in our personal beliefs (meaning-making), knowledge (sense-making) and relationships (connection-making). Organisations are moving from a performance and physical assets driven culture (and strategy) to a capability and intangible assets driven culture (and strategy) and person-based emergent leadership is at the centre of this shift. This is not about hierarchy being abandoned but operating , and being integrated with, wirearchy.

There has been an explosion of entrepreneurial activity focussed on the global consumer-driven marketplace. Consumption driven capitalism will need to achieve a balance with the interdependent natural order of things as part of its evolution which in turn will demand a conscious appreciation of people-based leadership. People are no longer "human resources" that are a cost of doing business.

In our capitalist consumer focused economy people are intangible balance sheet assets that create sustainable returns through innovation, adaptability and know-how. Capital investment is quickly beginning to reflect this 'tipping point' shift that has emerged from our real time connection to global challenges, notwithstanding the vested corporate interests at the apex of the hierarchy that still have great economic and political influence in maintaining the status quo. The management of these organisations is beginning to develop insight, adapt intentions and rediscover integrity as they meet these emergent challenges.

Connected people represent an emergent leadership paradigm shift where knowledge is the new capital and where there are no boundaries to interpersonal knowledge flows. Even though many still live in the old serial world of hierarchical position-based power, the new 'king' is personal and collective knowledge. "The king is dead, long live the king!" Humpty Dumpty would be happy that he may just be able to be put back together again!

Let's have a closer look at the nature of choice-making in hierarchy. The nature of hierarchy places power of position at the top and powerlessness of person at the bottom. The rapid emergence of wirearchy has created a distributed base of power based on collective interdependencies that enable the application of multi-disciplinary knowledge to solve complex problems. Hierarchy provides rules-based structure that puts us in boxes in a stable world.

Hierarchy loves a crisis so it can take 'top down' control, but it is now inadequate to deal with the complexity of the problems we have created. In the history of the planet we have been led to believe that big things eat little things, that then eat even smaller things. What we haven't observed that in a planetary crisis only the little things survive. Dinosaurs know that and human beings are next if we refuse to acknowledge that we are at a tipping point of never before experienced turbulence. The turbulence we are experiencing can be looked at as a series of transitional levels. The table below captures these levels and the understanding of them.

Turbulence Level	1	2	3	4	5
Context	Repetitive	Expanding	Changing	Discontinuous	Unpredictable
Events	Familiar	Predictable	Problematic	Unexpected	Emergent
Visibility of Future	Crystal Clear	Clear	Fuzzy	Obscure	Puzzling
Path to Future	An Open Road	A Gentle Climb	An Uneven Staircase	A Rock Climb	"Beam Me Up Scotty"
Typical Behaviour	Stable	Reactive	Proactive	Creative	Agile
If you like stability you will be	Content	Comfortable	Achieving	Anxious	Panicking
If you like turbulence you will be	Frustrated	Bored	Anticipatory	Excited	Curious
Leadership Evolution	Transactional/ Horizontal		Adapting	Transformational/ Vertical	

The present level of turbulence induced by significant global change and complexity is probably at level 4 and bordering level 5 while most people are operating at an experiential capacity of level 2 bordering level 3. The emergence of a wave of entrepreneurial activity also suggests that an increasing number of people are leveraging level 4 turbulence and paradoxically creating more turbulence for those operating in the lower levels. At level 4 and above the distinctive attribute of complex systems is the dynamic nature of the interaction of the individual parts.

Knowledge of the individual parts does not explain the nature of the whole. It involves the idea of emergence. The behaviours you will experience, if you like stability or like turbulence, can be used to identify the responses you may see in yourself and others in the present turbulent context. To put this into a time frame context we can see that the emergence of increasing turbulence has seen the evolution of leadership development between a transformational and a transactional focus over the last century.

INSIGHT INTENTION AND INTEGRITY

This evolution of leadership can be looked at in four reasonably distinct phases that reflect the leadership context and leadership focus over many years.

- Hero Leader – Transformational in low turbulence with a focus on my vision, charisma, and loyal followers in order to conquer the environment,
- Rational Manager – Transactional in low turbulence with a focus on strategy, systems, and structure in order to control the environment,
- Process Manager – Transactional in high turbulence with a focus on issues, processes and time in order to codify the environment, and
- Emergent Leader – Transformational in high turbulence with a focus on purpose, priorities, potential in order to connect in the environment.

The figure below illustrates these phases.

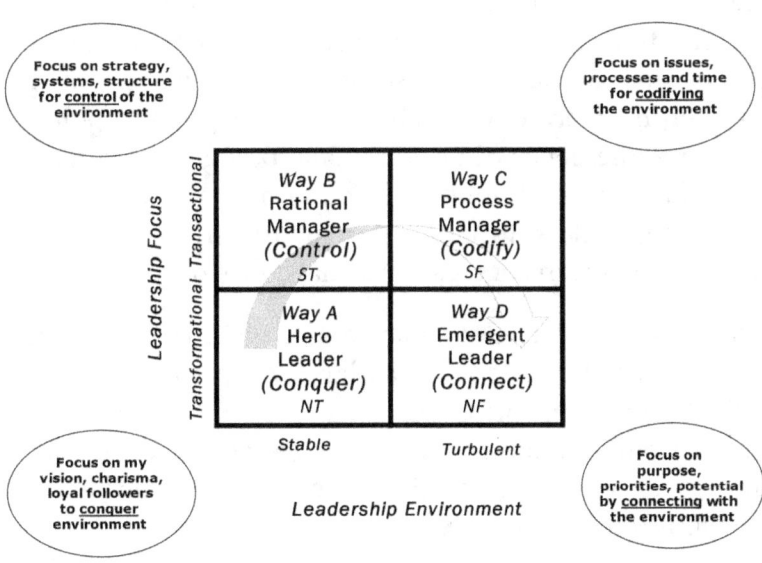

Figure 29: The Evolution of Leadership

Leadership focuses on context and nature of relationships between things (flow) and management focuses on the container and the control of relationships in that container (focus).

The idea of leadership in the hierarchy context made it largely an extension of management authority and it has resulted in a merging of the two. The growth of large organisations meant that the focus of leadership was almost always framed in that managerial context. The use of the term leader in job titles is never found at the top of the hierarchy. It only appears at the lower 'team leader' level otherwise you are known as a manager, general manager, executive director or managing director. In this context, choice-making is subservient to the control, order, prescribe (COP) mindset that unconsciously pervades organisations even to this day. The emergence of wirearchy has changed all of that and underpins the new transformational focus of choice-making using the adapt, create, engage (ACE) mindset.

The nature of hierarchy has kept the three roles of hero leader, rational manager and process manager firmly in place and this has led to the search for solutions in the form of a whole range of organisation development interventions that haven't worked largely because of the latent position-based choice-making power that underpins hierarchy. In a broader sense populist politics has seen the re-emergence of hero leadership, together with a reversion to blue tier conditions, as a solution to globalisation and it isn't working unless an authoritarian driven populist model is your preferred means of creating social cohesion.

We can reflect on the Gravesian model again to understand the *choice-making context* that we are largely experiencing in today's turbulent and transformational environment. We are seeing global red-blue-orange-green-yellow overlaps and our personal means drivers are being significantly challenged. The table below, demonstrates this challenge.

Level	STATE OF THE WORLD	SUCCESS STRATEGIES
First Tier		
Red - Level 3	Like a jungle where the tough and strong prevail, the weak serve; nature is an adversary to be conquered. Aggression and hostility are part of everyday life.	Power: Asserting self for dominance, conquest and power; exploitative. Be a hero by all available means.
Blue - Level 4	The law of the jungle has caused much suffering. The privileged have totally exploited the poor. The world is now controlled by a higher power that punishes evil and eventually rewards good works and righteous living.	Obedience: Dutiful as higher authority and rules direct; conforming; guilt driven. There is one truth that everyone follows.
Orange - Level 5	Progress affords opportunities for material wealth. The world is full of exploitable resources and affords the means to make things better and bring prosperity.	Achievement: Pragmatically achieve results and get ahead; test options; manoeuvre. It pays to conduct or be in a profitable business.

Green - Level 6	The material social development makes it possible to ask the question of meaning. The world is a habitat where humanity can find wholeness and purpose through affiliation and sharing.	Humanity: Responsive to human needs; affiliative; situational; consensual; fluid. People join together so that everyone can share equally in growth.
Second Tier		
Yellow – Level 7	Prosperity enables completely new thought, hopes and breakthroughs. The world is one big living organism where change is the norm and uncertainty an acceptable state of being.	Knowledge: Functional; integrative; interdependent; existential; flexible; questioning; accepting. Problems are solved from new perspectives and with a sense of flow.

At the highest *global* level of context the dominant state of the world for the second half of last century has been in the orange level 5 with about 25% of the population but who hold 50% of the power. While it is waning, the blue tier (with its religion-based centre) is still a substantial size (50%) and has about 30% of the power.

As mentioned earlier blue and orange tiers are first tier memes and so each believes that its worldview is the only true perspective. With increased global connectedness we are seeing some rapidly emerging signs of the green level meme (labelled by the lower tiers as "woke"). However, it will be some time before a qualitative leap in consciousness occurs when a larger proportion of the population moves into the green meme and begin to occupy the yellow level of the second tier.

While there is some evidence of the re-emergence of red behaviour, most organisations are historically designed around the blue-orange life conditions. They retain structures that come largely from military and religious ways of working combined with the ownership control of capitalism. Obedience and achievement tend to be the unconscious and somewhat contradictory bed fellows that underpin 'leadership' behaviour at these two levels.

What is emerging is a shift in overall context from a more national (blue-orange) level to a more global (green-yellow) level. We see this shift emerging in the areas of climate change, viral pandemics and trans-migration crises. The old dichotomy of leader versus manager will no longer serve us well in the new interconnected globalised world. Wirearchy provides the relationship-based structure that recognises the diversity of interconnected roles we play in a turbulent (VUCA) world. This emerging "in transition" environment, that exhibits both complexity and turbulence, requires a recognition of leadership (and followership) qualities that reflect a mindset shift from rational manager (blue-orange) to emergent leader (green-yellow).

The next level of context is at the *institutional* level where we see various forms of private and public sector organisations of varying sizes that, when they reach a critical mass, are designed as natural hierarchies with divisions of responsibilities, functions and positions. While these organisations, in cultural terms, variously mimic the red, blue and orange Gravesian hierarchy, they also take on 'industry' or sector attributes that reflect so-called blue-collar and white-collar qualities and related values.

In these institutional hierarchies the next level of context are the *divisions/functions* and associated position descriptions which describe job responsibilities and the personal knowledge and skills that are required to "perform". People are appraised using "performance management" as the entry point for conversations with managers. Individual performance is invariably attributed to the person's behaviour, skills and knowledge and ignores the impact of management behaviour, process shortcomings, lack of relevant tools and technologies, poor information access and competing goals.

Performance management in a hierarchy constrains choice-making and invariably gives little regard to the wider context and evaluates each individual against 'growth' goals, forecasts and budgets. These were rarely little better than good guesses at the time, based on extrapolating past financial performance, adding a growth percentage, and doing the same things to get there. Unfortunately, they represented senior management 'promises' to the shareholders that had to be delivered by 'subordinates' who had no involvement in the development of those 'growth' goals, forecasts and budgets. Worse still, the context was neutralised by performance measures that were established in an earlier timeframe and ignored the changes in context complexity and turbulence.

In general terms leadership and management had the same flavour and were based on a Control, Order, Prescribe (COP) mindset. Management development largely occurs by imitation of, and indoctrination by, those already in power under the COP hierarchy model, and has largely seen leadership development as an appendage of the position-based role of manager. What this meant was that performance management set up a defensive culture of compliance and only ever focused on mandatory effort. Those being evaluated were not able to direct attention to processes, tools, technologies and information access as contributors to performance success and failure.

In fact 'normal distribution curves' are used to ensure only a small percentage of people were more than 'satisfactory'. Invariably monetary consequences flowed from this "reward and punishment" approach to performance appraisal which further reinforced the choice-making (power) imbalance between the manager and employee. An unconscious 'master-servant' relationship from early in the twentieth century has been the culture driver of leadership behaviour once all the buzz words and values statements died a natural death.

INSIGHT INTENTION AND INTEGRITY

Harry Levinson in his book The Great Jackass Theory captures this narrow view of performance management and the associated motivation consequences very well when he says:

> *"Frequently, when conducting executive seminars, I ask the participants what the dominant philosophy of motivation in management is. Almost invariably, they quickly agree that it is the carrot-and-stick philosophy: reward and punishment. Then I ask them to close their eyes for a moment and to form a picture in their mind's eye with a carrot at one end and a stick at the other. When they have done so I ask them to describe the central image in that picture. Most frequently they respond that the central figure is a jackass.*
>
> *When the first image that comes to mind when one thinks 'carrot-and-stick' is a jackass, obviously the unconscious assumption behind the reward-punishment model is that one is dealing with jackasses, that people are jackasses to be manipulated and controlled. Thus, unconsciously, the boss is the manipulator and controller, and the subordinate is the jackass.*
>
> *The characteristics of a jackass are stubbornness, stupidity, wilfulness, and unwillingness to go where someone is driving him. These, by interesting coincidence, are also the characteristics of the unmotivated employee. Thus it becomes vividly clear that the underlying assumption management makes about motivation leads to a self-fulfilling prophecy.*
>
> *The consequences are increased inefficiency, lowered productivity, heightened absenteeism,*

> *and other modes of withdrawal from engagement, or covert engagement in a combative struggle."*

This remains the unconscious "jackass" dimension of the culture of many large and medium sized organisations. However, performance is, and has always been, a function of capability and context. Performance has three dimensions:

- setting goals with associated priorities and plans,
- getting results with associated rewards and reputation, and
- explaining variance with associated capability and context.

The challenge has been to see capability and context as legitimate explanations of variance rather than the myopic focus on the person in their position 'box'. This leads to a need to identify the many variables that impact on performance outcomes and how they can be seen in the context of wirearchy and hierarchy coexisting.

Capability comprises:

- management behaviour,
- personal behaviour, skills, knowledge and relationships,
- tools and technologies,
- processes, and
- access to real time information flows.

At the organisation level there are two context dimensions that impact variance between planned and actual performance:

- internal, and
- external.

The internal dimension comprises culture, strategy, systems, structure and policies. The external dimension comprises markets, customers, investors, competitors and regulators with the related turbulence and complexity. Little wonder performance reviews at the personal level are futile. If any of the variables are raised they are seen as excuses rather than opportunities for improvement.

Consequently, this traditional (blue-orange) personal performance evaluation approach also led to learning being bureaucratised and treated the same as training. Training is about knowledge acquisition of structured content and is anchored in sense-making. Learning is about skill building in a situational context and is anchored in meaning-making. Developing encompasses both and is focussed on the integration of capability – people, processes, tools and technologies, and real time information access - anchored in connection-making. The new mindset is Adapt, Create, Engage (ACE).

The figure below, while initially appearing a little complex, provides some insight into these relationships. Paradoxically, it is also a framework for organisation development.

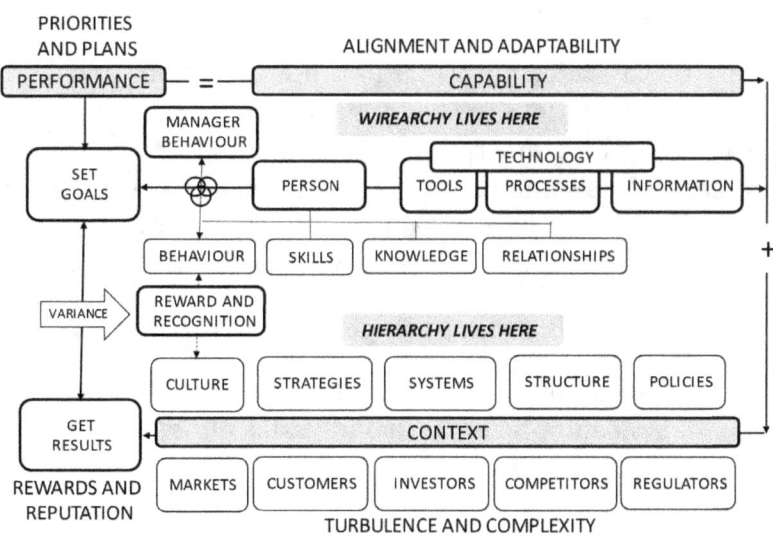

Figure 30: Performance, Capability and Context Framework

This performance framework also provides the pathway between hierarchy and wirearchy by recognising that knowledge sharing, in the connected space of each person, through multiple relationships, is the key to developing an innovation and development response to 'performance' variance. There is a reciprocity between performance and capability in the interaction that individuals, teams and organisations have with their context level.

At the *interpersonal* level of context we are experiencing the integration of people and digital technologies which has resulted in a shift from passive receivers to active broadcasters of information. The idiosyncrasies of people become the focus of much of content of the digital platforms. So it becomes important for those in position-based leadership roles to challenge their habit-based sense-making, meaning-making and connection-making mindsets and develop insight, intention and integrity that we have discussed in some depth in earlier chapters. More importantly however is to recognise the emergence of people centric leadership in that same wirearchy that demands the personal development of those same attributes.

Against those leadership evolution, life conditions and context level backgrounds, let's reflect on the development of our knowledge and skills that underpin choice-making in a hierarchy a little more depth. It is sometimes called as *horizontal* development. In essence there are three knowledge and skill categories that we progressively develop to become effective "performers" in hierarchy.

The horizontal skills and knowledge choice-making categories are:

- Professional and technical knowledge – the 'what',
- Task and process managing skills – the 'how', and
- Interaction and influence skills – the 'who'.

The figure below, without being comprehensive, illustrates the idea of horizontal development.

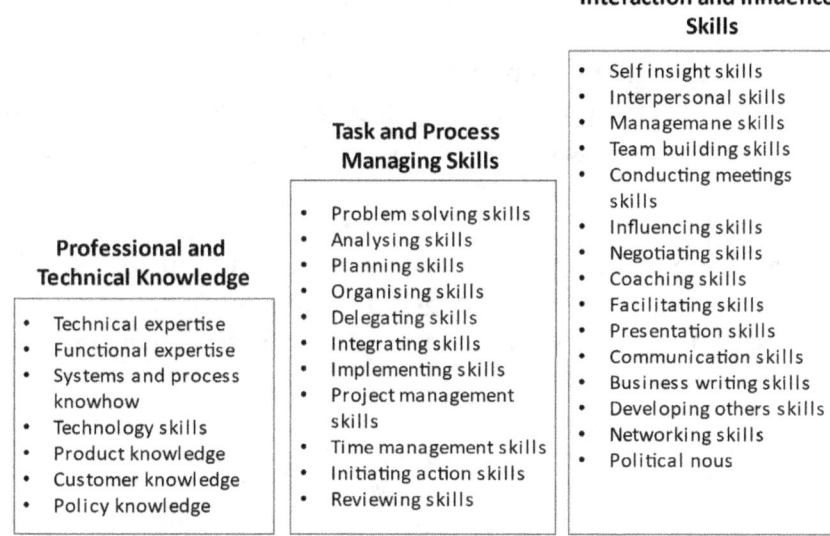

Figure 31: Horizontal Development

These *horizontal* management skills and knowledge are, paradoxically, also a hierarchy in that we begin by first developing broader professional and technical knowledge, and then gain organisation focused task and process managing skills, and then progress to interaction and influence interpersonal skills as we are 'promoted' through roles in the hierarchy. The emphasis is on 'objective' sense-making rather than 'subjective' meaning-making and 'integrative' connection-making.

Developing leadership skills were a subset of management development. Consequently we can capture the essence of traditional leadership development in a hierarchy by understanding the three transitions from technical knowledge to management skills to leadership responsibility and the associated levels of contribution to organisation success.

- Technical knowledge is focused on content – contributes to professional knowledge, process knowledge and own position-based responsibilities,

- Management skills are focused on constructs - contributes to business plans and performance management and embedded management practices, and
- Leadership behaviour is focused on context – contributes to developing strategy, shaping the prevailing culture and business growth.

This all happens in a closed system where the outside is only considered by the top of the pyramid and brought inside the organisation and deployed downwards through management to subordinates.

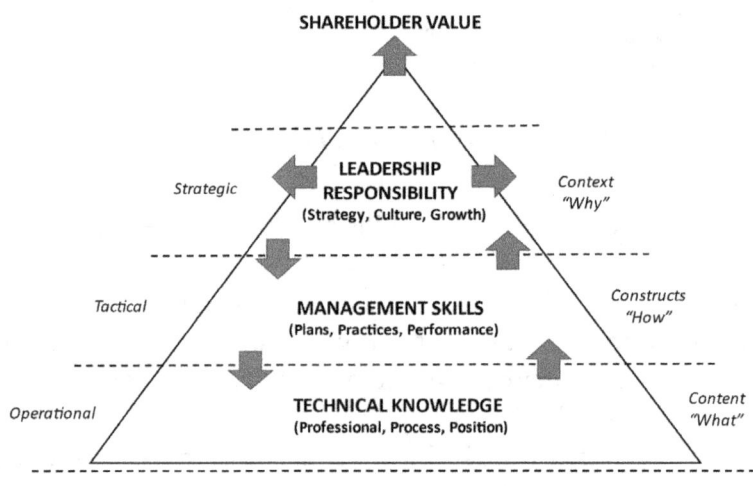

Figure 32: The Information and Knowhow Transitions

This traditional approach to leadership development is position authority power based and does not reflect the new reality of personal distributed power, based on know-how and idea generation, at any "level" of the hierarchy. It is fundamentally anchored in position-based choice-making power.

Let's again recall that the working definition of Wirearchy is *a "dynamic two-way flow of power and authority, based on knowl-*

edge, trust, credibility and a focus on results, enabled by interconnected people and technology". Power and authority in wirearchy are person-based. Whereas hierarchy is a system in which members of an organisation or society are ranked according to relative status or importance and are represented as being "above", "below", or "at the same level as" one another. Power and authority is position-based.

The interface between hierarchy and wirearchy involves *emergent or vertical* development. The emergent (vertical) development pathway is a reflection of our choice-making demands in a world of connection, turbulence and complexity. Emergent leadership in the context of the interaction between hierarchy and wirearchy is comprised of four roles that reflect the four Jungian function pair social styles we discussed earlier, that enable the organisation to maintain focus and direction and at the same time embrace innovation through universally connected knowledge sharing space.

The four descriptive characteristics of Jungian function pair social styles are:

- The Catalyst NT style - relating to initiative, expertise and ingenuity,
- The Synergist NF style - relating to optimism, ideas and empathy,
- The Harmonist SF style - relating to patience, duty, and cooperation,
- The Specialist ST - relating to correctness, predictability and standards.

Catalyst style - NT (Intuition and Thinking) - often with EJ temperament:

- are task-oriented and idea-focused,
- want to know the gist of what is expected, while having room to design their own logical systems and pursue their personal vision,

- place great value on competence, expertise, and the logical soundness of ideas,
- will critique and improve ideas and strategies, with an eye on the big picture and sound models,
- are single-minded and may struggle to see ideas, realities, and details that do not fit with their own,
- might struggle with interaction in emotionally charged situations and taking the emotions of others into account.

Synergist style - NF (Intuition and Feeling) - often with EP temperament:

- are people-oriented and idea-focused,
- want to know the gist of what is expected, while having room to do things in their own way, while helping others,
- will place great value on genuineness, empowerment, and meaning in work and in life,
- want to help others find their passions and reach their potential, while allowing others' voices and opinions to be heard,
- are sensitive to criticism and may react impulsively to feedback,
- might miss details and current realities while carrying out their own ideas and working towards desired change.

Harmonist style - SF (Sensing and Feeling) - often with IP temperament:

- are people-oriented and practical-focussed,
- want to know detailed expectations for completing tasks and helping others up front,
- will place value on consistency, harmony, and good relationships in their environment,

- want to help people get through their tasks with as little difficulty as possible,
- may take criticism too personally but will brood on it rather than reacting immediately,
- might avoid conflict to preserve harmony, even when conflict may improve the situation in the end

Specialist Style – ST (Sensing and Thinking) - often with IJ temperament:

- are task-oriented and practical-focussed,
- want to know detailed expectations for completing tasks and projects up front,
- will place value on having, knowing, and consistently following standard operating procedures for tasks that are to be repeated,
- want to know the outcome required and get things done in the most efficient, simple way possible… no fuss, no drama,
- may struggle to adjust to change that seems unneeded and/or happens quickly,
- might struggle with emotionally charged situations and considering others' emotions.

The figure below, without being comprehensive, illustrates the attributes of each role.

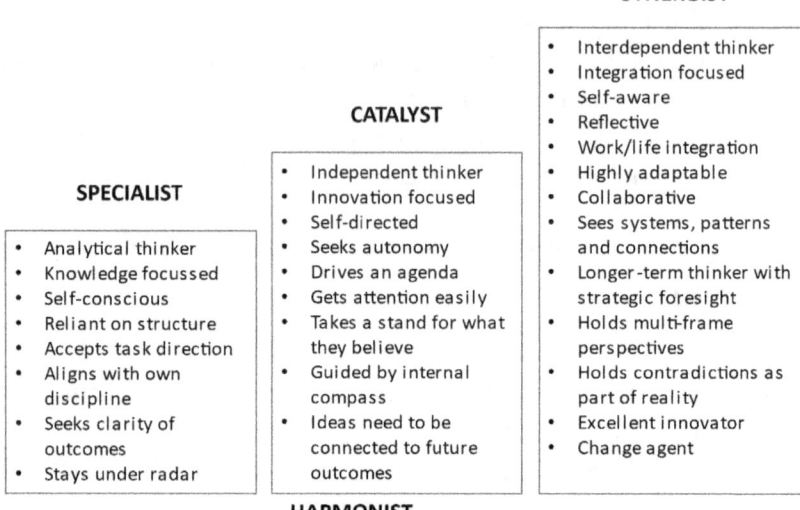

Figure 33: Emergent Leadership Development

The Harmonist role is embedded in horizontal development and plays a stabilising role in the choice-making space that underpins culture alignment pre and post transformation. They will be observers of the emergent culture and may be seen as "laggers" but are central to the embedding of change once they can see it has the potential for a new stability. They can also adopt an important "devil's advocate" role by advocating a people focused approach to change.

Each of the three emergent leadership roles (Specialist, Catalyst and Synergist) create a bridge between hierarchy and wirearchy in a way that allows the organisation to integrate interdisciplinary knowledge, get engagement in idea generation and enable universal connection. The bridge between hierarchy and wirearchy connects us to communities of practice and knowledge networks.

Communities of practice are voluntary groups of people (you can join and leave as you choose) who have a common interest in a specific technical or business domain. They cooperate to share information, improve their skills, and actively work on advancing the general knowledge of the domain. A community of practice usually evolves naturally because of the members' common interest in a particular domain or area. However it can be created deliberately by a small group of individuals with the goal of gaining knowledge related to a specific field. It is through the process of sharing information and experiences with the group that members learn from each other, and have an opportunity to develop personally and professionally.

Knowledge networks are collections of individuals and teams who come together more formally across organisational, spatial and disciplinary boundaries to innovate and share a body of knowledge. The collaborative focus of such networks is usually on developing, distributing and applying knowledge. Knowledge networks require a proactive, systematic approach to the planning and use of a formalised approach to knowledge creation and transfer. It includes promoting and improving conditions to cultivate informal and formal networking within a larger network of organisations.

The figure below illustrates these roles in the context of hierarchy and wirearchy:

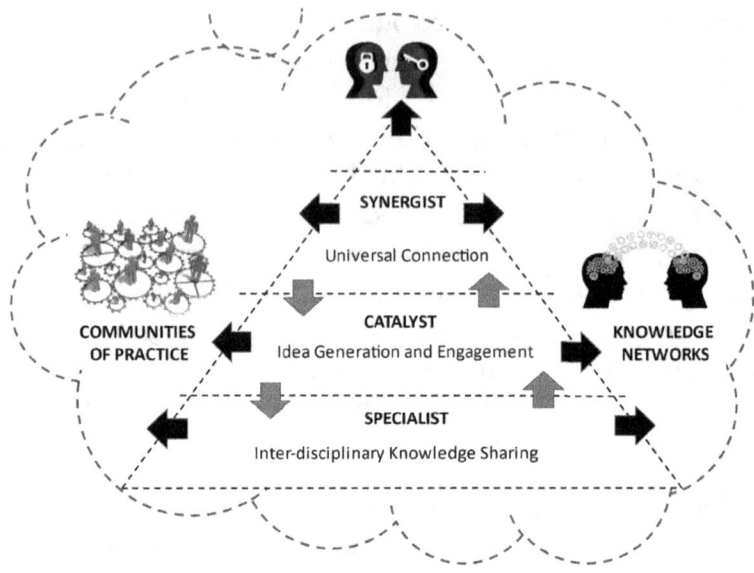

Figure 34: Emergent Leadership Role Development

You will recall that our Adaptive Learning Map© places choice-making at the centre which in turn is determined by our personal mindsets of meaning-making, sense-making and connection-making and the related three "eyes" – Insight, Intention and Integrity. These three mindsets and "eyes" become the development foundation of emergent leadership as you apply the Adaptive Learning Map©.

Emergent (vertical) development is fundamentally about choice-making and integrating your meaning-making, sense-making and connection-making capabilities and acting in more aligned and adaptable ways. It is about continuing to transform our habit-based mindsets and expanding our context-responsive behaviours to embrace the relationship between hierarchy and wirearchy. It is not any longer about whether the cup is half full or half empty and filling it (horizontal development) but about growing the capacity of the cup (vertical development).

INSIGHT INTENTION AND INTEGRITY

The essence of emergent leadership is about the central role of choice-making in all that we do as co-responsible creative agents of the system, and for leadership to be understood, in the universally connected open systems world of wirearchy, as a personal role open to all. The development of the three mindsets is directly related to the choice-making role of the emergent leader.

- the Specialist ST role is underpinned by the Thinking Centre, and needs to develop Insight and emotional intelligence to enhance application of sense-making,
- the Catalyst NT role is underpinned by the Moving Centre, and needs to develop Integrity and social intelligence to enhance application of connection-making, and
- the Synergist NF role is underpinned by Feeling Centre, and needs to develop Intention and intellectual intelligence to enhance application of meaning-making.

These relationships are illustrated in the diagram below:

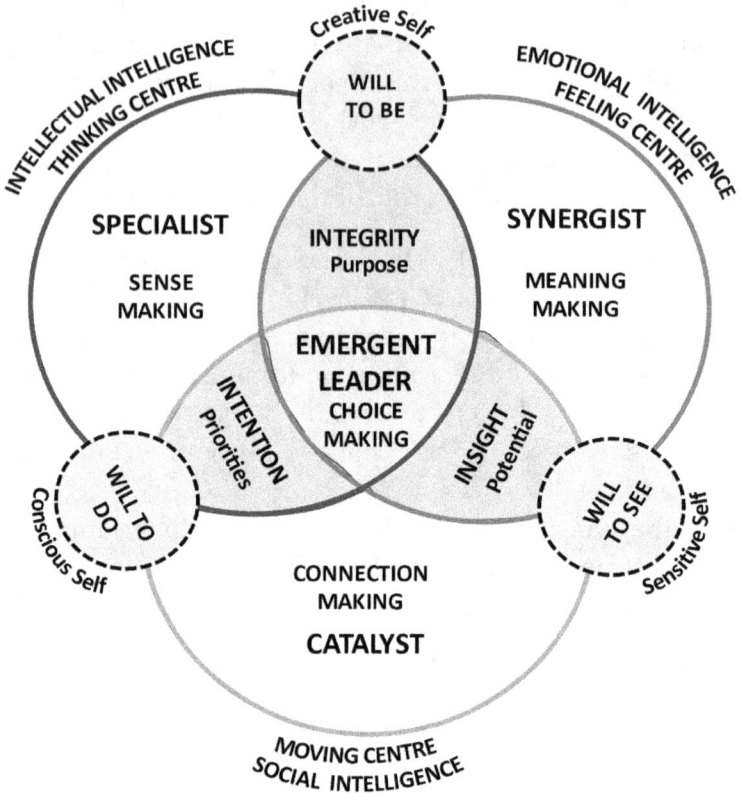

Figure 35: The Three Emergent Leadership Roles

This personal role of leadership is no longer a simple extension of management authority, in the closed hierarchic structures of command and control, that is experienced as position-based leadership. Consequently, person-based leadership, in a living adaptive system, requires three essential qualities. They are the three "eyes" of emergent leadership:

- insight (the capacity of seeing into a situation or the act or result of comprehending the inner and outer nature of things by seeing intuitively),

INSIGHT INTENTION AND INTEGRITY

- intention (**a commitment to carry out an action in the future** and involves mental activities such as planning and forethought), and
- integrity (the practice of being trustworthy and showing a consistent and uncompromising adherence to personal and collective principles and values).

The emergent leadership perspective recognises that there are multiple leaders and that leadership activities are widely shared within and between organisations and networks of like-minded people. Emergent leadership focuses upon the interactions, rather than the actions, of those in formal and informal leadership roles. It is primarily concerned with leadership practices and how leadership influences structure and culture integration. It is not about a particular role in a hierarchy.

An emergent perspective on leadership acknowledges the work of all individuals who con-

tribute to leadership practices, whether or not they are formally designated or defined as leaders. Emergent leadership is also central to organisation systems reconfiguration and organisation redesign which require lateral, cross functional decision-making processes.

Leadership development that recognises our present personal choice-making is essentially based on our meaning-making, sense-making and connection-making mindsets is the starting point. They are the blind spots that reinforce hierarchy and understanding them is the key to unlocking the door to the three 'eyes' of insight, intention and integrity as the foundations of emergent leadership. We need to start with improving our insight.

If we start from where we are at we can take a first simple step developing our insight by considering how we make statements, how we ask questions and how we reflect on our situation.

- advocacy: making our own sense-making and meaning-making mindset visible to others,
- inquiry: inquiring into others sense-making and meaning-making mindsets,
- reflection: becoming more aware of our own sense-making and meaning-making mindsets.

The four main approaches that arise from the relationship between advocacy and inquiry are:

- High advocacy, low inquiry is one-way communication - even if both people are doing it! It can be useful for giving information. It makes it difficult to take advantage of diverse perspectives or to build commitment to a course of action.
- High inquiry, low advocacy is one way in a different sense: the speaker does not state their thinking. It can be useful as a way of finding out information. It can create difficulty when the speaker has a hidden agenda and is using questions to get the other person to "discover" what the speaker already thinks is right.
- Low inquiry, low advocacy is useful when being an observer is useful. It is a low contribution approach. Sometimes people take a low-low approach on key issues while covering this up by advocating or inquiring on safe subjects, (the "Nice day we're having" syndrome).
- High advocacy, high inquiry is an approach for mutual appreciation and learning. I state my thinking, I inquire into your thinking, and I encourage you to question my thinking. To get into the high-high box, the quality of the advocacy and inquiry is crucial. For example, saying "That's a stupid idea, were you born that way?" is both a statement and a question, but it does not lead to mutual learning.

Each dimension has a destructive quality if it is not values balanced.

- High advocacy, low inquiry can be about dictating,
- High inquiry, low advocacy can about interrogating,
- Low inquiry, low advocacy can be about withdrawing,
- High advocacy, high inquiry can be politicking.

The relationship between advocacy and inquiry is shown in the figure below.

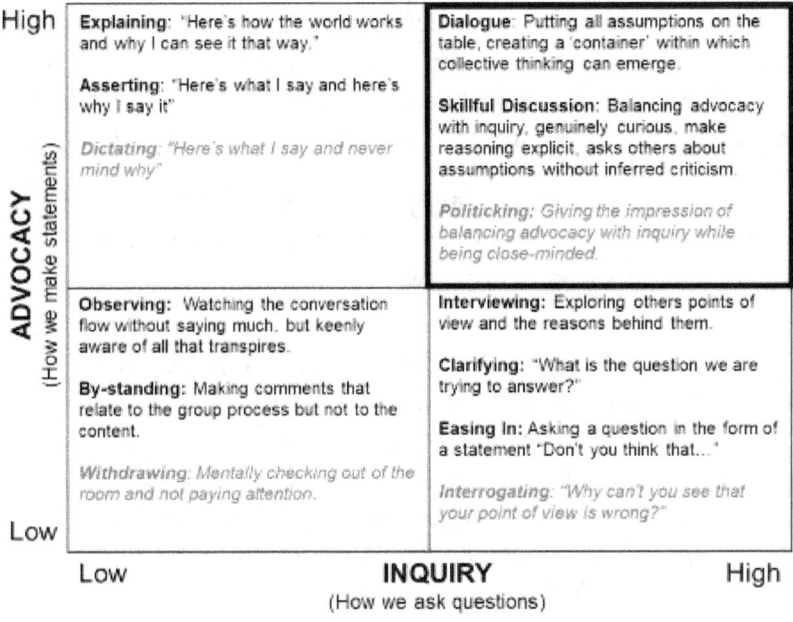

Figure 36: Advocacy and Inquiry Matrix

The idea of "balancing advocacy and inquiry" was first proposed by Peter Senge in his book, The Fifth Discipline: The Art and Practice of the Learning Organization. The practice of balancing advocacy and inquiry is intended to expose, or make visible, each person's thinking, and to open that thinking for examination. Through this practice, we expose and open our own thinking for examination; we also inquire into others sense-making and meaning-making mindsets in order to better understand their viewpoints and perspectives.

Each of us has a tendency, a conversational and thinking habit, to favour either advocacy or inquiry. The intent of this practice, as the name suggests, is to help us balance the propensity to assert our viewpoint and the willingness to show curiosity into other viewpoints.

Balancing advocacy and inquiry is known as dialogue. Dialogue is a form of conversation where people genuinely try to access different perspectives to enable a new understanding to emerge. Unlike debate, dialogue seeks to discover a new meaning that was not previously held by any of the participants in the dialogue.

The four dimensions of dialogue are deep listening, respecting others, suspending assumptions and beliefs and reflecting. Each of these skills is explained below.

> **Deep listening** - *In its most simple form deep listening derives from the conscious choice to listen. It involves quietening the voice in our heads so that we can hear the true story of the person to whom we are listening. As we listen to understand their context we literally stay quiet and just listen.*
>
> **Respecting others** - *This is particularly difficult to do when we interact with people who have contrasting views to our own. While respecting others does not mean that you have to agree with them, it does mean that you will allow them the time and space to have their say and you will see it as a perspective that, while you may not understand it, it is a perspective that is valid in the context that it contributes, even if only in a small way, to our understanding of*

the 'complete' picture of whatever is our area of focus at the time.

Suspending assumptions and beliefs - *The capacity to explain why we hold the views that we hold lies at the heart of suspending assumptions and beliefs. Much like we hang our clothes on a line for them to dry, suspending means that we 'hang out' the reasons for our points of view. This allows people to look at them, question them and assist us in developing a deeper understanding of our perspectives. To make visible your assumptions and beliefs illustrates a willingness to be vulnerable which is a key attribute of emergent leadership.*

Reflecting - *The capacity to reflect enhances our connection-making skills and capacity to engage in dialogue. In networked environments it is worth holding a reflection at the end of each knowledge sharing to embed the process of dialogue into your normal connection-making approach.*

In dialogue, people freely and creatively explore issues, listen deeply to each other and suspend their own views to enable ideas and approaches to emerge. People in dialogue have access to a larger pool of knowledge than any one person. The primary purpose of dialogue is to enlarge ideas, not to diminish them. It is not about winning acceptance of a viewpoint, but sharing knowledge and seeing what emerges. The table below provides some insight into advocacy and inquiry approaches that block and encourage dialogue.

ADVOCACY THAT BLOCKS DIALOGUE	ADVOCACY THAT ENCOURAGES DIALOGUE
That is how it is! (withholding your reasoning). Because I say so! (no discussion possible). Statements with "always" and "never".	When you do this, I …. It seems to me that ….. Because of …., I believe that …. My experience is that …. What I see is that ….
INQUIRY THAT BLOCKS DIALOGUE (DEPENDING ON TONE)	**INQUIRY THAT ENCOURAGES DIALOGUE**
Don't you agree? (Especially when said in an intimidating way) Did you do that because of X, Y or Z? Do you really think you did a good job? (When you think s/he did not) Why don't you just try what I'm suggesting? Why didn't you just tell me? Why are you so defensive?	How do you see this differently? What's your reaction to…? What led you to that conclusion/action? Say more about that… Why is that so? What makes you …? What kept you from telling me? How have I contributed to that? How can I/we…?

The advocacy and inquiry matrix provides a useful way of developing dialogue the foundations of our emergent (vertical) leadership capabilities.

INSIGHT INTENTION AND INTEGRITY

In the past, it may have been enough to get by on personal intelligence alone. But it's no longer enough to be brilliant on our own. Our pressing problems today require that we be 'smart' *together*, by harnessing our collective thinking and knowhow to contribute to the common good. The three emergent leadership transitions, from specialist to catalyst to synergist, can be aligned to the three dimensions of the advocacy and inquiry matrix of making statements, asking questions and reflecting. The diagram below seeks to capture these stages of role transition between hierarchy and wirearchy.

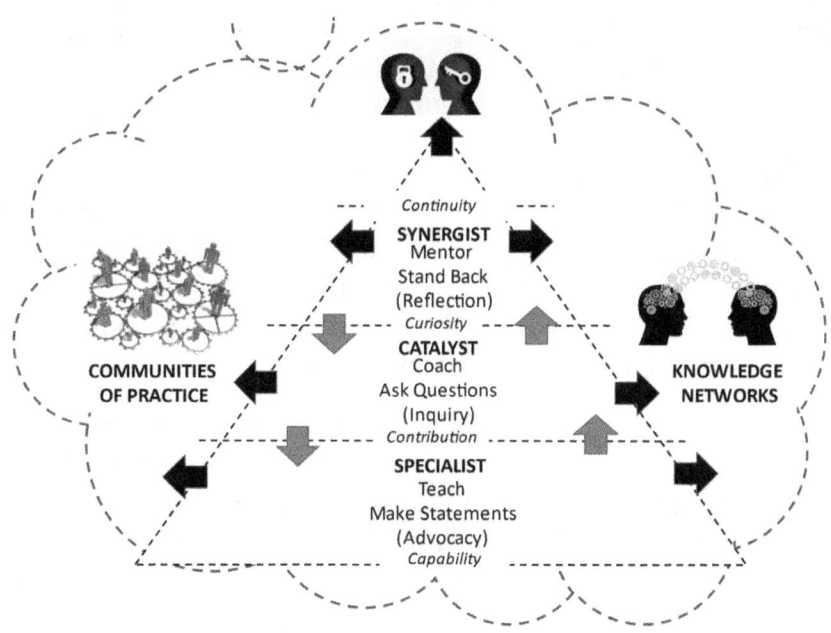

Figure 37: The Stages of Role Transition

The Specialist role sits between capability and contribution and supports and underpins the the development of interdisciplinay knowledge networks and requires advocacy skills. It is about emergent sense-making and the emergent leadership teaching role in knowledge sharing with others. The focus is on the knowledge content of each task and asks the question "what is it?".

The Catalyst role sits between contribution and curiosity and supports the development of ideas by engaging with internal and external communities of practice and requires inquiry skills. It is about emergent meaning-making and the emergent leadership coaching role in skill building of others. The focus is on the process and relationsip skills of people and asks the question "how do I?".

The Synergist role sits between curiosity and continuity and supports the universal connection between hierarchy and wirearchy and requires reflections skills. It is about emergent connection-making and the emergent leadership mentoring role in developing situational awareness in self and others. The focus is on the context and situational drivers of behaviour and asks the question "why is it so?"

At the top of the hierarchy is continuity and is about integrity; the core underpinning values of the business that pervades all roles. This is an open system where the outside turbulence is translated into opportunities for growth inside the organisation and at all levels of the hierarchy. It is the foundation for developing new capabilities that contribute to changing demands.

The behaviours you exhibit in making statements and asking questions, together with the thoughts and feelings that occur during reflection, will be shaped by your intentions and motivations that reflect each Social Style (Jungian function pair) that we discussed earlier. Let's refresh our understanding of them in the emergent leadership context.

NT Style: Catalyst	
Intention (What they want)	**Motivation** (What they desire for themselves and others)
- Seek solutions to problems - Get immediate results - Overcome objections - Accelerate efforts when competing - Show impatience - Take authority - Give orders	- Independence to act - Power and authority - Wide sphere of operation - Creative adventure tasks - Freedom from close supervision - Prestige and challenge - Opportunity for advancement
NF Style: Synergist	
Intention (What they want)	**Motivation** (What they desire for themselves and others)
- Use tactful communication - Persuade and convince others - Provide tension release with humour - Generate enthusiasm - Contact people - Accept varied opinions - Respond spontaneously	- Appreciation and positive feedback - New openings and better possibilities - Freedom of expression - Teaching and instructing roles - Connections with higher ups - Opportunities to showcase talents - Appreciation and positive feedback

ST Style: Specialist	
Intention (What they want)	**Motivation** (What they desire for themselves and others)
• Adhere to rules and regulations • Show diplomacy and tactfulness • Check for accuracy • Weigh actions against stated goals • Emphasise systematic procedures • Provide order and improved systems • Show concern for practical skills	• Task to determine cause of problems • Task of formulating goal or objectives • Expert role in long range planning • Reassurance • Sheltered environment • Chance to restore order • Answers about questionable assignments
SF Style: Harmonist	
Intention (What they want)	**Motivation** (What they desire for themselves and others)
• Develop unity with others • Expect security • Remain calm and composed • Build a reserve of strength • Give attention to details • Show loyalty	• Time to achieve methodical outcomes • Understanding of procedure changes • Opportunity to structure a plan • Sincere appreciation • Identification with team/group • Credit for successfully completed tasks

Having an appreciation of the intentions and motivations of yourself and others in the hierarchy and wirearchy spaces enhances the choice-making drivers of acumen, aspiration and autonomy.

Using the behaviour observation guide that we discussed in chapter 10, when we looked at Insight, will help you identify your dominant Social Style (Jungian function pair), and that of those you connect with, to provide insight into both your intentions and motivations and theirs.

INSIGHT INTENTION AND INTEGRITY

As emergent leaders we are situational and contextual. People are the key component of that situation and context in the connected space we now live in. When we have a good idea or knowledge to share, we connect with others without direction. We have a mature sense of the beliefs and the actions that flow from us. With insight and intention we can consider how we might use advocacy and enquiry and seek to understand the intentions and motivations that the person we are connecting with is operating from.

Leadership, in this new turbulent and interconnected context, emerges as it is required. The new role of emergent leadership is innovation and connected know-how driven, and is about the emergent developmental role of the three "I's" – insight, intention and integrity. Emergent leadership will occur naturally when these three "I's" are in place to support the transition from the old order to the new order and to ensure that the disenfranchised are supported through that turbulent transitional change.

Unfortunately, but predictably, we are already beginning to see the re-emergence of the new "Leadership Luddites" and that is what happens when those in power are disenfranchised by change. This is playing into the populist power based political game that has no insight, intention or integrity.

Emergent leadership is based on the idea that the very nature of universal connectedness has created "wirearchy", where leadership assumes a personal dimension based on voluntary association. You choose to be a leader in the way that you connect and share knowledge.

You can now use the Toolkit in the next section to develop your three 'eyes' of emergent leadership in the context of wirearchy, and reflect on each of them:

- insight to identify and develop your potential and provide the foundation for recovering your voice,
- intention to identify and develop your priorities and provide the foundation for uncovering your vision, and
- integrity to identify and develop your purpose and provide the foundation for discovering your values.

Your capacity to assume an emergent leadership role in the connected spaces you operate in, be it hierarchy or wirearchy, will be consistent with your potential, priorities and purpose. I trust you will enjoy applying to our Adaptive Learning Map© in breaking out of your limiting habits and in supporting the development of your choice-making role as an emergent leader as you get to see the 'tipping point' from a new perspective.

Humpty also didn't know the answer to the question "What came first the chicken or the egg?" Just as you won't be able to answer the question "What is emergent leadership?" until you take the steps to develop the individual qualities of insight, intention and integrity that it emerges from.

As Humpty Dumpty would say, "You can't make an omelette without breaking an egg!".

An egg is an omelette in disguise just as you are an emergent leader in disguise.

I invite you to break some eggs………and realise your emergent leadership potential.

Is that excitement or fear on Humpty's face! What about yours?

TOOL KIT

In the Tool Kit a range of tools are introduced to assist in developing insight, intention and integrity, with a significant focus on Jung's model. These approaches are meant to provide an insight into the questions you will be asking yourself as you are faced with challenging your present meaning-making, sense-making, connection-making and choice-making mindsets. These 'personality' constructs provide you with a framework of discovery rather than satisfactory answers to your personal complexity and uniqueness.

The tools provided to support your continuous self-development as an emergent leader are:

- Tool 1: The Adaptive Learning Map©
- Tool 2: The Instinctual Stack Questionnaire
- Tool 3: Temperament and Dominant Centre Questionnaire
- Tool 4: Functional Pair Behaviour Traits questionnaire and four main Social Styles
- Tool 5: Gravesian/Spiral Dynamics questionnaire and meme level descriptions

Tool 1: The Adaptive Learning Map©

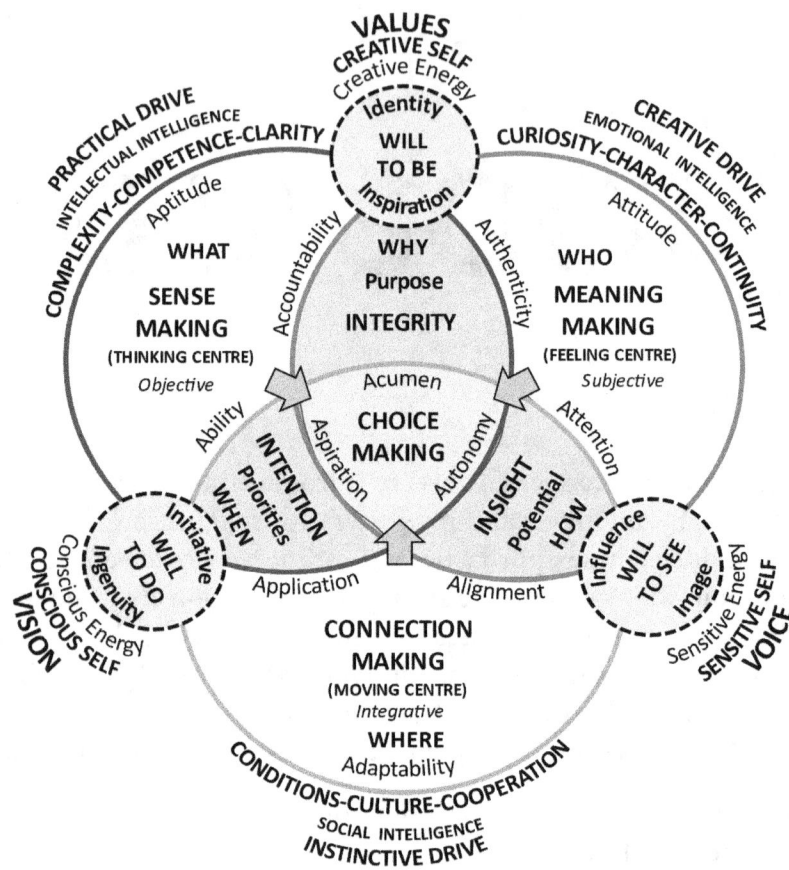

INSIGHT INTENTION AND INTEGRITY

Tool 2 - Instinctual Stack Questionnaire

Read the following three paragraphs and choose which is most, next most and least like you when you are alert to your surroundings and the people in them.

Paragraph A. *When you walk into a room at a party you notice that a number of presents have been left on a table and you leave your gift with them – it has a card with it so the guest of honour will know who it is from. You quickly become aware of the volume of the music and the brightness of the lighting. You help yourself to a drink and find a comfortable chair to sit in where you can observe what others are doing from a distance. You look out for someone you know as you think about the incessant chatter of conversations in the background. You try not to be conspicuous. You notice that the room temperature is quite cold and wonder how you might get the temperature increased. The food is set out on a table and when you notice it you need to try it. When you get to the table with the food on it you notice there are some unusual looking items you have not seen before. You think about smelling them but don't want to be seen to be bad mannered. Your sixth sense tells you that they may not be safe to eat – you avoid them and find something familiar. After about an hour you think about how you can leave early without offending the person that invited you. As you prepare to leave you think to yourself "I don't know why I keep accepting invites to parties, they are always noisy and full of people I don't know".*

Paragraph B. *When you walk into the room at a party you are immediately aware of just how many people are there. You are late because of the time you spent on your presentation – your clothes, your appearance and your accessories. You scan the whole group and notice a person across the room – there is something about them that creates a sense that you are going to enjoy the evening by getting to know them. They have energy about them that you can almost feel from a distance. You make your way toward the person and they look toward you and smile. You smile back and say "Hi" and introduce yourself. The other person does the same and there is a feeling of connection that you always seem to recognise on those occasions when it happens. You begin a conversation about a recent trip that you went on and talk about how you enjoyed the buzz of the place. The other person connects your conversation to* *their personal experiences in a refreshingly open way. You become unaware of others at the party. The other person notices that you haven't got a drink and you are still holding the present for the guest of honour in your hand. Your sixth sense tells you that this person enjoys your company but you sense you should step back as you experience déjà vu – you are getting in too deep too quickly again! You notice someone you know nearby and introduce the other person to them and then charmingly disengage yourself to get a drink and give your present personally to the guest of honour. As you walk away you think to yourself "A little bit of flirting doesn't do any harm, after all we may never meet again".*

Paragraph C. *When you walk into the room at a party you immediately feel amongst friends. You look for the guest of honour so you can share in the pleasure you hope they will get when they open your present. You find a way to mingle with the group that is talking with the guest of honour, firstly by engaging with a person in the group then by expanding the circle they are in. You enjoy being with a familiar crowd and those congregated around the guest of honour are people you like to be with. The conversation is largely undirected and you are easily able to pick up the threads of what is happening and join in the conversation. You go with the flow and then you notice one person is not being included so you cleverly shift the conversation to them and feel good that everybody is now part of the conversation. Your sixth sense tells you that now is not the time to make a big deal of your gift but it's too late as another person prompts you to hand it over. You give the gift to the guest of honour with the comment "You are really hard to buy for, so I hope you like it". You feel a little conspicuous, but you are able to move the conversation to another topic. You relax again and chat about whatever comes up, "after all we are all friends".*

My probable instinctual **stack** is:

Most like   Paragraph ____ Instinct name* _____

Next most like Paragraph ____ Instinct name* _____

Least like Paragraph ____ Instinct name* _____

INSIGHT INTENTION AND INTEGRITY

*The key to the paragraphs is:

    Paragraph A   Self-preserving Instinct

    Paragraph B   Self-renewal Instinct

    Paragraph C   Social Instinct

The following descriptions developed by Katherine Fauvre provide a deeper understanding of each instinct.

- **Self-preserving instinct:** is driven by the ongoing search or survival and well-being. Anything that could possibly damage, endanger, or exploit the self is of concern. The focus of attention is subtly on "the self" and "my world." The primary desire is for security, which is manifested by a continual perceived quest for well-being and for the "essential" needs of life, such as food, comfort, safety, protection, and resources.

    The concern of the self-preserving instinct involves issues of living and compromise – for example, "to be or not to be present" or "how to be present" The survival strategy places an intense emphasis on either caution or self-destruction. The focus is to aggressively go after what one needs and/or to defensively hold onto what one has. The common theme statements reflect the attention to "self," such as "how am I?" with this type often defining itself by "how comfortably and successfully I experience my body" – i.e., issues dealing with "what are my physical needs and desires?"

    The energy projected is described as "conserved energy" and is often experienced as "grounded," as if it were tightly contained around the body like a spiral coil. The energy is usually sombre, heavy, and serious in nature, as if the person is attempting to function while carrying some great weight on his or her shoulders, and is thus conserving energy for later personal use. The self-preserving Instinctual Subtypes will "sacrifice for self" to ensure survival. Rather than looking to the group or a mate to "solve problems," these types tend to "look inward" based upon an inherent recognition that "I'm on my own" and "I have to take care of myself."

- **Self-renewal instinct** is driven by the ongoing search for intimacy and one-to-one relationships. The focus of attention is on "the beloved" and "our intimate world." The primary desire is for a mate, which is manifested by an imbalanced perceived need for wholeness, affinity, and closeness in a continual search for "the other half." The concern of the self-renewal instinct involves issues of intimacy – for example, "to be intimate or not to be intimate" or "how to be intimate."

- The survival strategy is abstinence or promiscuity. The common theme statements reflect an inclination to define oneself in terms of the mate and the relationship, such as "what am I?", with this instinct being defined by "how comfortably and successfully I experience my relationship" i.e. issues dealing with "how am I perceived by my intimate partner?"

- The energy projected is described as "high energy" and is often experienced as "intense" and laser-like, appearing to be intently focused, and is usually playful and light, yet penetrating in nature. There is a sense of energy and vibration, the search for the mate, the need to display their strength and beauty, like the peacock showing its feathers or, in some manner, acting out the mating ritual or dance.

- The self-renewal instinct will "sacrifice for the relationship" to ensure connection. Rather than looking inward or to the group for security to "solve the problem," these types tend to "look to the mate," based upon a belief that "I cannot be whole unless I find my other half".

- **Social instinct:** is driven by the ongoing search for groups and community, akin to the herd instinct in animals, where there are safety and security in numbers. The focus of attention is on "the group" and "our greater world." The primary desire is for groups, which is manifested by an imbalanced perceived need for people, recognition, popularity, honour, status, and social acceptance.

The concern of the social instinct involves issues of relating – for example, "to relate or not to relate" or "how to relate." The survival strategy is an emphasis on sociability or unsociability. The common theme statements reflect an inclination to categorize oneself in terms of others, such as "who am I?", with this type being defined by "how comfortably and successfully I experience my group" – i.e., issues dealing with "how am I perceived by the group?"

The energy projected is described as "split energy" and is often experienced as "scattered" and projected outward, appearing personable, superficial, and cursory in nature. It is imperative that "a good impression is made" and that "nothing important is missed." The social instinct will "sacrifice for the group" to ensure status. Rather than looking inward or to a mate for security and to "solve problems," these types tend to "look outward," based upon a belief that "my value is dependent upon how I am perceived by the group".

Tool 3: Temperament and Dominant Function Pair Social Style

Step 1. Review each pair of the following traits and respond to each pair based on how each statement best describes your behaviour on a day-to-day basis.		
Your *choices* are to be scored as follows:	A	B
If you definitely prefer statement A, your score should be	2	0
If you definitely prefer statement B, your score should be	0	2
If you find it difficult to decide which statement you prefer, your score should be		
either	2	1
or	1	2
Note that 2-0, 0-2, 2-1 or 1-2 are the only possible score combinations		

Step 2. Add the score for each Set

Step 3. Transfer your scores to the appropriate box at the end of the questionnaire

SET A	A	B	SET B
Gregarious - drawn to large number and variety of relationships.			**Intimate** - most comfortable in small groups and with one-on-one relationships.
Enthusiastic - being energetically with the "action" and at the centre of things.			**Quiet** - present yourself modestly, drawn to the calm away from the centre of action.

Initiator - social facilitator, assertively outgoing, build bridges among people. **Expressive** - easy to know, approachable, warm, readily show feelings. **Auditory** - learn through listening, active dialogue, and involvement with others.		**Receptor** - content to let others initiate social activities - even to the point of being overlooked. **Contained** - well controlled, calm exterior, often difficult for others to "read.". **Visual** - learn through observation, reflection, reading, and more solitary means.
TOTAL A SCORE		**TOTAL B SCORE**
SET C	C | D	**SET D**
Concrete - depend on verifiable, factual information and direct perceptions. literal, mistrust fuzzy information **Realistic** - value being practical, cost-effective, and exercising common sense. **Pragmatic** - highly value the usefulness or applications of an idea - more interesting than idea itself.		**Abstract** - comfortable with and inferring meaning from ambiguous and non-literal information. **Imaginative** - enjoy being ingenious, clever and novel . . . for its own sake. **Intellectual** - learning, acquiring knowledge, mental challenges are valued as an end in itself.

Experiential - heavily grounded by first hand, past experience. Reluctant to generalize beyond direct experience.			**Theoretical** - conceptual, automatically search for patterns in observed facts, comfortable with theories and inventing new ones.
Traditional - trust what is familiar, support established groups and methods, honour precedents.			**Original** - value initiative and enterprising, inventive, and novel solutions. Often mistrust conventional wisdom.
TOTAL C SCORE			TOTAL D SCORE
SET E	E	F	SET F
Critical - comfortable making distinctions, categorizing, making win/lose choices, being in adversarial situations.			**Accepting** - tolerant towards human failings, see positive side of others, instinctually seek win/win resolutions of problems.
Tough Minded - results oriented, ends justify the means, stick on task.			**Tender Hearted** - use gentle persuasion to influence, reluctant to force compliance..
Questioning - intellectually independent, resistant to influence, self-confident.			**Accommodating** - seek consensus, deferential, conflict avoiding, seeks harmony.

Logical - value and trust detached, objective, and logical analysis. **Reasonable** - is clear-thinking, objective, reasoned, and logical in everyday decision-making.		**Affective** - trust emotions and feelings, value human considerations, in touch with feelings. **Compassionate** - make decisions on overall impressions, patterns, and feelings (including emotional likes and dislikes).
TOTAL E SCORE		**TOTAL F SCORE**
SET G	G | H	**SET H**
Early Starter - focused. Structure activities to work on one thing at a time, allowing adequate time for proper completion. **Systematic** - prefer orderly, structured and programmed responses. Like formal contingency planning. **Scheduled** - create and easily follow standardized and familiar routines.		**Pressure Prompted** - prefer variety and multi-tasking. Most effectively energized when working close to deadlines. **Casual** - comfortable making adjustments as situation requires. Prefer informal guidelines vs. structured rules.. **Spontaneous** - dislike repeatedly following the same routines. Seek variety and change.

Planful - like to schedule future commitments far in advance, use dates and deadlines to organize your energies.

Methodical - implement projects in a planned, organized, and step-by-step manner..

TOTAL G SCORE

Open-ended - strongly value preserving flexibility and freedom, dislike being tied down by long range plans. Make flexible plans.

Emergent - ad hoc planner. Move quickly into action without detailed plans, plans on the go.

TOTAL H SCORE

Step 4. Record your scores for each Set in the table below.

FUNCTION	SCORE	FUNCTION	SCORE
Set A – E (Extraversion)		Set B – I (Introversion)	
Set C – S (Sensing)		Set D – N (Intuition)	
Set E – T (Thinking)		Set F – F (Feeling)	
Set G – J (Judging)		Set H – P (Perceiving)	

Step 5. Your temperament is one of the two top pairs (Set A - Extraverted or Set B - Introverted) and one of the two bottom pairs (Set G - Judging or Set H - Perceiving).

Record them here by name e.g. EJ (Extraverted Judging) ………………………………………………..

Step 6. Your dominant function pair is the one of the first two pairs - S (Set C - Sensing), N (Set D - Intuition), and one of the

other two pairs of T (Set E - Thinking) or F (Set F - Feeling) with the highest score.

Record it here by name e.g. SF (Sensing-Feeling)
....

Step 7. Combine the temperament letters e.g. EJ with the function pair letters, e.g. SF to obtain your personality profile, e.g. ESFJ ....

Step 8. Revisit your earlier observations about your temperament and dominant function pair in the relevant chapters.

Functional Pair Social Styles

The four Social Styles (Jungian functional pairs) and the key qualities that they each bring to leadership.

NT: CATALYST

Behaviour Tendencies: Takes advantage of opportunities; relishes difficult situations; sets priorities; gives orders; holds people accountable for their actions - measures results, rewards and punishes; resists the slower, more deliberate path of cooperation, preferring win-lose situations; demonstrates fast reaction time and ability to move decisively.

Task Accomplishment: Gets things done quickly; projects strong views on what should be accomplished; reaches objectives by any and all means; identifies a symbol or enemy to be confronted and overcome; achieves high personal performance.

Primary Focus: To control events and personal destiny.

Motivated By: Opportunities to satisfy personal need to exercise mastery, individuality and assertiveness. Works well when: in an ever-changing environment.

Personal Values: Advancement, challenge, competition, independence.

Persuades Others By: Speaking assertively; employing precise logic and a precise choice of words; using expert testimony and visual aids with authority; asking for a firm commitment. Has a high success in selling tangibles, medium success in selling intangibles.

Handles Conflict By: Challenging; reacting with urgent intensity; caring little about acceptance or being liked; trying to get others to give up their goals.

Responds to Pressure By: Becoming more productive, viewing stress as a tool to initiate action.

As a Team Leader: Emerges as a directive leader, giving the team needed direction in highly competitive situations; rewards faithful followers; establishes a chain of command.

As a Team Follower: Accepts changes that make sense; often plays the role of devil's advocate; expects to be told what to do; resists a weak leader.

Preferred Task Functions:

- Imagining, as in figuring out new ways to do things.
- Distinguishing important from unimportant, as with examining proposals.
- Showing foresight, as in planning ahead, predicting consequences

Strategies for Self-Development: Use empathy and understanding; listen without interrupting; use others' objections as opportunities; rethink the idea of persuasion as a 'battlefield'; involve others as willing rather than compliant participants; form alliances with individuals who have complimentary skills in team cooperation.

NF: SYNERGIST

Behaviour Tendencies: Vies for attention, seeking centre stage; shares advice, materials, and success with others; establishes immediate rapport with people through emotional appeal and persuasiveness; encourages others to speak out; finds it difficult to discipline others; avoids an 'eye for an eye' approach; depends upon goodwill of others for assistance.

Task Accomplishment: Uses whatever resources are available; believes that new situations demand new methods; gravitates toward tasks requiring interpersonal skills and a positive attitude; believes in maintaining a happy, friendly atmosphere; lets efficiency take care of itself.

Primary Focus: To engage in a variety of activities.

Motivated By: Opportunities to satisfy personal need to exercise acceptance, belonging and contentment. Works well when: free of control and detail.

Personal Values: Personal contact, recognition, status/prestige, variety.

Persuades Others By: Putting people at ease; showing interest; exuding charm and self-confidence; talking, joking, making many promises; dismissing objections as unimportant. Has low success in selling tangibles, high success in selling intangibles.

Handles Conflict By: Ameliorating; believing that conflict hurts people; promoting harmony; desiring to be accepted and liked by all.

Responds to Pressure By: Renewing influential contacts; using wit and charm to fend off criticism.

As a Team Leader: Emerges as a tension-releasing leader, meeting the team's need for pleasure, activity and social creativity; willingly shares leadership.

As a Team Follower: Builds bridges between people, reducing tension; relies on a strong leader to keep all team members on a productive and disciplined course.

Preferred Task Functions:

- Promoting, as in making inspirational speeches; counselling and supporting others.
- Acting on gut reactions, as in exploring a hunch; deciding on basis of interpretation.
- Drawing out people, as with eliciting unspoken facts.

Strategies for Self-Development: Concentrate on the task; meet time obligations; speak assertively and directly; be objective in decision making; meet objections head on; form alliances with individuals who have complimentary skills in developing an organised approach.

SF: HARMONIST

Behaviour Tendencies: Sets a consistent pace and sticks to it; demonstrates patience; fulfils commitments; expects and shows loyalty; gives attention to important details; states and defends personal convictions and values; shows enthusiasm for nature and beautiful surroundings;

Task Accomplishment: Acquires expertise in a specialty; uses common sense to solve problems; uses step-by-step approach to become familiar with new methods; finds it difficult to refuse excessive responsibility.

Primary Focus: To achieve success through cooperation.

Motivated By: Opportunities to satisfy personal need to exercise cooperation, contentment and non-assertiveness. Works well when: has time to use orderly methods.

Personal Values: Friendships, security, service, appreciation.

Persuades Others By: Involving committed people similarly modest, quiet and sincere; readily asking others for help in getting across the benefits of an idea/product. Has medium success in selling tangibles, low success in selling intangibles.

Handles Conflict By: Compromising; seeking a solution where both sides gain; finding the middle ground between two extremes.

Responds to Pressure By: Taking responsibility willingly; seeking the best route to long-term security.

As a Team Leader: Emerges as an accommodating leader, allowing the team to resolve struggles among assertive contenders for leadership; excels in redirecting uncooperative people.

As a Team Follower: Identifies with individuals who respond to firm leadership; works effectively in a traditional niche; develops expertise in understanding processes.

Preferred Task Functions:

- Using follow-through, as in sending out materials on time.
- Taking orders, as in accepting and following instructions without hesitation.
- Following well tried processes and systems.

Strategies for Self-Development: Stay in control even though pressured by others; immediately reproach those who are irresponsible; set guidelines for accomplishing tasks; become proactive; taking the initiative rather than reacting to people or events; form alliances with individuals who have complimentary skills in building variety into tasks.

ST: SPECIALIST

Behaviour Tendencies: Tends to compete with things rather than with people; aims to please others; directs efforts toward winning cooperation rather than demanding it, compromising when necessary; complies with respected authority; believes that hard work and fairness will pay off; seeks responsibilities that require solitude and concentration;

Task Accomplishment: Displays a serious, quiet, but determined approach to reach objectives; develops standards; becomes an expert in at least one task; prefers assignments requiring analytical and critical skills in problem solving.

Primary Focus: To bring order out of chaos.

Motivated By: Opportunities to satisfy personal need to exercise expertness, conscientiousness and self-discipline. Works well when: Developing plans along structured lines.

Personal Values: Ethical/moral code, knowledge, precise work, recognition.

Persuades Others By: Relying upon a line of reasoning; building confidence in the message by projecting a thoughtful, precise and reserved image; downplaying emotion. Has high success in selling tangibles, medium success in selling intangibles.

Handles Conflict By: Avoiding; staying away from the issues over which conflict is taking place; believing it may be useless to attempt to solve conflict.

Responds to Pressure By: Becoming more conscientious and careful; eventually complying with reasonable requests.

As a Team Leader: Emerges as a technical leader, helping the team deal with specialised problem areas; provides dignity and ritual; uses a formal style.

As a Team Follower: Treats decisions as complex; fills roles in critical thinking and information gathering; uses extensive analysis; concentrates more on tasks than team relationships.

Preferred Task Functions:

- Keeping financial or numerical records, as with statistics or charts.
- Assembling, as with kits.
- Organising, classifying categories of objects, as with books

Strategies for Self-Development: Make new people connections; develop a tolerance for conflict; speed up decision making; recognise that not all issues are complicated; practice making snap decisions in less important areas; form alliances with individuals who have complimentary skills in dealing with people on a personal basis.

Tool 4: Gravesian/Spiral Dynamics Meme Levels and Descriptions

This tool was developed by Beck and Cowan to identify the "meme" level you are anchored in. It provides the "flavour" that your Reactive Self gives to the way that level is expressed in your personal needs driven behaviour. Rank the statements in Parts I and II below to identify your present personal coping means and life conditions levels.

Part I – Personal Coping Means

	In my normal relaxed state I seek to be…..	Your ranking – 1st to 7th
1.	Safe, like a member of an extended family that looks after its own	
2.	A successful, independent, innovative and competitive winner	
3.	Functional and flexible within my own personal principles	
4.	A responsible being, aware of community and the planet	
5.	Strong and powerful, because they are respected most	
6.	Warm and supportive so that all can grow and be fulfilled	
7.	Purposeful and disciplined as directed by a rightful higher authority	

INSIGHT INTENTION AND INTEGRITY

Part II – Life Conditions

I believe that in my organisation or cultural context….	Your ranking – 1st to 7th
1. Loyalty earns security now and guarantees future rewards	
2. Others stay off my back so I can do what I need and like to do	
3. The primary concern is with our role in the larger eco-system	
4. People feel safe and honour our traditions and rituals	
5. The opportunity exists for people to excel and become winners	
6. People and their feelings come first creating a sense of community	
7. Natural differences, inevitable conflict and constant change energises people	

Now you can look at the following table that matches the numbers with the likely Spiral level and place your ranking alongside each level.

Part I			Part II		
No.	Level	Your ranking	No.	Level	Your ranking
1.	Purple		1.	Blue	
2.	Orange		2.	Red	
3.	Yellow		3.	Turquoise	
4.	Turquoise		4.	Purple	

5.	Red		5.	Orange	
6.	Green		6.	Green	
7.	Blue		7.	Yellow	

What is your highest ranked Spiral level –

- in your relaxed state? (Part I) ....
- for your organisation or cultural context? (Part II) ....

You can now review the descriptions that follow to understand the key elements of your meme levels.

The Meme Level Descriptions

Beige "Survival" meme: The first is the Beige "Survival" meme. This first arrived on the scene, or "awakened," 100,000+ years ago. Its basic premise is: *Do what you must to stay alive.*

The characteristic beliefs and actions of the Beige meme are:

- An individual uses instincts and habits just to survive,
- The distinct self is barely awakened or sustained,
- Food, water, warmth, sex, and safety have priority over anything else,
- Individuals form into family survival bands/tribes to perpetuate life.

The Beige meme includes approximately 0.1 percent of the world's adult population and zero percent of the power.

Purple "Safety" meme: As human consciousness evolves it next goes into the Purple "Safety" meme. This second "awakening" occurred approximately 50,000 years ago. The basic theme for the Purple meme is: *Keep the spirits happy and the tribe's nest warm and safe.*

The Characteristic beliefs and actions of the Purple meme are:

- Thinking is animistic; magical spirits - both good and bad,
- Obeying the desires of spirit beings and mystical signs,
- Showing allegiance to chief, elders, ancestors, and the clan,
- Preserving sacred objects, places, events, and memories,
- Observing rites of passage, seasonal cycles, and tribal customs.

The typical qualities seen in the Purple "Safety" meme are:

- *Characteristics:* mystical spirits, signs; safe clans and nests; powerful elders; our people vs. "them",
- *Decision making:* custom and tradition; elders' counsel; signs or the shaman; clan gets the spoils,
- *Education:* paternalistic teachers; rituals and routines; passive learners; family-like learning; oral history to pass down the stories,
- *Family:* extended kinships; rites of passage; strict role relations; protects bloodline,
- *Community:* respects folk ways; honours ethnicity; lets group be itself; guards magic places,
- *Life space:* old country ways, focus on subsistence; fearful, mystical, superstitious; full of spirit beings.

Red "Significance" meme: The Red "Significance" meme, the third "awakening," occurred about 10,000 years ago. Its basic theme is: *Be what you are and do what you want regardless - "Nobody tells me what to do."*

Many teenagers are at the Red meme. The characteristic beliefs and actions of this meme are:

- The world is seen as a jungle full of threats and predators,
- The individual breaks free from any constraints to please self as self-desires,

- The individual stands tall, expects attention, demands respect, calls the shots,
- The individual enjoys himself to the fullest, right now without guilt or remorse,
- The individual conquers, out-foxes, and dominates other aggressive characters,
- An overly developed ethnic identity can lead to genocidal wars, slavery, and racism,
- The individual believes that: *"I am special, I'll live forever, I am immortal, not like the others."*

The typical qualities seen in the Red "Significance" meme are.

- *Characteristics:* raw power displays; immediate pleasure; unrestrained by guilt; colourful and creative,
- *Decision making:* tough-one dictates; what gets respect; what feels good now; powerful grab the spoils,
- *Education:* rewards for learning; tough-love tactics; work on respect; controlled freedom,
- *Family:* gang-like battles; builds us vs. them walls; tests of worthiness; struggles with the system,
- *Community:* predators in control; danger to the outsiders; forms fiefdoms; turf wars and vendettas,
- *Life space:* unconstrained; might makes right; winners and dead losers; attention-seeking.

Blue "Order" meme: After the very individualistic Red meme, the next level goes back again to the more community-focused orientation. The Blue meme, as the fourth "awakening," began about 5,000 years ago. The basic rules for the Blue meme are: *Life has meaning, direction and purpose with outcomes determined by an all-powerful Other or Order.* This meme brings discipline to the spiral because you are now "following a higher order."

The characteristic beliefs and actions of the Blue meme include:

- Sacrificing of the self to the transcendent Cause, Truth, or righteous Pathway,

- Allowing the Order to enforce a code of conduct based on eternal, absolute unvarying principles of "right" and "wrong - there is one right way to live and deviations from the path are punished,
- Following the right path produces security now and guarantees future reward; if you don't follow the path, well, you've made your choices,
- Displaying missionary zealotry, which can be short on evidence and long on belief and faith, as well as closed minds. When you run into people with very rigid thought structures, you are dealing with someone who is residing at the Blue meme,
- Engaging in pleasurable acts is seen as frivolous; humour is rare; actions are based in judgment not compassion, although there is a lot of talk about compassion,
- Operating from a fundamentalist, conventional, traditional, and conformist worldview.

The typical qualities seen in the Blue "Order" meme are:.

- *Characteristics:* only one right way; purpose in causes; guilt in consequences; sacrifice for honour,
- *Decision making:* orders from authority; do right, obey rules; adhere to tradition; righteous earn the spoils,
- *Education:* truth from authority; traditional stair steps; moralistic lessons; punishment for errors,
- *Family:* seat of truths and values; proper places for all, respect for parents; codes of conduct; teaches moral ways,
- *Community:* peace-and-quiet; cautious and careful; tidy, green, and neat; born into society,
- *Life space:* law abiding citizen, places for everybody; seeks peace of mind; rewards to come.

Orange "Prosperity" meme: The Orange "Prosperity" meme, the fifth "awakening" began only 300 years ago. Its basic rule is: *Act in your own self-interest by playing the game to win.*

Some of the characteristic beliefs and actions of this meme include:

- Strongly expressed individualism; Orange breaks away from the "herd" of the Blue meme,
- Developed human rights, legal freedoms, free markets, capitalistic democracies,
- Strong faith in science and rationality, which eclipse superstition,
- Seeking to live the "good life" with material abundance,
- Believe that optimistic, risk-taking, and self-reliant people deserve their success,
- Play to win and enjoy competition; very success driven,
- Basing principles on ethics, not religion,
- Ignoring of inner spirituality to a high degree; the subsequent loss of the sacred.

The typical qualities seen in the Orange "Prosperity" meme are:

- *Characteristics:* competes for success; goal-oriented drive; change to progress; material gain/perks,
- *Decision making:* bottom-line results; test options for best; consult experts; successful win the spoils,
- *Education:* experiments to win; high-tech, high status; how to win niches; mentors and guides,
- *Family:* upwardly mobile; demands attention; high expectations; image conscious,
- *Community:* caters to prosperous; displays affluence; buys into society; security for the elite,
- *Life space:* wants to prosper now; competition always; leverages influence; seeks material things.

Green "Community" meme: The response to the somewhat singularly driven Orange meme is found in the Green "Community" meme, the sixth "awakening," which first appeared nearly 150 years ago. The basic theme for the Green meme is: *Seek peace within the inner self and explore, with others, the caring dimensions of community.*

Some of the characteristic beliefs and actions of the Green meme include:

- Becomes more aware of the suffering of the world, of other sentient beings,
- The human spirit must be freed from greed, dogma, and divisiveness,
- Feelings, sensitivity, and caring supersede cold rationality,
- Share the Earth's resources and opportunities equally among all,
- Reach decisions through consensus processes,
- Anti-authoritarian and against hierarchy; establishes lateral bonding and linking,
- All values are pluralistic and relativistic; no one should be marginalised,
- Environmentalism becomes a socio-political movement,
- A fundamental belief is "All people are good; it's society that makes them bad.",
- Create cults of censorship through politically correct thinking; may be politically dogmatic.

The qualities inherent in the Green "Community" meme are:

- *Characteristics:* seeks inner peace; everybody is equal; everything is relative; harmony within the group,
- *Decision making:* reach consensus; all must collaborate; accept any input; community get the spoils,
- *Education:* to explore feelings; shared experiences; social development; learn cooperation,
- *Family:* grouping of equals; participative activities; highly accepting; all feelings processed,

- *Community:* social safety-nets; "politically correct"; open for insiders; invests in self,
- *Life space:* thrives on belonging; needs acceptance; sacrifice feels good; renews spirituality.

Yellow "Interdependence" meme: The first level within the Second Tier is the Yellow "Inter-dependence" meme, which is the 7th "awakening," and it occurred about 50 years ago. The Yellow mneme's basic tenet is: *Live fully and responsibly with authenticity.*

Some of the characteristic beliefs and actions of the Yellow meme are:

- Pursuit of learning for its own sake,
- Systems thinking,
- Viewing life as a kaleidoscope of natural hierarchies, systems, and forms,
- Valuing the wonder of existence over material possessions,
- Prioritising flexibility, spontaneity, and functionality,
- Valuing knowledge and competency over rank, power, and status,
- Integrating complex systems with ease.

The qualities that typify the Yellow "Inter-dependence" meme are:

- *Characteristics:* big picture views; integrative structures; naturalness of chaos; inevitability of change,
- *Decision making:* highly principled; knowledge centred; resolved paradoxes; competent get the spoils,
- *Education:* becomes self-directed; whole-day package; tuned to interests; non-rigid structure,
- *Family:* shifting roles; expects competence; takes each as is; as an information base,
- *Community:* does more with less; appropriate technologies; power is dispersed; integrated systems,
- *Life space:* life is learning; intrigued by process; freedom to just be; rarely fearful.

Turquoise "Harmony" meme: Beyond the largely individualistic Yellow meme, the Turquoise "Harmony" meme, as the 8th "awakening," began expressing about 30 years ago. This meme's basic premise is: *Experience the wholeness of existence through mind and spirit.*

Some of the characteristic beliefs and actions of the Turquoise meme include:

- Experiencing the world as a single, dynamic organism with its own collective mind,
- Acknowledging the Self as both distinct and a blended part of a larger, compassionate whole,
- Viewing everything connected to everything else as incredibly beautiful ecological alignments,
- Experiencing energy and information as permeating the Earth's total environment,
- Thinking that is holistic and intuitive, with an expectation of cooperative actions,
- Synthesising science and religion into a universal spirituality.

The qualities that define the Turquoise "Harmony" meme are:

- *Characteristics:* scans the macro; synergy of all life; safe, orderly world; restores harmony,
- *Decision making:* blend natural flows; look up/downstream; plan for long-range; life gets the spoils,
- *Education:* access to world; blends feelings and technology; bring past to life; maximise the brain,
- *Family:* global awareness; grows consciousness; broad interest ranges; seeks outreach,
- *Community:* interconnected; highly diversified; not isolationist; information rich,
- *Life space:* belong to universe; fit into chain of being; do something here; as one with life-force.

REFERENCE SOURCES

Deeper Man: J.G. Bennett: Bennett Books: Santa Fe
Energies: J.G. Bennett: Claymont: Charlestown
Transformation: J.G. Bennett: Bennett Books: Santa Fe
Hazard: J.G. Bennett: Bennett Books: Santa Fe
A Spiritual Psychology: J.G. Bennett: Bennett Books: Santa Fe
The Roots of Self: Robert Ornstein: Harper: San Francisco
Integrity in Depth: John Beebe: Texas A&M University Press:
Pathways to Integrity: Blake Burleson: Centre for Application of Psychological Type: Gainesville
What We May Be: Piero Ferrucci: Tarcher Pengiun: New York
The Open Mind: Dawna Markova: Conari Press: Berkeley
The Evolving Self: Robert Keegan: Harvard University Press: Cambridge Mass
Power of Now: Eckhart Tolle: Hodder: Sydney
Stillness Speaks: Eckhart Tolle: Hodder: Sydney
Thriving in Mind: Katherine Benziger: KBA LLC: Carbondale
The Whole Brain Business Book: Ned Herrmann: McGraw Hill
The Attention Economy: Thomas Davenport John Beck: Harvard Business: Boston
Understanding Yourself and Others: Linda Berens: Telos: Huntington Beach
The Keirsey Stratagem: John Fudjack
Energetics of Personality: John G Geier, Dorothy E Downey: Aristos Publishing House
Personality Type: Lenore Thomson: Shambala: New York
Understanding Your Personality: Patricia Hedges: Sheldon Press: London

Spiral Dynamics: D.E. Beck and C.C Cowan: Blackwell Publishing: Malden MA
The Intelligent Enneagram: A.G.E. Blake: Shambala: London
Personality Types: Don Richard Riso with Russ Hudson: Houghton Mifflin: New York
Enneagram Instinctual Subtypes: Katherine Chernick-Fauvre
Our Inner Conflicts: Karen Horney: Norton: New York
Building Blocks of Personality Type: Leona Haas and Mark Hunziker: Telos: Huntington Beach

AUTHOR BIO

Ian Cogdell is a leadership and team development mentor, facilitator and executive coach. Ian has had extensive practical experience in senior human resource management, information technology and sales and marketing roles in national and international organisations. He is a former Director of Knowledge Management at the then Mt Eliza Centre for Executive Education, Melbourne Business School and has taught on their Executive MBA program. He is highly regarded for his insightful, engaging, facilitative, challenging and theoretically sound yet practical approach to learning and development. He is the author of The Nine Dots – Discovering the three faces of self using the Enneagram.

www.ingramcontent.com/pod-product-compliance
Lightning Source LLC
Chambersburg PA
CBHW052009070526
44584CB00016B/1678